The Golde

The Golden Rule

The Ethics of Reciprocity
in World Religions

Edited by

Jacob Neusner and Bruce Chilton

continuum

Continuum International Publishing Group

The Tower Building   80 Maiden Lane
11 York Road   Suite 704
London   New York
SE1 7NX   NY 10038

www.continuumbooks.com

British Library Cataloguing-in-Publication Data
A catalogue record for this book is available from the British Library.

ISBN: HB: 1-8470-6295-4
             978-1-847-06295-6
        PB: 1-8470-6296-2
             978-1-847-06296-3

Library of Congress Cataloging-in-Publication Data
A catalog record for this book is available from the Library of Congress.

Typeset by Newgen Imaging Systems Pvt Ltd, Chennai, India
Printed and bound in Great Britain by Cromwell Press Ltd, Trowbridge, Wiltshire

Contents

List of Contributors

Robert Berchman is professor of philosophy and religious studies at Dowling College and a fellow of the Institute of Advanced Theology at Bard College. He has published numerous books and articles in the fields of ancient philosophy and ancient Mediterranean religions and is the author of *Porphyry Against the Christians*. He is the coeditor, with John F. Finamore, of *Plato Redividivus History of Platonism*, and *Metaphysical Patterns in Platonism: Ancient, Medieval, Renaissance, and Modern Times*. Berchman is an editor of the *Encyclopedia of Religious and Philosophical Writings in Late Antiquity* and serves as editor of *Ancient Mediterranean and Medieval Texts and Contexts: Studies in Platonism, Neoplatonism, and the Platonic Tradition*. He is also the past president (U.S.) and international general secretary of the *International Society for Neoplatonic Studies*.

Bruce Chilton, Bernard Iddings Bell Professor of Philosophy and Religion, executive director of the Institute of Advanced Theology, and chaplain of the College, is a scholar of early Christianity and Judaism and the author of the first critical translation of the Aramaic version of Isaiah (*The Isaiah Targum*, 1987). He has written academic studies that put Jesus in his Jewish context (*Rabbi Jesus: An Intimate Biography*, 2000; *Pure Kingdom*, 1996; *The Temple of Jesus*, 1992; and *A Galilean Rabbi and His Bible*, 1984). Doubleday recently published his book, *Abraham's Curse: The Roots of Violence in Judaism, Christianity, and Islam*, and has released his other volumes, *Mary Magdalene: A Biography, Rabbi Paul: An Intellectual Biography*, and *Rabbi Jesus: An Intimate Biography* in paperback. Chilton has taught in Europe at the universities of Cambridge, Sheffield, and Münster, and in the United States at Yale University (as the first Lillian Claus Professor of New Testament) and Bard College. Throughout his career, he has been active in the pastoral ministry of the Anglican Church; he is currently rector of the Church of St. John the Evangelist in Barrytown, New York.

Mark Csikszentmihalyi is associate professor, East Asian Languages and Literature, University of Wisconsin-Madison. He researches early China, and is chiefly concerned with questions that come out of the fields of comparative ethics and religious studies.

Richard H. Davis is professor of religion and director of the Religion Program at Bard College. He is the author of *Ritual in an Oscillating Universe: Worshiping Siva in Medieval India* (1991) and *Lives of Indian Images* (1997), winner of the

1999 A. K. Coomaraswamy Prize. He is also editor of *Images, Miracles, and Authority in Asian Religious Traditions*, and *Picturing the Nation: Iconographies of Modern India*. Davis has contributed to journals such as *History and Anthropology, Journal of Asian Studies, Journal of Ritual Studies, Journal of Oriental Research*, and *History of Religions*. He is the recipient of fellowships from the Guggenheim, Fulbright-Hays, and Mrs. Giles Whiting foundations, and the National Endowment for the Humanities.

Carolyn Dewald, is professor of classical and historical studies and director of the Classical Studies Program at Bard College. She received a BA degree from Swarthmore and a PhD from the University of California at Berkeley. Dewald taught at Stanford University from 1975–77, USC from 1977–2003, and at Vassar College from 2001–02 as Blegen Distinguished Professor. She was a NEH Fellow from 1984–85 and Phi Beta Kappa National Lecturer from 2002–03. Dewald is the author of numerous articles on Herodotus, Thucydides, and Greek historiography. Her publications include *Herodotus: The Histories* (introduction and commentary, tr. Robin Wakefield, Oxford University Press, 1998) and *Thucydides' War Narrative: A Structural Study* (University of California Press, 2005). She is coeditor of the *Cambridge Companion to Herodotus* and author of a forthcoming study of narrative organization in the history of Thucydides. Dewald received an American Council of Learned Societies fellowship for a new edition of *Herodotus Book I—critical apparatus, introduction, and commentary*.

Olivier du Roy, of Paris, France, retired following a career of 35 years as a consultant for humanitarian organizations and resources. He was born in Brussels in 1933 and, in 1966, received a PhD in Theology from Strasbourg with a thesis, titled *L'intelligence de la foi en la Trinité selon saint Augustin, Genèse de sa théologie trinitaire* (*Intelligence of the Faith in the Trinity According to Saint Augustin, Genesis of his Theology Trinitaire*), which was presented under the direction of Maurice Nédoncelle. As a graduate student at the École pratique des Hautes Études (5° section : Sciences Religieuses), he attended seminars by H. I. Marrou, Jean Pépin, and Pierre Hadot. He received a PhD in philosophy in 2007 from the University of Paris-Est Marne la Vallée, after 30 years of study that began in 1968 under the direction first of Paul Ricoeur, then Pierre Hadot. His philosophy dissertation was *La règle d'or. Histoire et portée d'une maxime éthique* (*The Golden Rule: History and Range of an Ethical Maxim*). His other publication in this field is *La réciprocité, Essai de morale fondamentale* (*Reciprocity, Test of Fundamental Morals*).

William Scott Green is senior vice provost and dean of undergraduate studies at the University of Miami. In the newly created position, he has overall responsibility for enhancing the quality of the undergraduate experience and strengthening the integration of university-wide undergraduate curricular and cocurricular initiatives. Green also holds an appointment as professor of religious studies and senior fellow in the Sue and Leonard Miller Center for Contemporary Judaic Studies. Green earned an AB in religion at Dartmouth

College and a PhD in religion from Brown University. He has held fellowships from the National Endowment of the Humanities, the American Council of Learned Societies, and the Andrew Mellon Foundation.

Charles Hallisey, formerly associate professor in the Department of Languages and Cultures of Asia at the University of Wisconsin-Madison is now on the faculty of the Harvard Divinity School. Since January 2005 he served as director of Wisconsin's Religious Studies Program. Earlier he taught at Amherst College and at Harvard, where he was John L. Loeb Associate Professor of the Humanities and member of the Committee on the Study of Religion and the Department of Sanskrit and Indian Studies from (1996 to 2001). His research centers on Theravada Buddhism in Sri Lanka and Southeast Asia, Pali language and literature, Buddhist ethics, and literature in Buddhist culture. He is currently working on a book project entitled *Flowers on the Tree of Poetry: The Moral Economy of Literature in Buddhist Sri Lanka*. Hallisey has received a AB degree from Colgate University, MDiv from Harvard Divinity School, MA from University of Pennsylvania, and a PhD from the University of Chicago.

Th. Emil Homerin is professor of religion in the Department of Religion and Classics at the University of Rochester, where he teaches courses on Islam, classical Arabic literature, and mysticism. Among his many publications are *The Wine of Love & Life: Ibn al-Fârid's al-Khamrîyah and al-Qaysarî's Quest for Meaning* (2005), *From Arab Poet to Muslim Saint* (2001), *Ibn al-Fârid: Sufi Verse & Saintly Life* (2001), and several chapters on Islam in the volume *The Religious Foundations of Western Civilization* (Abingdon Press, 2006).

Baruch A. Levine is Skirball Professor Emeritus of Bible and Ancient Near Eastern Studies, New York University. His research interests include the biblical cult and religion, and is author of commentaries on Leviticus and Numbers. He adopts a political approach to the rise of Israelite monotheism and a comparative approach to biblical exegesis. Parallel track: ancient Semitic epigraphy, primarily in Aramaic and Ugaritic.

Mahnaz Moazami is an associate research scholar at Columbia University. She studied Old and Middle Iranian languages at the University of Tehran (MA) and religious anthropology and history of religion at the Sorbonne University (DEA and PhD). Moazami has held postdoctoral research fellowships at Harvard and Yale Universities. Her research is focused on ancient Iranian religion and she has published several articles on different aspects of Zoroastrian traditions in pre-Islamic Iran. She is currently preparing an edition (text, translation, and commentary) of the *Pahlavi Videvdad*, a critical text for the understanding of purification laws in ancient Iran (circa 500 C.E).

Jacob Neusner is Distinguished Service Professor of the history and theology of Judaism, and Senior Fellow, Institute of Advanced Theology at Bard College. He also is a Member of the Institute for Advanced Study, Princeton NJ, and Life

Member of Clare Hall, Cambridge University in England. He has published more than 1,000 books on the history of Judaism.

Kristin Scheible earned a PhD from Harvard University in 2006, holds an MTS from Harvard Divinity School, and a BA from Colby College. She is assistant professor of religion at Bard, where she has taught for the past five years. Formerly, she was a lecturer at Brown University and senior teaching fellow at Harvard. Her area of expertise is Theravada Buddhism, and her work revolves around the genre of historical narrative literature (*vamsas*) in the Pali language.

Preface

To make comparisons we must begin with shared traits, then proceed to contrast. But for the comparative study of religions where are we to find shared traits? Religions by their nature contend about truth. Comparative religions can find no more suitable arena for its work than the Golden Rule in world religions. That is for a simple reason. The Golden Rule—"do to others as you would have them do to you" "what is hateful to you to your fellow don't do," to take the two most familiar formulations—defines a meeting place for many fields of learning. There the study of comparative religion, philosophy and ethics, anthropology and sociology, and the whole range of cross-cultural studies carried on in the social sciences and the humanities intersect. That hardly presents a surprise, since the Golden Rule finds a place in most religions and is universally acknowledged to form a part of the shared heritage of human wisdom.

But even if it is one thing on which religions concur, that does not mean the Golden Rule is simple or self-evident. Its ubiquity presents us with tough questions of context and difficult problems of content. Both the Golden Rule itself and how it attests to the human condition demand study. Defining the rule and explaining its universality in religion and culture require attention. The role of the Golden Rule in various systems of thought, both religious and philosophical, invites study. How the logic of a given system interprets the Golden Rule demands analysis. Objective data deriving from empirical study of nature and society deserve close examination. Specialists in a wide range of disciplines have a contribution to make out of their particular disciplines and areas of expert knowledge.

In these pages specialists in various fields of the study of religion respond to a program of questions addressed to all divisions of the history and comparison of religions. The questions, formulated by Professor William Scott Green, secure a common program for the presentation of the several religious traditions of humanity.

The essays collected in this book derive from an academic conference presented in April 2008, by the Institute of Advanced Theology (IAT) of Bard College. The project was organized by Professor Bruce Chilton, Director of IAT, and this writer, together with Mrs. Emily Darrow, executive assistant of IAT. Numerous offices at Bard College cooperated in practical ways to facilitate our meeting.

Those who read papers at the conference participated in this project in an exemplary manner, providing their papers on the deadline and otherwise facilitating work on the project. We thank them for sharing their learning with our students and faculty at Bard.

Undergraduates at Bard College participated in a seminar at which the papers were read and discussed and joined in the discussion of the papers at the conference.

The conference was supported by the Templeton Foundation through the good offices of Dr. Stephen G. Post, Case-Western Reserve University. Dr. Post was responsible for advising the Institute of Advanced Theology on the names of specialists in various aspects of contemporary study on the Golden Rule.

On behalf of the Institute of Advanced Theology I express thanks to all who helped bring the project to realization.

Jacob Neusner

Distinguished Service Professor of the History and Theology of Judaism

Senior Fellow, Institute of Advanced Theology, Bard College

Annandale-on-Hudson, New York 12504

jneusner@frontiernet.net

Chapter 1

Parsing Reciprocity: Questions for the Golden Rule

William Scott Green
University of Miami

The Golden Rule is perhaps humanity's most familiar ethical dictum. In conventional usage, the term refers to "the precept that one should do as one would be done by."[1] The *Oxford English Dictionary*'s fifth definition of the word "golden" provides the following elaboration: Of rules, precepts, etc.: Of inestimable utility; often *spec.* with reference to the precept, "whatsoever ye would that men should do to you, do ye even so to them" (Mt. 7.12).[2] The rule also can be stated "negatively," as in the Aramaic saying assigned in the Babylonian Talmud (*Shabbat* 31a) to the first century B.C.E. Jewish sage, Hillel: "What is hateful to you, do not do to your comrade. This is the entire Torah. And the rest is commentary. Go and study." The Golden Rule appears in both religious and secular systems, and it has attracted the attention of sages and philosophers alike. Jeffrey Wattles[3] admirably captures the Golden Rule's virtues:

> The golden rule is, from the first, intuitively accessible, easy to understand; its simplicity communicates confidence that the agent can find the right way. The rule tends to function as a simplified summary of the advocate's moral tradition, and it most commonly expresses a commitment to treating others with consideration and fairness, predicated on the recognition that others are like oneself.

The purpose of this project is to give the Golden Rule a fresh look in an unprecedented intellectual setting. For the first time, scholars of religion, philosophers, and scientists gather to share and compare their perspectives on the meaning and significance of the Golden Rule. Participants will examine the formulation

---

[1] *The Chambers Dictionary* (Larousse, 1994), p. 718.
[2] *The Compact Edition of the Oxford English Dictionary* (Oxford: Oxford University Press, 1971), Vol. I, p. 280
[3] Jeffrey Wattles, *The Golden Rule* (Oxford: Oxford University Press, 1996), p. 188. Wattles' book serves as an intelligent, thoughtful, and extremely useful foundation for the work of this project. The questions proposed at the end build on Wattles' work.

and significance of the Golden Rule in the world's major religions, and philosophers and scientists will assess a new how the Golden Rule works and what it
implies, particularly as part of systems of morality and collective life. The goal
of this brief introductory exercise is to supply the barest structure of a common
agenda so that, at some level, we all can be part of a collective inquiry. Our hope
is that a shared framework of description and analysis will facilitate and even
generate a productive exchange among us.

On the basis of the definitions and formulations listed at the outset, we can
take the term "the Golden Rule" to refer at least to a general statement that
instructs us to treat others as we want, and would want, others to treat us. Thus,
the Golden Rule is an abstract mandate to use an ethic of reciprocity as the
fundamental guide to the way we consider, conceive, carry out, and assess our
actions toward other people. The Golden Rule does not discuss particular
actions, nor does it guarantee rewards for following it. Rather, it prescribes reciprocity as the foundational conceptual framework and context of consistency
for shaping and evaluating our actions toward others.

Though the attachment of the adjective "golden" to the rule of reciprocity—
suggesting its superiority over other rules—occurred in mid-sixteenth century
Europe,[4] statements recommending or at least approving reciprocity
as a principle of behavior appear across humanity's religions and cultures.
J. O. Hertzler[5] lists at least twenty-five variations of an RR, from the Yoruba to
Kant, and contemporary websites provide comparable exhibits.[6] The virtual
ubiquity of the Golden Rule has led to judgments about its signal importance
in ethics. Consider the following comment of Marcus G. Singer[7]:

> The golden rule has been widely accepted, in word if not in deed, by vast
> numbers of greatly differing peoples; it is a basic device of moral education;
> and it can be found at the core of innumerable moral, religious, and social
> codes . . . The nearly universal acceptance of the golden rule and its promul-
> gation by persons of considerable intelligence, though otherwise of divergent
> outlooks, would . . . seem to provide some evidence for the claim that it is
> a fundamental ethical truth.

An alternative perspective is offered by ethicist Bernard Gert, who approves
the Golden Rule's sentiment but doubts its practical value. He suggests that
a "straightforward reading" of the Golden Rule reveals its basic inability to help

---

[4] *The Encyclopedia Britannica, Micropedia,* (1978) IV, p. 608.
[5] J. O. Hertzler, "On Golden Rules," *International Journal of Ethics,* 44/4 (July 1934), 418–36.
[6] See, for example, the website of Prof. Harry Gensler, S. J., of John Carroll University, and
the links listed there: http://www.jcu.edu/philosophy/gensler/goldrule.htm.
[7] Marcus G. Singer, "Golden Rule," *Encyclopedia of Philosophy* (Macmillan, 1967), III, New York,
pp. 365–67.

people decide what to do, so it cannot effectively inform conduct. Gert concludes that[8]

> the Golden Rule is not really a very good guide to conduct. It seems to require conduct that everybody admits is not required and sometimes seems to require conduct that is clearly wrong. If followed literally, and how else are we to understand it, it requires all normal policemen not to arrest criminals, and all normal judges not to sentence them. Assuming that normal judges and policemen want neither to be caught nor sentenced, according to the Golden Rule, it follows that they ought not to arrest or sentence others. The Golden Rule also requires, and students might like this, that teachers not give flunking grades to students even if they deserve it. If you were a student you would not want to be flunked. But it also seems to require that a student get a better grade than those who do not deserve it, because if you were a student and deserved a better grade, you would want a better grade. So it now seems that the Golden Rule is really pretty useless if you are trying to find out what you ought to do.

The Oxford English Dictionary suggests that the rule of reciprocity is called "golden" because of its "inestimable utility," that is, because it is supremely useful. Singer thinks that the Golden Rule's extensive cross-cultural presence lends plausibility to its status as a "fundamental ethical truth." In sharp contrast, Gert demonstrates that, when read "literally," the Golden Rule is "a useless and pointless rule to use as a guide to your conduct." From one perspective, the Golden Rule appears as universal and supremely useful. From another perspective, it has no value as a guide to actual behavior. The contrast between these assessments can help to shape the agenda for our collective work on this project.

The conflicting views outlined above show that the Golden Rule is easier to endorse than to enact. As a general moral principle or as an abstract statement of ethical value, the Golden Rule makes intuitive sense and enjoys wide acceptance across religions and cultures. But the generality and abstraction that enable its broad appeal make the Golden Rule problematic as a directive for practical action. Indeed, on Gert's analysis, it is possible that the Golden Rule must be read figuratively or very expansively in order to be used, surely a challenge for any basic moral principle. The Golden Rule can be accepted unambiguously but applied only after considerable reflection and qualification. The Golden Rule's basic formulations—either positive or negative—require the constraints of context and interpretation to achieve the "inestimable utility" the OED ascribes to the rule. Consider the following problem: The core value of

---

[8] Bernard Gert, "Morality versus Slogans," http://aristotle.tamu.edu/~rasmith/Courses/251/gert-paper.html

the Golden Rule is reciprocity, but the positive formulation of the Golden Rule ("Do unto others . . .") is unclear about how reciprocity actually works. Are we to conceive the other in terms of ourselves, ourselves in terms of the other, or some combination of the two? This ambiguity is particularly troublesome if we and the other inhabit conflicting moral universes. To achieve reciprocity, does the rule require or imply that we should respect moral positions we oppose and shape our actions around them? For instance, must a person who is "pro-life" imagine herself as holding the values of someone who is "pro-choice" in deter-mining whether or not to close a women's health clinic in which abortions are performed? Since the "pro-choice" person would not want the clinic closed, should the "pro-life" person allow it to remain open? Is the basic reference point of the Golden Rule the actor or the recipient of the action, the self or the other? Does the Golden Rule allow me to "do" what I believe to be good "unto others" who do not want it or value it because I would want that good "done" to me? Are there limits to the reciprocity of the Golden Rule? If so, then in what sense is the Golden Rule a general moral principle?

This kind of conundrum is not merely theoretical. There are historical exam-ples with real-life consequences. In the eighteenth and nineteenth centuries, abolitionist and proslavery Christian clergymen debated the question of slavery. Abolitionist preachers used the Golden Rule to argue that slavery should be eliminated. Proslavery ministers—who did not regard slavery as a sin—employed the Golden Rule to support the very opposite position. They argued in essence that ending slavery would disrupt the social and economic order and harm more people than it would benefit. On this view, rather than mandating the abolition of slavery, "The Golden Rule demands that free men ask themselves what they would consider reasonable and just if they were slaves."[9] James Henry Thornwell put it bluntly: "We are not bound to render unto them what they might in fact desire. Such a rule would transmute morality into caprice. But we are bound to render unto them what they have a right to desire—that is, we are bound to render unto them what is 'just and equal.'"[10] For Thornwell and others, apparently, rather than eliminating slavery, the reciprocity of the Golden Rule meant understanding how to endure it. In the end, the Golden Rule served the arguments of both sides, and the matter was settled on the battlefield rather than in the pulpit. This episode seems to add weight to Gert's concern about the rule's practical value in guiding conduct. If the Golden Rule could not help resolve the question of slavery, what kind of moral dilemmas can it actually settle?

The conundra described above are not unique in scholarship on the Golden Rule; they are part of a tradition of honest intellectual scrutiny of the

---

[9] Elizabeth Fox-Genovese and Eugene Genovese, *The Mind of the Master Class: History and Faith in the Southern Slaveholders' Worldview* (Cambridge: Cambridge University Press, 2005), p. 621. For a fuller account, see pp. 618–24.
[10] Ibid.

rule's meaning. That the basic formulation of the Golden Rule so easily generates and fails to solve basic problems about its practicality suggests that our
project should focus less on the rule itself than on the preconditions, contexts,
settings, frameworks, stipulations, etc. that give the Golden Rule its concrete
and substantive significance. To appreciate and evaluate the Golden Rule's
importance, it will help to understand the constraints that focus its meaning
and the circumstances to and in which it actually applies. Jeffrey Wattles suggests that "The Golden Rule . . . has more than a single sense. It is not a static,
one-dimensional proposition with a single meaning to be accepted or rejected,
defended or refuted. Nor is its multiplicity chaotic. There is enough continuity
of meaning in its varied uses to justify speaking of the golden rule."[11] Freshly
examining the Golden Rule's "utility" in a broad comparative and analytic context can help us chart in detail the Golden Rule's "varied uses," sharpen our
picture of its "continuity of meaning," and assess if, how, and why the Golden
Rule matters in human cultures and societies.

To achieve these elemental scholarly goals, we might organize our collective
investigation of the Golden Rule around four basic and fairly broad topics:
In the religion, culture, or philosophy you study, what does the Golden Rule say?
What does the Golden Rule mean? How does the Golden Rule work? How does
the Golden Rule matter? The questions listed beneath each topic are suggestive
rather than normative. Their goal is to stimulate inquiry. It is difficult to devise
a single set of questions that will work equally well in the study of religions and
in philosophy. The questions below probably are better suited to the former
than the latter. That is in part a reflection of the author's intellectual limitations
and in part because this is the first collective study of the Golden Rule in the
context of comparative religion. Treating each religion similarly will yield useful comparative results. The questions assume that a religion is a system with
interacting and mutually reinforcing elements. One goal of our study is to show
how the Golden Rule works in a discrete religion, how it affects and is affected
by the system of which it is a part. It is hoped that philosophers will be able to
adapt the questions' concerns to their own materials. Let us now turn to the
four topics.

What does the Golden Rule say?

In the religion, culture, or philosophy you study, is the Golden Rule formulated
positively, negatively, or both? Is it formulated as a narrative, a work of art, or
a ritual practice? Why was this formulation chosen? What is the semantic range
of its language and formulation? How does the Golden Rule emerge and where
does it appear? If the Golden Rule is not specifically mentioned or formulated,
are there approximations?

[11] Wattles, p. 5

What does the Golden Rule mean?

Literature

In the materials you study, is there a literary context for the Golden Rule? If you study a religion, does it appear in the religion's scripture? If there is a literary context, what in that context provokes the Golden Rule's appearance? Does the literary context constrain the Golden Rule's meaning by, for example, glossing it or embedding it in a highly particular setting or circumstance?[12]

Interpretation

How important is the Golden Rule in the interpretive tradition of the religion, culture, or philosophy you study? How much interpretive attention does the Golden Rule receive relative to other doctrines, practices, precepts, etc.? How has the Golden Rule been interpreted and applied over time? Does the tradition advance some understanding(s) of the Golden Rule at the expense of others? Does the interpretive tradition distinguish between reciprocity and retaliation? Does it (and if so, how) constrain excessive or ridiculous inferences from the Golden Rule, i.e., the idea that evildoers should not be punished because we, in their shoes, would not like to be punished?

How does the Golden Rule work?

Social consequence

In the materials you study, to which segments of society is the Golden Rule directed? Does it apply uniformly across genders and social classes? Is it limited to a particular group, or does it apply to people in general? Does it presuppose literacy or a certain level of education? Who is the author of or authority behind the Golden Rule? Does it apply all the time or only in particular circumstances?

Actor and recipient

Who is the Golden Rule's assumed actor and recipient of the action? Does the Golden Rule assume that the actor is an autonomous moral agent whose subjective and individual desires are the basis for the actions taken toward the other? Alternatively, are the actor's desires prescribed by some other authority?

---

[12] See, for example, Alan Kirk, "'Love Your Enemies,' The Golden Rule and Ancient Reciprocity," (Luke 6.27–35), *Journal of Biblical Literature* 122/4 (Winter 2003), pp. 667–86, which discusses Luke's glossing the Golden Rule with the mandate to love our enemies.

Does the actor determine how s/he wants or would want to be treated or does the tradition supply that content? Does the Golden Rule apply to a deity or other superhuman beings?

Reflexivity and reciprocity

Does the Golden Rule include reflexivity as a component of reciprocity, i.e., the notion of treating others as you would treat yourself?[13] In the materials you study, is the Golden Rule equivalent to the precept to "Love your neighbor as yourself?" Is the Golden Rule's basic reference point the actor or the recipient of the action, the self or the other? Does the Golden Rule presuppose or require empathy? Are there limits to the Golden Rule's conception of reciprocity?

Violence and oppression

Does the Golden Rule sanction violence or oppression against others? If so, which circumstances make such behavior acceptable?

How does the Golden Rule matter?

Systemic significance

How important is the Golden Rule in the system of the religion or culture you study? Is it central or peripheral? How does the Golden Rule work with the religion's other component parts—parts we often classify as myths, beliefs, rituals, ethics, etc.—to produce coherence? What are the Golden Rule's prerequisites? What must be assumed in order for the Golden Rule to make sense both as a principle and a potential or actual practice? Do other teachings and practices depend on the Golden Rule? Does the religion or culture identify specific teachings or actions as particular applications of the Golden Rule? Are there other rules, precepts, or values that always supersede the Golden Rule? Within the religion or culture, are there major alternatives or challenges to the Golden Rule?

Consequences of failure and success

What are the consequences of ignoring, disobeying, or otherwise failing to implement the Golden Rule? Are there social sanctions, negative religious

---

[13] See Bo Mou, "A Reexamination of the Structure and Content of Confucius' Version of the Golden Rule," *Philosophy East and West*, 54/2 (April 2004), 218–48, which discusses this issue in detail within the Confucian tradition.

judgments, punishments in the next world, etc.? What are the consequences of fulfilling the Golden Rule? Are rewards or benefits promised or assumed?

Exceptions

Does the religion, culture, or philosophy you study justify flouting the Golden Rule? Is it permissible to treat others as you do *not* want them to treat you? How are exceptions to the Golden Rule justified, and what do the exceptions reveal about the importance of the Golden Rule in the system you study?

At the conclusion of his book on the Golden Rule, Jeffrey Wattles points to the stakes in the collective work of this project. He writes, "The rule is an expression of human kinship, the most fundamental truth underlying morality."[14] In an age in which people across the planet encounter one another—both in person and electronically—with unprecedented concentration and intensity, and in which technology has made our capacity to inflict pain and death on one another easier than ever before, and in which engagement with difference is an unavoidable and often uncomfortable fact of everyday life, understanding the nature of our "human kinship" is an essential activity of mind and spirit. To such activity, nothing could be more relevant than the critical study of the Golden Rule.[15]

[14] Wattles, p. 188.
[15] I am grateful to Stephen Sapp, Michael McCullough, Irene Koukios, and Dexter Callender—all colleagues at the University of Miami—for helpful criticism and conversation. My thanks also go to Eugene Genovese for good counsel and wise perspective.

Chapter 2

The Golden Rule in Ancient Israelite Scripture

Baruch A. Levine
Emeritus, New York University

The Hebrew Bible on human cognition

For their part, the ancients knew relatively little about the neurological functions of the brain. In fact, there is no term for "brain" in the Hebrew Bible. The Hebrew word *mōaḥ*, which came to mean "brain" in postbiblical Hebrew, occurs only once in the Hebrew Bible, in Job 21.24, within the phrase "and the marrow of his bones" (*ûmōaḥ 'aṣmôtâw*, and cf. the related term *mēḥîm* "fatty (animals)" in Ps. 66.15). In the biblical mentality, it was the heart, Hebrew *lēb, lēbāb*, and also other internal organs such as the kidneys and the liver, which were variously identified as seats of both emotion and cognition. Very often in Biblical Hebrew usage, words for "heart" are best taken to mean "thoughts, feelings." It is the heart that either "knows" (the Hebrew verb *yāda'*) or fails to know what is right and what is wrong. Similarly, Hebrew *nepeš*, the word usually translated "soul" more accurately means "breathing mechanism, esophagus," and *pars pro toto* "the person, the life," even "feelings." Hebrew *nepeš* likewise locates the center of emotion and thought in the upper thorax, and neck, not in the cranium. One could also cite the transactions on the Hebrew word *rûaḥ* "wind, spirit" in the same vein.

It is true that certain organs located in the head have a role in human behavior. Thus, the eyes either perceive or fail to perceive, just as the ears either heed or fail to heed. Thus, Deut. 29.3:

> And yet, Yahweh has not given you a heart to know, nor eyes to see, nor ears to hear until this very day.

Or, Isa. 6.10:

> Encase the "heart" of this people with fat, stop-up his ears, and avert his eyes, lest seeing with his eyes and hearing with his ears, he will (also) discern with his "heart"; then repent, and heal himself.

I dwell on the above facts of language because the best method of investigating biblical notions of human behavior is precisely, to follow the philological trail. It is the human mind, represented as the heart, which most often accounts for human behavior, especially in the ethical dimension, where choice and decision are crucial. To illustrate usage of Hebrew *lēb, lēbāb* to connote thought and emotion in the process of balancing between aggression and ethical conduct we had best examine two paraphrases on human behavior in the flood narratives of Genesis. They explain that God had decided to undo his creation because of violence by humans (and animals!), which had overrun the earth. Thus, Gen. 8.21:

> Then Yahweh said in his thoughts (lit. "to his heart"): I will never again curse the earth on account of the human being, for the predisposition (*yēṣer*) of the "heart" of the human being is evil from his youth; (therefore), I will never again destroy all living things as I have (now) done.

Cf. the slightly expanded statement in Gen. 6.5–6:

> Then Yahweh saw that the evil (perpetrated) by the human being is extensive, and that the entire predisposition (*yēṣer*) of his "heart's" intentions is only evil all day long. So, Yahweh regretted that he had made the human being on the earth, and he became agitated in his "heart."

So, first off, we note that God also has a heart, which is also the seat of his cognition! The key term is Hebrew *yēṣer*, usually translated "inclination" which has here been rendered "predisposition." In Hebrew, the verb *yāṣar* means "to form, mold," and the noun *yôṣēr* actually means "potter, one who molds" (Isa. 29.16, 64.7). Like a potter, God molded the human being from earth. On this basis, *yēṣer* would mean "something molded," and when the Bible says that the human being possesses a *yēṣer* it is saying that he is formed so as to behave in a certain way that this is his "makeup," hence: "predisposition." Another expressive translation would be "temperament," taken to mean a sustained pattern of traits. This is perhaps the closest we come in biblical literature to the notion of the innate or genetic. To put it in neuropsychological terms, God spared Noah from extinction because Noah had balanced his aggressive *yēṣer* with his moral instinct; he was *ṣaddîq tāmîm* "faultlessly just" (Gen. 6.8).

The narrative of the Garden of Eden (Gen. 2.4–3.24) also comes to mind. It is replete with toned-down mythological themes and has been interpreted in diverse ways, so that any particular line of interpretation inevitably omits alternative possibilities. In the present context, we can see this tale as an etiology on human nature, intended to explain how the human animal came to be as we humans are. More specifically, how is it that human beings became capable of knowing the difference between good and evil, a way of saying that we possess a "moral instinct?"

God had planted a garden with beautiful trees, including the tree of knowledge (Hebrew *da'at,* from the verb *yāda'* "to know"), and the tree of life (Gen. 2.9). Note the admonition to Adam, before Eve had been constructed from his rib:

> Then Yahweh-Elohim commanded the human being (=Adam) as follows: Of every tree of the garden you may surely eat. However, from the tree of knowledge of good and evil you may not eat, for on the day you eat from it you shall surely die. (Gen. 2.16–17)

Later, after woman had been created, the two creatures disobeyed God's command, and ate of the forbidden fruit. In the course of tempting them, the snake had the following to say:

> Then the snake said to the woman: You most assuredly will not die. It is only that the Elohim knows that on the day you eat from it your eyes will be opened so that you will become like Elohim (or: "like divine beings"), knowing good and evil (*yōd'ê ṭôb wāra'*). Gen. 3.4–5

Once again, the eyes have a role in human behavior; opening the eyes becomes a way of describing awareness. It is as though the eyes receive a message and transfer it to the "heart." This is exactly what happened, as we read further in Gen. 3. The point of the tale is that the human creature was initially animal-like, able only to obey or disobey and to be tempted by lovely appearances, but unable to make judgments as to right and wrong. Previously, the two humans had seen the tree's enticing beauty; but now that their eyes were opened, they perceived the effects of eating its fruit. We are to understand that the outcome of the story places the human creature only slightly below the divine, to paraphrase Ps. 8; humans are mortal like animals, but possessed of "knowledge" like Elohim. They know right and wrong and are capable of fulfilling the Golden Rule.

The classic, biblical formulation of the Golden Rule

Biblical pronouncements on fairness and reciprocity show the Golden Rule to be complex in its realization. It generates spirals of action and reaction, rewards and penalties, and hardly simplifies human behavior. This is true of the covenant relationship between Israel and God, so often characterized as turbulent and disappointing. Perhaps the clearest paradigm of reciprocity in the Hebrew Bible is the vow, Hebrew *neder,* a conditional, covenantal agreement between an individual Israelite and his God, usually with cultic accompaniments. As expected, reciprocity is an active principle of biblical law, a predicate of justice, and a tenet of wisdom. The virtues of fairness pervade the biblical ethos. It was decided, therefore, to focus on selected epitomes, of diverse types, which provide insight into the applications of the Golden Rule in the Hebrew Bible. We begin by examining the formal statement of reciprocity, the positive commandment: "Love your fellow as yourself," in Hebrew: *we'āhabtā lerē'akā kāmôkā* (Lev. 19.18). It is the comparative "as yourself, equal to yourself" that conveys the notion of reciprocity, and we will observe elsewhere that the prefixed, comparative particle, Hebrew: *k-*, regularly appears in statements to the same effect. To understand the import of this statement we must put it in context.

Leviticus 19 opens with the words: "You shall be holy, for I, the Lord your God, am holy." This mandate is addressed to the entire community of Israel, and expresses what in theological circles is known as *imitatio dei* "emulation of God." The chapter then proceeds to specify what the Israelites, individually and collectively, are instructed to do so as to fulfill the commandment to be holy, and in the process, presents a portrait of a holy community. Leviticus 19 is the centerpiece of what is known as the Holiness Code, consisting of Lev. 17–27. In its entirety, the Holiness Code is one of three, major collections of laws in the Torah, the earliest being the Book of the Covenant (Exod. 20–23). At that point, disagreement arises as to whether the Deuteronomic code (Deut. 12–28, also with additions) or the Holiness Code comes next. It is the view taken here that Leviticus is a response to Deuteronomy, which preceded it, and that the Holiness Code is a primary statement of priestly law composed in the postexilic period beginning in the late sixth century B.C.E. It reflects the situation of the restored Jewish community in the Land of Israel during the Achemenid-Persian period after the end of the Babylonian Exile, when Cyrus, the Great, in 538 B.C.E. had issued a charter granting the Judeans the right to rebuild their temple in Jerusalem.

In its totality, the Holiness Code outlines the priestly agenda, and at times incorporates earlier legal and social norms, often paraphrased, while also innovating and reforming law and worship. It opens with a statement on the proper sacrificial worship of the God of Israel (Lev. 17), followed by regulations governing the family (Lev. 18 and 20), and affecting the priesthood (Lev. 21). These are followed by a festival calendar (Lev. 23), and by laws of land tenure, indebtedness, and taxation within a temple-centered institutional structure (Lev. 25 and 27). Additional particulars are dealt with elsewhere in the Holiness Code. Within this larger framework, Lev. 19 functions as a mini-Torah covering areas of activity that concern the entire community, not only the priesthood. At least six of the Ten Commandments are resonated in Lev. 19, a feature already noted in the Sifra, an ancient Midrash on Leviticus.

Leviticus 19 is quite clearly a compilation, at times repetitious and resumptive, wherein cultic dictates alternate rather abruptly with ethical imperatives. In the first category, we find emphasis on the banning of idolatry and forms of divination and magic associated with paganism. The ethical material, which predominates, is presented in clusters of divine dictates, each ending with the declaration: `*anî YHWH* "I am Yahweh," or a longer form "I am Yahweh, your God." The first series of ethical-legal statements covers verses 11–12; the second, verses 13–14; the third, verses 15–16; and the last in this part of the chapter covers verses 17–18. It is in verse 18 that the commandment to love one's neighbor occurs, and one has the impression that this statement was intended to cap the preceding clusters, all the way back to verse 11. Thus, Lev. 19.11–18:

> You shall not steal; you shall not deal deceitfully or falsely with one another. You shall not swear falsely by my name, profaning the name of your God. I am Yahweh. You shall not defraud your fellow (*rē̄ʿakā*) . You shall not commit robbery. The wages of a day-laborer shall not remain with you until (the next) morning. You shall not curse the deaf, or place a stumbling block in front of the blind. You shall be in fear of your God; I am Yahweh. You shall not render an unfair judgement; do not favor the poor or show deference to the rich; judge your neighbor (*ʿamîtekā*) equitably. Do not deal basely with your kinsman. Do not profit by the blood of your fellow (*rē̄ʿakā*); I am Yahweh. Do not hate your kinsfolk in your heart. Reprove your neighbor so that you will not incur guilt on his account. You shall not take vengeance or bear a grudge against your kinsfolk Love your fellow (*rē̄ʿakā*) as yourself. I am Yahweh.

The terminology alternates between kinship terms and those we might call "social terms." In the kinship group we find Hebrew `aḥ "brother, kinsman," and *ʿam* "kinsfolk, clan, people." The social terms are *rē̄ʿa* "fellow, associate, companion," a positive term of wide distribution, and a second term that is virtually limited to Leviticus, namely, (*ʿamît*) "neighbor" literally, a person whom one regularly encounters. It is the term *rē̄ʿa* that commands our attention in particular. Although it is not a kinship term it applies in the present context only to Israelites—a conclusion that is not necessitated by etymology, but rather indicated by usage in all three law collections in the Torah. These texts are all addressed to the Israelites, specifically, and their prescriptions are binding only on Israelites. I stress the social context of Hebrew *rē̄ʿa* because it is the key to understanding what comes later on in Lev. 19.33:

> And if a resident alien (Hebrew *gēr*) should dwell with you in your land, you shall not wrong him. The *gēr* who dwells with you shall be to you as one of your own natives, and you shall love him as yourself (*we'āhabtā lô kāmôkā*), for you were resident aliens in the land of Egypt; I am the Lord, your God.

We note the same syntax, expressive of reciprocity, as obtained in the commandment applicable to fellow Israelites. If we backtrack to Lev. 19.9–10, we read that the gleanings of vines and farms must be left for "the poor and the *gēr*." So it is that if an enactment is meant to apply to non-Israelites as well, this must be made explicit. Hebrew *gēr* allows of diverse definitions, depending largely on context and perspective, but in Torah law it necessarily connotes a non-Israelite, and evokes the memory of when the Israelites were, themselves, aliens in Egypt, and had to rely on the rulers and native population for protection under the law. Leviticus 19 is just one of many sources that require care for, and fair treatment of non-Israelites who were attached to Israelite communities.

It would be worthwhile, at this point, to probe our understanding of the Hebrew verb `*āhab* "to love." It is only to be expected that verbs with this meaning in any language will exhibit far-ranging connotations. Closest to usage in Lev. 19 is Deut 10.17–19:

> For Yahweh, your God, is God of the gods, and Lord of the lords, the God who is great, heroic, and awesome; who does not show favoritism nor accept a bribe. He takes up the suit of the widow and orphan, and loves the *gēr*, giving him bread and clothing. You (too) shall love the *gēr*, for you were resident aliens in the land of Egypt.

The repeated references to the Egyptian experience (cf. Exod. 22.20) epitomize empathy, the placing of one's self in another's place, most clearly spelled out in Exod. 23.9, from the Book of the Covenant:

> Nor shall you oppress a *gēr*, for you know (*yedaʿtem*) the feelings (*nepeš*) of the *gēr*, since you were resident aliens in the Land of Egypt.

To love someone, in these terms, means to be kind and caring, and to be fair. It should strike us as significant that in the very commandment to love the resident alien the Torah is mandating reciprocity; the Israelites might have perished as a group had the Egyptians not granted them the basics of life, at least for a time. In effect, an Israelite who did what the Holiness Code prescribed, and avoided doing what it prohibited, was acting with love toward his fellow Israelite and toward the resident alien as well. The list of "do's and don't's" in Lev. 19.11–18 (resumed with some interruptions in Lev. 19.26–36) effectively defines reciprocity by example, and teaches that a holy community is one in which the expectation of fairness is fulfilled.

Some epitomes of reciprocity in biblical literature

The theme of reciprocity in biblical literature can be traced in several ways, both as regards relations on the human level, and as a factor in the human-divine encounter. This theme is pervasive, and cuts across all literary genres and agendas. Very often, key concepts will be conveyed by specific terms of reference so that an exploration of the language of reciprocity will lead us to an understanding of how it was perceived.

Biblical narratives

Stories told and retold often reveal more about the ethos of a society than its laws and formal beliefs. Here we will contrast two narratives, each of which embodies notions of reciprocity, but in different ways: the story of Ruth (in the Book of Ruth), and the Joseph Cycle (in Gen. 37.39–50). Both of these narratives address multiple themes, to be sure, but the principle of reciprocity which operates drives them quite noticeably. The story of Ruth epitomizes the blessings of kindness; in Hebrew *ḥesed*. Simply put, it is a story in which kindness shown by one human being to another is warmly reciprocated, by the other person and by God. The Joseph Cycle, in contrast, shows how the expectation to be treated fairly, when it meets with disappointment, can morph into anger and vengeance. Joseph retaliates to the limit against his brothers until both he and they come to realize how close they were to tragedy. At that point, Joseph, the originally aggrieved party, desists, after his brothers confess their guilt. Reciprocity had run its course!

The story of Ruth

Ruth was a Moabite woman married to a Judean from Bethlehem, named Elimelekh, who had migrated to Moab with his family during a famine. Later, when her Judean mother-in-law, Naomi, decided to return from Moab to Bethlehem after her husband and two sons had all died, Ruth returned with her, pledging never to leave her. This was Ruth's first act of *ḥesed*:

> Wherever you go, I shall go, and wherever you lodge, I shall lodge. Your kinsfolk are my kinsfolk, and your God is my God. Wherever you die, I shall die, and there shall I be buried. Thus and more may Yahweh do to me if anything but death separates me from you. (Ruth 1.16–17)

With her sons gone, there would have been no way for Naomi to secure the continuity of her family or to hold on to her late husband's estate, but with Ruth returning with her there was a chance. Ruth could marry a Judean and bear children who would carry on the "name," which is what eventuated, after all.

Enter Boaz, a family relative, who showed *ḥesed* to Ruth from the outset. Both as a *gōʾēl* "restorer," whose duty it is to redeem family land and keep it in the family, and undoubtedly as a romantic figure, Boaz maneuvers affairs so as to marry Ruth. Here is a bit of dialogue between Boaz and Ruth:

> Then she (= Ruth) said to him: "How is it that I have found favor in your eyes, since I am (only) a foreign woman?" Then Boaz replied, saying to her: "I have been duly informed of all that you have done for your mother-in-law after

your husband's death; how you abandoned your father and mother and the
land of your birth, and came to a people whom you did not know before. May
Yahweh fully pay the reward of your deeds (*yešallēm YHWH po'alēk*), and
may your recompense be complete from Yahweh, God of Israel, under whose
wings you have sought shelter." (Ruth 2.10–12)

The key term in this exchange is the Hebrew noun *po'al*, whose meaning is
subtle. It often comes as the object of *šillēm* "to pay out," as here, and as such,
connotes both "act , deed," and "the consequence of the deed"—either reward
(as in the present case) or more often in biblical usage—punishment (conceived
as the inevitable consequence of misdeeds). In other words, it expresses reciprocity on both the human-to-human level, and in the human-divine encounter, and is central to the wisdom tradition (Jer. 50.29, Prov. 24.10, 29–and see
further). The story of Ruth expresses the symmetry between human and divine
kindness, as if to say that God also holds to the Golden Rule!

The Joseph cycle (Gen. 37, 39–50)

The cycle of stories about Joseph and his brothers is the closest we come to a
prose novel in biblical literature. The plot centers on vengeful reciprocity on
the human level, as the unwitting actors play out the roles assigned to them by
a watchful deity who has his own agenda. As the plot "thickens" there are
repeated incidents of reciprocity. The brothers set the process in motion by
punishing Joseph for his egocentric dreams and disloyal behavior; they sell him
into slavery in Egypt. Although Judah and Rueben (symbolizing southern Judah
and Northern Israel, respectively) intervened to prevent fratricide, the separa-
tion of Joseph from his family, and the lies told about his fate, aggrieve the
Patriarch, Jacob, so that reciprocity has already exceeded proportionality. The
effects of action and reaction by the brothers on their father are repeatedly
emphasized, making the point that vengeful reciprocity often outpaces its
intended targets, and harms third parties as well (Gen. 37).
    Meanwhile, in Egypt, while in the household of the royal courtier, Potiphar,
Joseph spurns the sexual advances of the courtier's wife. Here is what Joseph
says to her:

Behold! My lord knows nothing about how I manage the household, and he
has placed everything he owns under my control. There is no one greater in
this household than I, and he has denied me nothing except for you, in that
you are his wife. How, then, could I commit this great evil by sinning against
God? (Gen. 39. 8–9)

To betray a trust is not only a sin against others, it is a sin against God. Joseph
remains committed to fairness, both out of pragmatic considerations, no doubt,

but also out of regard for mutuality. As a result, God is with him, so that even when he is not believed and is falsely imprisoned, he fairs well. Soon after, Joseph brought closure to the two courtiers imprisoned with him by interpreting their dreams, which was an act of kindness on his part. For two years, however, his kindness was forgotten but then, the courtier whom Pharaoh spared just as Joseph had predicted, recalled the wisdom of the Hebrew youngster and recommended him to Pharaoh, who had just experienced frightening dreams of his own. The rewards of reciprocity are often slow in coming, but soon thereafter, Joseph was appointed viceroy over all Egypt as that country prepared for the oncoming famine (Gen. 39–41).

Returning to the primary plot of the Joseph Cycle, we see the brothers engaging Joseph under radically different circumstances, as the once spurned brother begins his cycle of "payback," of vengeful reciprocity. Without reviewing all of the interactions in the story, we can refer to key points as the brothers make repeated trips to Egypt to purchase grain. The brothers bow down before Joseph in fulfillment of his dreams (see Gen. 42.6). When Joseph, unrecognized by his brothers, orders them to bring Benjamin with them next time they come for grain, here is what they say to one another after pleading unsuccessfully with Joseph:

> Then they said to each other: We are truly culpable in the matter of our brother, when we perceived his inner anguish as he pleaded with us, but did not take heed. It is for this reason that all of this anguish has come upon us. (Gen. 42.21)

In a punitive frame of mind, Joseph even accuses the brothers of breaking reciprocity by stealing objects of value. Here is what his men are to say to the brothers when they catch up with them: "Why have you repaid (*šillamtem*) evil in place of good?" (Gen. 44.4)

After successive acts of vengeance, Joseph finally broke down and was reconciled with his brothers. In the several exchanges that took place in the interim, the effect of Joseph's cruel actions on their father, Jacob, is referred to repeatedly. To lose Benjamin after believing that he had lost Joseph would be too much for the old Patriarch. The reader agonizes as Joseph persists in tormenting his brothers, time after time, by threatening to hold Benjamin hostage so that we cannot miss the point. Just as they had sought to separate Joseph from his father and family, so was he now seeking to separate Benjamin (Gen. 43–44).

The chain of vengeful reciprocity is broken when Joseph reveals his identity to his brothers. This is part of what he says:

> Now then, be not distressed, or reproach yourselves for having sold me here, for God sent me as a life-sustaining force in advance of you . . . Now, then, it is not you who sent me here, but rather God. (Gen. 45.5, 8)

The theme of forgiveness is repeated later on, after Jacob's death, when the brothers feared that Joseph would once again try act to avenge himself against them. When Joseph's brothers learned that their father had died, they said to each other:

> "What if Joseph still bears a grudge against us, and surely repays us for all the evil that we paid him (`ašer gāmalnû `ôtô)?" Then they sent a message to Joseph as follows: "Your father left instructions before his death as follows: 'So shall you say to Joseph: Please! Pardon the sin of your brothers and their offense, for they repaid you (kî gemālûkā) evil.' Now, then, pardon the sin of the servants of the God of your father." (Gen. 50.15–17)

The Hebrew verb *gāmal* "to pay, repay" connotes reciprocity. It is on this basis that it often assumes the meaning "to repay"—both out of a sense of indebtedness, and out of a desire to penalize or retaliate. Thus, Prov. 3.30:

> Do not dispute with another person without cause, if he has done nothing to harm you (`im lo' gemālekā rā'āh).

In other words, do unto others as they have done unto you! Usage of Hebrew *gāmal* suggests that the recipient of the kindness (or the harmful act) deserves it, and what is more, it may at times imply that the kindness done to a person exceeds just deserts; that it was granted out of love or compassion (e.g. Isa. 63.7). In fact, the virtuous wife of Prov. 31.12 may be a case in point: "She repaid him with goodness (gemālathû ṭôb), not evil, all the days of her life." Thus, Ps 103:10:

> He (=God) has not dealt with us according to our offenses (kaḥaṭṭā'ênû), nor has he repaid us (gāmal 'ālênû) according to our sins (ka'awônōtênû).

A *quid pro quo* calculation pursuant to the Golden Rule would have left us much worse off! A cognate of Hebrew *gāmal* is Akkadian *gamālu* which, in its verbal forms, is consistently irenic and beneficent "to be obliging, to perform a kind act, to come to an agreement" (*Chicago Assyrian Dictionary*, vol. 5, "G" 21–23). Both Hebrew and Akkadian attest nominal derivatives, Hebrew *gemûl*, and Akkadian *gimillu*, and related forms. (For Akkadian see *Chicago Assyrian Dictionary*, vol. 5, "G" 73–75.) More often than not, Akkadian *gimillu* bears a positive connotation, namely, "an act of kindness," but in the combination *gimilla turru* literally: "to return the act, repay" it assumes a negative connotation: "to wreak vengeance." This is semantically equivalent to Hebrew *hēšîb gemûl* "to return payment, to repay," namely, "to punish reciprocally, to avenge" (Ps. 28.4, 94.2; Prov. 12, 14; Lam. 3.64; etc.). In Hebrew generally, *gemûl* more often than not bears a negative connotation, and serves to expose the downside of reciprocity. Thus it is that the Joseph Cycle, like the story of Ruth, epitomizes reciprocity and utilizes key biblical terms of reference that convey this principle, in both its positive and negative effects.

Reciprocity in the wisdom tradition

Upholding the Golden Rule: wise counsel

Do not withhold good from one who deserves it, when you have the power to do it (for him). Do not say to your fellow (*lerēʿakā*): "Come back again; I'll give it to you tomorrow," when you actually have it with you. Do not devise harm against your fellow (*rēʿakā*) who lives trustfully with you. Do not quarrel with a person for no cause, when he has done you no harm. Do not envy a lawless person, or choose any of his ways. For the devious person is an abomination to Yahweh, but he bonds with the straightforward (*yešārîm*). The curse of Yahweh is upon the house of the wicked, but he blesses the abode of the righteous. At scoffers, he scoffs; but to the humble—he is gracious. (*Prov. 3.27–34*)

This passage resonates with the Golden Rule of Lev. 19. It speaks of the proper treatment of one's *rēʿa*, urging the proverbial disciple to avoid doing quite precisely what the Holiness Code forbids. Of particular interest is the contrast drawn between various sorts of evildoers, and "the upright, straightforward" (*yešārîm*), a characterization often associated with fairness toward others.

God holds to the Golden Rule

Therefore, thoughtful men, listen to me: Wickedness is anathema to El, and wrongdoing to Shaddai. For he (*=God*) fully pays a person the reward of his deeds (*pōʿal ʾādām yešallem lô*), and according to the conduct of a man he provides for him. For El does not act wickedly, and Shaddai does not pervert justice. (*Job 34.10–12*)

The belief that God will repay us according to our just desserts is here stated in wisdom terms, as a reasonable expectation. It comes as a response to the cynic, who has just been quoted as saying: "Man gains nothing by being in God's favor" (Job 34. 9). The speaker reassures us that this is not so; that man can count on God's fairness, stated in the well-known reciprocal terms.

A rite of entry: The ethical agenda of Psalm 15

Yahweh! Who may sojourn in your tent; who may dwell on your holy mountain? One who conducts himself innocently, and who acts justly, and acknowledges the truth in his heart. He has no slander on his tongue; he does no evil to his fellow (*lerē ʿēhû*), nor has he ever borne disgrace (for acts) against his neighbor. For whom a contemptible person is abhorrent, but who honors those who fear Yahweh. Who does not renege on his oath even when it has turned to his disadvantage. He does not lend his silver at interest, nor accept a bribe against the innocent. One who does these things shall never falter!

A comparison of the virtues and transgressions enumerated in Ps. 15 with the provisions of Lev. 19 reveals, once again, how this cultic declaration of innocence resonates with the Golden Rule. It details the mandates of reciprocity, as well as its breaches.

A plea for the punishment of those who violate the Golden Rule

1') Do not drag me along with the wicked, and with evildoers, who profess goodwill toward their fellows (*rē̂ êhem*), but have malice in their heart. Pay them back according to their acts (*kepo'alām*) and according to the evil of their deeds. According to their handiwork pay them; bring back on them their deserts (*gemûlām*). For they do not understand Yahweh's acts, nor his handiwork. May he tear them down, never to rebuild them. (*Ps. 28.3–6*)

The plea to be rescued from evildoers resonates with Lev. 19, in its usage of Hebrew *rē̂a* "fellow." The language of reciprocity is once again echoed by Hebrew *gemûl* "payback," and the noun form *pō'al* "deed, the consequences of a deed." Evildoers do not love their fellows!

2') How you boast of your evil, oh you (would-be) hero! El's kindness seems never to end! Your tongue plots mischief, like a sharpened razor that cuts furtively. You love (*'āhabtā*) evil more than good; the lie more than speaking truthfully. *[Selah]* You love (*'āhabtā*) all destructive words, treacherous speech. Surely, El will tear you down forever, he will break you and remove you from your tent. He will uproot you from the land of the living. (*Ps. 52.3–7*)

The resonance with Lev. 19 is to be found in repeated usage of the verb *'āhab* "to love." This person loves the wrong things! The emphasis on deceitful speech also resonates with Lev. 19, where many of the "don't's" refer to false and foul speech. God allows evildoers to persist for a while but punishes them in good time.

Covenant as a reciprocal bond

In no subject have we seen more progress during the twentieth century than in the investigation of the biblical covenant as a form of agreement between designated parties, both on the human level and in the human-divine encounter. The reader will find an informative summary of biblical covenant traditions by

Moshe Weinfield in: *Theological Dictionary of the Old Testament*, ed. G. J. Botterweck and H. Ringgren (Grand Rapids, MI: Eerdman's Publishing Company, 1975) vol. II, pp. 253–79, under: "*berith*," the most frequent Hebrew term for "covenant." Weinfeld presents extensive comparative information from ancient Near Eastern societies that reveals both the ramifications of covenant–enactment in the Hebrew Bible, and its forms and phenomenology.

Interest here is limited to the observation that on analysis, the essential, biblical covenant is reciprocal. It is structured around the fulfillment of mutually binding obligations, undertaken by the parties to the covenant. It bears mention that in some of its versions, the covenants between Yahweh and the people of Israel are declared to represent an unconditional commitment by the deity to the survival of his people, Israel. We read of *berît 'ōlām* "an eternal covenant" (e.g. Gen. 17.7–19, Exod. 31. 16), one never to be annulled. Genesis 15, which turns out to be a relatively late text, records a covenant in which Yahweh promises the land of Canaan to Abram and his descendants, with no stated conditions (see Gen. 15.18– 21). Such covenant promises are best understood as progressive adaptations, not as representative of the basic, reciprocal structure of the biblical covenant. To understand that structure it would be best to begin by reviewing several individual covenants recorded in Genesis as part of the Patriarchal Narratives, after which we will examine the Epilogue to the Holiness Code, preserved in Lev. 26.

Abraham and Abimelekh (Gen. 21.22–34)

In order to resolve a dispute over a well that had been taken over by Abimelekh's agents, Abraham and Abimelekh take an oath and "cut" a covenant between them. The formula *kārat berît* "to "cut" a covenant," harks back to symbolic physical acts of incision performed as a way of confirming the agreement. Previously, the two had an altercation involving Sarah, Abraham's wife, during which the Philistine had occasion to learn through fear that Abraham was protected by divine providence (Gen. 20). This text may be outlined as follows:

a. Abimelekh expresses goodwill toward Abraham, and bids Abraham take an oath of friendship to him and to his descendants: This is what he says:

> Therefore, swear to me here, by God, if (`im) you ever deal falsely with me or with my kith and kin; and that you will act toward me, and toward the land where you have sojourned, according to the (same) kindness (*kaḥesed*) that I have shown to you. Then Abraham said: "I will take the oath." (Gen. 21.22–23)

b. The text recapitulates, informing us that Abraham had aired a grievance to Abimelekh on the matter of the well that he, Abraham, had dug. Abraham was only a sojourner in Philistia, and reliant on the protection of the local ruler. For his part, Abimelekh protests that he knew nothing of the actions of his men in seizing the well, and that not even Abraham, himself, had ever complained about this before. At that point, the two cut a covenant, with Abraham offering sheep and cattle to Abimelekh as a gift of good will (Gen. 21.24–27).

c. In what appears to be a parallel account (Gen. 21.28–34) this incident turns etiological, explaining the name Beer Sheba as "the well of the "seven" of the swearing," a *double entendre* on the seven ewes that were set aside to celebrate the covenant, and on swearing the covenant oath (Hebrew *hiššābaʿ* "to take an oath").

Present concern focuses on the wording of the promissory oath, and on the comparative particle, prefixed *k-* in: *kaḥesed* "according to the (same) kindness." Abimelekh had released Abraham's wife out of obedience to God, and had showered gifts on Abraham, inviting him to continue his sojourn and now Abraham was gifting him and joining an alliance with him. What is clearly evident is that the pledges of the two parties to the covenant are regarded as reciprocal and conditional: "If (*'im*) you ever deal falsely" (Gen. 21.23)—the covenant is annulled!

Isaac and Abimelekh (Gen. 26)

Like father like son! Isaac perpetrates the same subterfuge on Abimelekh, who becomes aware that Rebekah is Isaac's wife, not his sister, as he observes the two of them making love. Just in the nick of time, Rebekah is released, but there remain issues regarding wells that cause continuous friction between the two camps, added to the fact that the land could not sustain so much sheep and cattle. Once again, the two chieftains cut a covenant between them:

> Then they said (= Abimelekh and his company): We see clearly that Yahweh has been with you, so we said: Let there be a sworn treaty (Hebrew *ʾālāh*) between (all of) us, between us and you, and let us cut a covenant with you. If (*ʿim*) you ever do any harm to us, seeing as we have not afflicted you, and seeing as we have always dealt kindly with you, then we shall send you away in peace. From now on, may you be blessed by Yahweh! Then he made them a feast, and they ate and drank. They arose early in the morning, and they swore to each other. Joseph sent them away and they parted from him in peace. (Gen. 26.28–32)

In this "couplet" of Gen. 21, we are introduced to the Hebrew term *ʾālāh* "sworn treaty," at times a synonym of *berît* (e.g. Deut. 29.11, Ezek. 16.59). It conveys a punitive nuance, alluding to what will happen if the covenant is violated.

Jacob and Laban (Gen. 31)

Against a background of subterfuge and deceit, Genesis 31 relates how Jacob escaped from his Aramean father-in-law, Laban, stealing away much of his livestock, along with his daughters, their children, and even the household, family gods, the teraphim. This happened after Jacob had outwitted Laban on the distribution of livestock claimed by Jacob as compensation for his years of service to him. Laban pursues Jacob and overtakes him in flight, threatening to wipe him out. The two exchange hostile accusations and make irreconcilable claims, and then, to our surprise, Laban offers to cut a covenant with Jacob instead of going to war:

> "Now, then, let us cut a covenant (*berît*), I and you, and let it serve as witness between me and you." Then Jacob took a stone and erected it as a stele. Jacob then said to his kinsmen: "Gather up stones," and they took stones and made a mound. Then they feasted there, at the mound. Laban called it "mound of testimony" [in Aramaic], whereas Jacob called it "mound of witness" [in Hebrew] ... (And as for the name) Mizpah, it is because he (=Laban) said: "May Yahweh monitor between me and you whenever we are out of sight of each other. If ('im) you ever abuse my daughters, or if (*we'im*) you ever take wives additional to my daughters. Though no one is here with us, beware! For God is a witness between me and you. . . . This mound is a witness, and this stele is a witness that I will not cross over to you past this mound, and that you will not cross over to me past this mound and stele with hostile intent. May the God of Abraham and the God of Nahor judge between us, their ancestral God." Then Jacob swore by the deity revered by his father, Isaac. Then Jacob prepared a sacral feast and invited his kinsmen to eat bread. They partook of bread, and spent the night on the mountain. (Gen. 31.44–54, with omissions)

This unusually elaborate narrative has a busy agenda, with numerous themes interacting. It is an etiology of the land of Gilead, in Transjordan, justifying borders between the Arameans and the Israelites, and hence validating the Transjordanian Israelite settlement of Gilead. Present concern focuses on the reciprocity that informs the treaty between Jacob and Laban, who are eponyms of the Israelites and Arameans, respectively. This passage introduces us to the importance of witnessing in covenant enactment, in addition to that of the covenant oath. God is witness when there are no human witnesses. At the same time, the emphasis on commemorative monuments brings us into the discipline of archeology.

The epilogue to the Holiness Code (Lev. 26): A priestly rendition of the covenant between Yahweh and Israel

For a literary-historical analysis of Lev. 26, the reader may wish to consult my interpretation of this text in: *The JPS Torah Commentary, Leviticus* (Philadelphia: Jewish

Publication Society, 1989); Excursus 11, 275–281: "A Priestly Statement on the Destiny of Israel." In its literary context, the Epilogue is addressed by Yahweh to the Israelites as they were about to enter the Promised Land, warning them that their right to the land was contingent on obedience to his commandments. Historically, it is best dated to the period of the Babylonian Exile and the early period of the return, in the late sixth century B.C.E. In effect, it is an explanation of the exile, *ex eventu.*

It is possible to show, based on earlier studies by H. L. Ginsberg, that as the Babylonian Exile progressed, and the prospect of return to the Israelite homeland seemed remote, the original version of the covenant promise was adapted so as to allow the exiles to hold onto their hopes. Of interest here is the primary Epilogue (Lev. 26.3–33a, 37b–38) which is a paradigm of the binary contrasts of blessing and curse, between the bountiful effects of obedience to the covenant versus violation of it, and a phased escalation of punishments if Israel persists in its disobedience. Here is how the blessing is presented:

> If (`*im*) you follow my laws and faithfully observe my commandments, I will grant your rains in their season, so that the earth shall yield its produce and the trees of the field their fruit . . . and you shall eat your fill of bread, and dwell securely in the land. I will grant peace in the land, and you shall lie down with none to threaten . . . You shall give chase to your enemies, who will fall before you by the sword . . . I will turn to you in favor, and make you fertile and cause you to multiply. I will fulfill my covenant (*berîtî*) with you . . . I shall establish my residence in your midst, and I will not reject you. I will continually walk in your midst. I will be your God, and you will be my people. I am Yahweh, your God, who brought you out of the land of Egypt, no longer to be their slaves. I broke the bars of your yoke, and lead you forth at full stature. (Lev. 26.3–13 with omissions)

The curse projects the opposite prospect, and portrays what will happen if the Israelites persist in disobeying their God, and violate the covenant:

> But if (*we'im*) you do not heed me, and do not observe all these commandments, and if (*we'im*) you reject my laws, and spurn my judgments, so that you fail to perform all of my commandments, and you break my covenant. Then I, in turn, will do the following to you. (Lev. 26.14–16a)

The Epilogue projects an antiphonal litany of horrible consequences escalating the catastrophe as it proceeds. Every blessing has its accursed counterpart and there is symmetry to the binary contrast. It is just such symmetry that expresses reciprocity. How much more suffering would Israel have to endure before it could be restored to its land! The cycle ends only when Israel atones for its sins, at which time God, who had never given up on his people, will remember his covenant with the ancestors.

An afterword

What we call the Golden Rule is truly a pivotal principle in human behavior. Neuroscientists have shown great interest in the ethical dimension of human behavior, seeking to explain what leads certain people to harm others while others act to be of help to others. Formulations of the Golden Rule, both positive and negative, represent attempts to pinpoint what it is that we're after in life. Most of all, we want to be treated fairly; we expect reciprocity. What often escapes us is that reciprocity imposes responsibilities on the self as well as the other. By examining biblical epitomes and applications of reciprocity we become aware of what happens when human beings fail to live up to their responsibilities. We might as well admit the truth of what the Hebrew Bible illustrates. The Golden Rule works well for good people, but not so well for the selfish and unkind. "For the paths of Yahweh are straight; the righteous can walk on them, but the sinful stumble on them" (Hos. 14.10).

Chapter 3

Alternatives to the Golden Rule:
Social Reciprocity and Altruism
in Early Archaic Greece

Carolyn Dewald
Bard College

Call your friend to a feast, but leave your enemy alone; and especially call him who lives near you. . . A bad neighbor is an evil, as much as a good one is a great advantage. . . Take fair measure from your neighbor and pay him back well, with the same measure and better, if you can, so that when you need him afterward you may find him there for you.

Hesiod, Works and Days, 342–51 (Evelyn-White, modified)

I know the art of loving him that loves me, hating my hater and foulmouthing him with an ant's venom.

Archilochus fr. 23 (West)

But I do have one good skill, that's to repay whoever hurts me with a corresponding ill.

Archilochus fr. 126 (West)

Then may the great wide bronze sky fall on me from above—a terror to earthborn human beings—if I do not help those who love me, but vex and become a great pain to my enemies.

Theognis fr. 869–72 (Edmonds, modified)

Zeus grant I may repay my friends . . . and even more my enemies. I'd feel then like a god on earth, could I but get revenge before my appointed death-day comes.

Theognis fr. 337–40 (West, modified)

Grant me that I have fortune from the blessed gods, and good repute from all men all the time; may I be sweet to my friends, bitter to my foes, honored on sight by the former, and, for the latter, fearful to see.

Solon fr. 13 (West, modified)

That's what a man prays for: to produce good sons—a household full of them, dutiful and attentive, so they can pay his enemy back with interest and match the respect their father shows his friend.

Sophocles Antigone 641–44 (Fagles)

The injustice of these men only caused me a moderate annoyance, as I considered it ordained that one should harm one's enemies and serve one's friends.

Lysias IX.20 (Lamb)

All societies are based on some form of the principle of reciprocity; the word "society" itself is an Anglicization of the Latin word *societas*, the abstract noun formed from the stem *socius*, or "ally"—the person who is reciprocally able and willing to show up, who can be counted on to take my interests as well as his own into account.[1] In its very etymology, a society is formed on acts of mutual, responsive trust and generosity. I can count on my *socii*, and they can count on me in return. This is why we can as a species form stable communities that endure over a number of years.

As the quotations at the head of this chapter indicate, however, the ancient Greeks did not articulate the bonds of mutual trust and sociability that held their communities together in the form we know of as the Golden Rule. Not until Aristotle in the fourth century B.C.E. and then more fully the Epicureans and the Stoics in the couple of generations after him, did the idea of a generalized, reciprocal altruism, "do unto others as you would have them do unto you," even come into discussion as a possibility.[2] Much more common—in fact, pervasive in the culture—was the expectation that the whole point of social engagement was to reward one's friends and take revenge on those who had done one wrong.[3]

For the purposes of this volume, I think it would be of some interest to look closely not only at the various Greek philosophical articulations of altruism, as Professor Berchman has done, but also at the social practices that lay behind

---

[1] Socius is cognate to the Latin sequor, "follow," as in the English derivatives "sequence," or "consequence" (Watkins 74); an "ally" follows or gives allegiance to one's own männerbund or Indo-European warrior band. Much of the misogyny of early Greek and Roman culture comes from the fact that in such a structure women were often perceived as something men in the warrior band exchanged among themselves; they were usually not seen as participants in the act of reciprocal exchange. Penelope's role in the *Odyssey*, though, shows us that in practice women could be accepted in positions of authority and (often as representatives for absent menfolk) actively participate in their culture's complex web of social exchange.

[2] See further, Berchman (this volume); cf. Konstan (1997), pp. 108–14.

[3] Reciprocity as calibrated vengeance is known as the lex talionis, popularly "an eye for an eye, a tooth for a tooth," found in the Code of Hammurabi, and in the Hebrew Bible (Exod. 21.23–27, Lev. 24.18–20, Deut. 19.16–21).

and informed the expressions of both reciprocity and altruism found in the epic poetry of the earlier archaic era—at least insofar as the ancient extant literary evidence allows us to discern them—since these continued to shape basic Greek attitudes well into the later classical and Hellenistic eras. A literary description, even when it is the product of a traditional oral poetics, is not a transcript of social practices in the "real world." It give us rather a composite picture whose working background assumptions its original audiences would have been expected to find reasonable in themselves, and whose problems would have been of interest to them. As the corpus of extant archaic and classical literature makes clear, in practice the ancient Greeks recognized the value of both reciprocity and altruism; they did not, however, use the Golden Rule to articulate the practice of these values. Their different ways of construing both reciprocity and altruism obliquely puts into high relief some of the difficulties other cultures too might find in taking the Golden Rule seriously as a practical guide both in other times and in our own culture, in the here and now.

The Greek *polis* or city-state of the archaic and classical period (eighth through fourth centuries B.C.E.) was a development from the late Dark Age warrior culture that followed upon the collapse of the Mycenaean world. Homer's epics, the *Iliad* and the *Odyssey*, must have taken their final shape in approximately 750–700 B.C.E. Some controversy exists about whether a poet by the name of Homer brought the *Iliad* and *Odyssey* to their final form, or whether "Homer" was rather a quasilegendary stand-in for an ongoing oral tradition. Whatever the reality of Homer as a person, it is now generally accepted that the Homeric epics are neither an idealized fantasy picture of a world that never really existed nor a realistic representation of the world of the early city-state taking shape as the *Iliad* and the *Odyssey* assumed their final form. It is much more likely that the world they depicted reflected a general cultural background and some of the working customs and assumptions of the hundred-and-fifty-year period immediately prior to the creation of the archaic *polis*, that we call late Dark Age or early Iron Age Greece.[4]

The Homeric poems depict a stratified male warrior society organized roughly around regional clans, based on loose kinship ties. Their leadership was of the "chief" or even occasionally what is sometimes called the "big man" type.[5] (The difference between these two forms of prestate organization is that the

---

[4] See Donlan (1998), pp. 52–53, and (1999), pp. 1–34. Articulations of our evidence for Greek ethical values appeared earliest in literature (especially Homeric epic, but also lyric poetry) rather than in what we could call religious contexts per se; the gods in Greek thinking enforced community social values but did not embody or expressly generate them.

[5] van Wees (1998), pp. 42–44. See also Donlan (1999), pp. 249–64 for a fuller analysis of structures of authority in the Homeric poems. One of the most important aspects of suspense in the *Iliad* focuses on the conflict between the chief, Agamemnon, who has inherited his status, and the threat to group solidarity posed by the potential rival, Achilles, who is the superior warrior and leader and triumphs at the end (though at a terrible price), but also ultimately accepts Agamemnon's leadership.

"big man" must both earn his place of leadership and maintain it by continuing demonstration of his superiority in battle, in leadership skills, or in his ability to call in favors from those he has benefited in the past, whether these are his own followers or other leaders, that is, his peers. The "chief," on the other hand, represents a more developed form of social organization. Like Agamemnon or Hector in the *Iliad*, he has to some extent inherited a stable leadership structure. He must exhibit a basic competence to preserve his leadership role, but others in his group assume that the job is his, provided that he has not committed mistakes that put the group itself at risk.[6]) In both forms of tribal society of this type, there is no state, so no automatic institutional control of an authorized, legitimated violence. The chief or big man is expected to lead his men into battle successfully and to allot the spoils at the end fairly, in a way that effectively honors the efforts of everyone. If more than one chief is involved (as in the *Iliad*), careful regard for an equitable distribution of war booty is also expected between leaders.

In such prestate societies, reciprocity is the glue that maintains group cohesion, so it is of immense importance and often very precisely calibrated. Three different types of reciprocity at least bind together tribal societies similar to that described in the *Iliad* and the Odyssey. The most basic form Marshall Sahlins calls "balanced reciprocity," the principle that the Romans later gnomically represented with the tag *do ut des*, "I give so that you give," i.e., articulating a systematic quid pro quo.[7] Many of the poetic excerpts at the beginning of this paper articulate the importance of balanced reciprocity in Greek culture generally: in order to remain friends, I am fair to you, you are fair to me; we keep careful track of the running balance of favors done between us. But also in play, especially in the archaic age, is a second form, a "generalized reciprocity," often exhibited by a chief or big man when he rewards his followers not because of the need for a specific repayment but in order to insure continuing loyalty, and sometimes precisely to demonstrate his own position of leadership and continuing ability to control the distribution of goods. The systematic exercise of generalized reciprocity, when widely practiced in a culture, can become very diffuse, so that eventually it creates expectations that if I do a good deed in the present, someone else will in the indefinite future repay me. This can create over time a far-reaching net of reciprocity that in practice can begin to look like the operation of the Golden Rule: everybody flourishes when generosity reigns from the top down.[8] Danger to group cohesion comes, of course, when the third type,

---

[6] See below, note 11.

[7] Sahlins (1965/1972), pp. 193–96, cited by van Wees (1998), pp. 21–24; see also Donlan (1998), pp. 51–53.

[8] See Herman (1998), pp. 199–225 for the relevance of the Prisoner's Dilemma, and the superiority of the "tit for two tats" model of social interaction. See also van Wees (1998), p. 22: "(t)he more diffuse forms of indirect reciprocity include all sorts of behavior inspired by the injunction to do as one would be done by." But see also below, pp. 33–35.

"negative reciprocity," prevails, and the normally expected returns for a favor done are denied. This is the situation that determines the major plot line of the *Iliad*; at the beginning of the poem, Agamemnon's refusal to give the outstanding Greek warrior, Achilles, his due leads to Achilles' anger and consequent refusal to fight, so that the whole Greek cause at Troy is put at risk (1.122–244).

In a succinct description of the theory of prestate patterns of reciprocity, Hans van Wees states, "(t)he more central to a culture reciprocity is, the greater its impact in shaping identity and defining status."[9] It is interesting to see how thoroughly both the Homeric poems instantiate this observation—in effect, their plot lines explore ways in which traditional Greek patterns of reciprocity are anything but altruistic. Instead, they define and reinforce the power relations that exist among the various prominent warriors in the Trojan War in the *Iliad*, and among the band of men trying to return home from the Trojan War with Odysseus in the *Odyssey*. A second general observation is relevant here as well, before we turn to the poems themselves. Warriors must identify enemies and firmly oppose them; that is what they do. I put it out tentatively (this is not a topic whose issues I am in any sense expert in) that members of a society whose self-identity and status within the group was profoundly shaped around war-readiness and the need for loyal deployment against the enemy *could not have* thought about reciprocity and altruism in terms of the Golden Rule, at least as we articulate it. To begin with an obvious general point, thinking about others in terms of one's own feelings makes little sense in a culture in which to be an adult male means being part of one's tribal fighting force, doing one's duty, that is, subordinating one's own feelings, whatever they may be, to the need for group cohesion.[10]

The two long epic poems of Homer flesh out what I have so far presented as rather abstract sociological observations; they allow us to see more concretely how and why Greek culture did not use the Golden Rule as a basic ethical standard. In both the *Iliad* and the *Odyssey*, the men who would later become Greek citizens, that is, members of a *polis*, are still organized along tribal and military lines. In the *Iliad*, Priam's Troy is a city under attack from Agamemnon's loosely organized band of Greek chieftains (*basileis*) and their followers. On the Greek side the strategists, Nestor and Odysseus, keep the Greek troops remembering the necessity for their loyalty to Agamemnon. They know that if they do

---

[9] van Wees (1998), p. 30. The most extreme expression of this truth comes in a "potlatch" culture, where generalized reciprocity becomes conspicuous consumption and a ruinous competitive sport (van Wees, pp. 31–32).

[10] The idea of distrust of emotions and the need for a rational, disciplined control over them continued well into the classical period. Plato's image in the *Phaedrus* (253–54) of the soul as a charioteer (reason) managing the reins that guide the two horses of moral sensibility (the disciplined white horse) and emotions/base appetites (the unruly, out-of-control black horse) is a vivid, although elaborated, illustration of the earlier principle.

not stay united the ten-year effort will collapse, and even if they succeed in slinking home to Greece, they will find great difficulties there because of their loss of status and the resentment they will incur at home because of the lives lost of their fallen comrades.[11] At Troy, army discipline must be maintained; when Thersites, an ugly, crippled, and loudmouthed commoner, complains in Book Two about Agamemnon's leadership, Odysseus ruthlessly bludgeons him about the head and shoulders with humiliating language, and the onlookers, noble and commoners alike, laugh merrily (2.211–77).

On the Trojan side too, Hector is crown prince and army leader, but it is clear that he owes his position to his competence and ability to maintain order at least as much as to his status as eldest son of Priam. He must fight off the doubts, suspicion, and anger both of his own seer, Poulydamas, and of his Lycian allies (12.223–50, 13.726–40, 765–73, 17.140–68), not to mention his ongoing need to remind his feckless brother Paris of his martial responsibilities (6.326–31; 13.768–73). When Hector finally goes out to fight Achilles, after Patroklos' death has driven Achilles back into the Greek fighting force, Hector knows that he will probably die —as he tells his beloved wife Andromache earlier, on the walls of Troy in Book Six, "I would feel deep shame before the Trojans, and the Trojan women with trailing garments, if like a coward I were to shrink aside from the fighting . . . for I know this thing well in my heart, and my mind knows it: there will come a day when sacred Ilion shall perish, and Priam, and the people of Priam of the strong ash spear" (6.440–49).[12] Hector knows that he must remain an effective warrior and war leader or he must die in battle; no other option remains open to him.

The leader in such a society must lead; his followers, on the other hand, must follow. One basic theme of both the *Iliad* and the *Odyssey* is the high cost of refusing loyalty and obedience to the leader, against the enemy and in the face of manifold perils. In the *Iliad*, Achilles' refusal to fight almost costs the Greeks their victory and costs Achilles himself the loss of his dearest friend. In the *Odyssey*, Odysseus' men rebel on the return voyage home and his home is invaded by young local aristocrats who dishonor his wife and threaten his son. The result is that only Odysseus himself survives to homecoming, and on doing so he takes bloodthirsty, comprehensive revenge on the suitors.[13] Those who are in power exact loyalty and exert control over their inferiors. The justification for such social stratification into leaders and followers, aristocrats and

---

[11] Problems of the sort that, even in victory, will be experienced by Agamemnon and Odysseus on homecoming, as Aeschylus' *Agamemnon* and Homer's *Odyssey*, Book Twenty-Four, make clear; see also Donlan (1998), pp. 67–68.

[12] All translations of the *Iliad* in this paper are those of Richmond Lattimore (1951); the line numbers are Lattimore's but also generally correspond to those of the Greek text.

[13] The group tensions are well analyzed in Donlan (1998), pp. 58–67.

commoners is famously summed up by Sarpedon, the leader of the Lycians, talking to his second-in-command, Glaukos, in Book Twelve of the *Iliad*:

> Glaukos, why is it you and I are honored before others/with pride of place, the choice meats and the filled wine cups/in Lykia, and all men look on us as if we were immortals,/and we are appointed a great piece of land by the banks of Xanthos,/good land, orchard and vineyard, and ploughland for the planting of wheat?/ . . . (I)t is our duty in the forefront of the Lykians/to take our stand, and bear our part of the blazing of battle,/so that a man of the close-armored Lykians may say of us:/"Indeed, these are no ignoble men who are lords of Lykia,/these kings of ours, who feed upon the fat sheep appointed/and drink the exquisite sweet wine, since indeed there is strength/ of valour in them, since they fight in the forefront of the Lykians." (12.310–21)

What possibility is there for a generalized altruism in such a culture, so alert to the necessity for social stratification, and to the obligations of obedience from one's inferiors and tit-for-tat reciprocity among one's peers? Does it exist at all—the impulse to benefit others as human beings, without regard for inherited status obligations or the need at all times to assure appropriate reciprocal benefit for oneself? In the Homeric corpus, the space for this question is occupied by the figure of Achilles. Much of the tension of the *Iliad's* plot is connected to the picture of this one superlatively gifted warrior and his struggle to negotiate the constraints of his culture but also to escape their limitations. In Book One, Agamemnon has taken Achilles' beautiful war captive, Briseis, and has dishonored him in doing so. As Achilles tries to explain to his uncomprehending comrades in Book Nine, no amount of reciprocity, balanced or generalized, from Agamemnon can make up the injury already done to him—especially because he knows that if he returns to battle, his life will be demanded of him; his goddess mother has told him so (9.410–16). Because of the combination of these two things, the dishonor shown him by his commander-in-chief and the certainty of his own death if he joins the battle, Achilles begins in Book Nine to question the whole warrior ethos described here: what is the point of obedience to one's warlord or of a glorious death in battle? What is it all for? In asking these questions, Achilles also might be approaching what we would call an articulation of a form of the Golden Rule, that is, a more generalized altruism than that normally expressed in the world of the Homeric poems. Two passages in particular merit discussion in this context.

The first occurs in Book Twenty-One, where Achilles in his rage at Patroklos' death begins to slaughter everyone on the Trojan side he can find, including the unfortunate Lykaon, a young half-brother of Hector. Lykaon had just been home at Troy twelve days, after being captured earlier by Achilles and sold as a slave to Lemnos and then ransomed home to Priam (21.34–135). On Lykaon's first day back in battle he sees Achilles approach, falls to his knees, and begs for mercy, but Achilles refuses it with the following words (21.99–113):

> Poor fool, no longer speak to me of ransom, nor argue it/. . . Now there is not one who can escape death, if the gods send/him against my hands/. . . So, friend, you die also. Why all this clamour about it?/Patroklos also is dead, who was better by far than you are./Do you not see what a man I am, how huge, how splendid/and born of a great father, and the mother who bore me immortal?/Yet even I have also my death and my strong destiny,/and there shall be a dawn or an afternoon or a noontime/when some man in the fighting will take the life from me also/either with a spearcast or an arrow flown from the bowstring.

Achilles' rage in Book Twenty-One is not pretty, and his wholesale slaughter of the enemy becomes so disgusting that even the river Scamander revolts and rises up against him. But in his speech to Lykaon we discern a curious form of empathetic reciprocity in play as well. Achilles tells Lykaon that death is coming to all of them. If one puts this sentiment together with the words of Sarpedon to Glaukos in Book Twelve, a curious paradox emerges: it is the enemy, after all, who gives the warrior a heroic death and therefore the glory that is the compensation for death and the justification for an exalted social status. The fact that Achilles killed Lykaon is what gives Lykaon a place in the poem; one could not be an eminent warrior and receive a warrior's enduring glory without enemies to fight, who will perhaps kill one. In one sense, to be killed by an outstanding warrior is, precisely, to receive what that warrior would wish for himself; thus, as Achilles articulates it to Lykaon, the reciprocity entailed in a noble death in battle at points suggests an identification of self and other that is deeper than mere conventional reciprocity of either the balanced or generalized sort.[14] It is difficult to construe it as altruism, however—Achilles' speech to Lykaon has to do rather with reciprocal dignity and the respect extended to enemies, the men at whose hands one might die playing the cultural game as it must be played.

The second way that the figure of Achilles indirectly develops in the *Iliad* the theme of an empathetic reciprocity that might approach the Golden Rule has given rise to genuine controversy among Homeric scholars. In Book Twenty-Four, Achilles compulsively, day after day, drags Hector's body around the walls of Troy. Priam, Hector's aged father, is stirred up by the gods to drive a mule cart laden with gifts under cover of night to Achilles' tent and to beg for the body of his son so that he can give it an honorable burial. When Priam kneels before

---

[14] Part of Achilles' pathos is that he will not die at the hands of a worthy opponent but be shot in the heel by Paris' arrow, a fact alluded to but not explicitly narrated as part of the *Iliad* (22.358–60).

Achilles and kisses the hand of the man who has murdered his son (24.506), Achilles remembers his own father Peleus alone in Phthia and he joins Priam in grieving both for Peleus and for Patroklos, the dear friend Hector had killed. He gives Priam Hector's body back, carefully wrapped for burial, and also protects Priam from being taken for ransom by Agamemnon, urging him to eat, and then to sleep, in his own tent.

Are Achilles' actions in Book Twenty-Four a form of the unconditional altruism articulated in the Golden Rule? One set of scholars argues that in Book Twenty-Four, although Achilles is certainly moved by Priam's suffering, he is basically still engaged in his status contest with Agamemnon.[15] His generosity to the king of Troy, father of his fallen enemy, in this reading is primarily undertaken to demonstrate his own refusal of ties of dependency, since Achilles is here engaging in precisely the generalized reciprocity that is the privilege of a chief magnanimously distributing favors—favors that show his superior status and are the mark of his own power to give or deny gifts as he chooses, ignoring the claims of his putative commander-in-chief, Agamemnon. In Book Nine he has rejected the gifts that Agamemnon has tried to foist on him to induce him to return to fighting; in Book Nineteen, he has returned, but makes it clear that he only does so to avenge Patroklos and that he remains utterly indifferent to Agamemnon's gifts. In Book Twenty-Three, Achilles himself celebrates Patroklos' funeral games and in that context distributes gifts to the other Greek warlords, including even Agamemnon (23.890–94). One can speculate that in effect Achilles here becomes in fact, if not in theory, the leader of the Greek fighting force; he has triumphed over Agamemnon in the reciprocity game.

In this reading, when it is regarded as part of an elaborate early archaic sociology, Achilles' generosity to Priam in Book Twenty-Four is not so much a sign of empathetic altruism to an enemy as it is a continuing marker of his refusal of Agamemnon's leadership. Achilles is now beyond gifts, beyond reciprocity itself—he only accepts Priam's gifts for form's sake and to placate Patroklos' spirit (12.592–95):

> Be not angry with me, Patroklos, if you discover,/though you be in the house of Hades, that I gave back great Hektor/to his loved father, for the ransom he gave me was not unworthy./I will give you your share of the spoils, as much as is fitting.

He hides Priam's presence from Agamemnon and the other Greek leaders because, as he tells Priam, Agamemnon would complicate the release of Priam with Hector's body back to Troy (24.650–55). Achilles is now outside Agamemnon's sphere of influence, and in this reading his generosity to Priam is an extreme expression of this fact, not a critique of the culture of generalized

---

[15] See Postlethwaite (1998), pp. 93–104 and Gill (1998), pp. 312–13.

reciprocity per se. There is clearly something to this interpretation, especially because Achilles' heart has not entirely softened toward Priam, either, in Book Twenty-Four. He threatens the old man when he expresses eagerness to receive Hector's body (24.560–70), and he carefully does not let Priam see Hector's body as he loads it himself in the ox-cart, for fear Priam's grief would make him lose his own self-control and violate Zeus' laws of guest-friendship by abusing Priam, although he is a guest in Achilles' own tent (24.581–86).

My inclination, however, is rather to privilege the moment of Achilles' identification with Priam, bound as they are in shared suffering and grief, and to regard the other elements of competitive reciprocity rather as a realistic social backdrop to this transcendent climax of the poem.[16] In this second, alternative reading, the ethical heart of Book Twenty-Four is Achilles' sudden and empathetic acceptance of oneness with Priam, stirring in him "a passion of grieving for his own father" (24.501–08). Achilles goes on to tell Priam about the two urns that sit at Zeus' threshold that distribute blessings and ills to men. Human beings, he says, are never given only blessings; they are either given only evils or a mixture of evils and goods (24.527–33). He tells Priam about his own father, Peleus:

> There was not/any generation of strong sons born to him in his great house/ but a single all-untimely child he had, and I give him/no care as he grows old, since far from the land of my fathers/I sit here in Troy, and bring nothing but sorrow to you and your children./And you, old sir, we are told you prospered once . . . But now the Uranian gods brought us, an affliction upon you,/forever there is fighting about your city, and men killed./But bear up, nor mourn endlessly in your heart, for there is not/anything to be gained from grief for your son; you will never/bring him back; sooner you must go through yet another sorrow. (24.538–51)

Here, as in the passage from Book Twenty-One concerning Lykaon, it is the universality of death, but also of suffering and loss, that makes men, even enemies, brothers; so Achilles will give Priam what his own father in Phthia will not receive—his son's body back, for burial.

A large part of the *Iliad's* depth, I think, stems from a genuine doubleness of values that emerges in Book Twenty-Four. Both readings that we have explored can be sustained. Achilles does triumph in the reciprocity game, both in his refusal to accept the generalized reciprocity (the gifts and apology offered by Agamemnon) and also in demonstrating his own ability to extend it (independently and on his own) to the king of Troy, his enemy. Just as certainly, in Book Twenty-Four Achilles existentially refuses to buy into the elaborate web of

---

[16] See Zanker (1998), pp. 73–92 and the interesting discussion of the passage in Farenga (2006), pp. 95–108, in terms of what it says about developing Greek notions of individual selfhood.

self-interested reciprocity mandated by his culture, and because of the acknowl-edgment of his own heart's emotion, he extends compassion and something like the Golden Rule to Priam as a sorrowing father who has lost his son.

If we had to fix on one question about this complex of sociological patterns that is of particular relevance to a volume about the Golden Rule, it might be this: at what point, if any, does reciprocity of the sort exhibited by a chieftain like Achilles to Priam blend into altruism of the sort embodied in the Golden Rule? Part of the controversy over the meaning of Book Twenty-Four comes down to differing scholarly opinions on this issue. Those scholars who see Achilles as basically still working within the boundaries of his culture's ethics would say that the Golden Rule itself in archaic Greek culture only emerges insofar as it is a logical but extremely sporadic extension of the generalized reciprocity model, and that it has to do only with evanescent moments like that in which Achilles weeps with Priam. The scholars who, on the other hand, see the *Iliad* as testing (and perhaps even implicitly critiquing) the reciprocity rules of the late Dark-Age and early Archaic culture also see a model for *homonoia* or a more profound fellow-feeling emerging at the climax of the poem as it intro-duces ideas that will not perhaps be fully articulated until the time of Aristotle three centuries later. These ideas about empathetic reciprocity to one's enemy, however, inchoate as they are, clearly also play their part in the role the *Iliad* later assumes as a basic expression of Greek cultural values.

The basic attitudes toward reciprocity that I've described in detail as those of the Homeric poems continued to shape the values of the developing Greek city-states of the later archaic, classical, and Hellenistic worlds. In the Greek popu-lar morality of the later classical period, a *philos* or "intimate" was either someone in your family or a friend so closely bound by multiple ties of reciprocity that you had stopped keeping track of who owed whom what: the Homeric models would be Achilles' relation with Patroklos, for instance, or Odysseus' with Penelope. It was also generally true, as the quotations at the head of this paper suggest, that reciprocity among Greek male citizens continued at times to exhibit the tensions that prevailed between Achilles and Agamemnon. As the Hesiod quotation at the very beginning of the paper indicates, the emphasis remained on a basic usefulness to oneself underlying one's ties of *philia*. If, as Aristotle famously put it in Book Nine of the *Nichomachean Ethics* (1166a30), "a friend is another self"—then, one's deep self-interest is engaged in the act of benefiting a *philos*.[17]

Since even in the *poleis* of the classical period social services remained quite primitive by our standards, the need to reciprocate to one's friends was what assured that they in turn would be there for you—a crucial factor to assure your

---

[17] Berchman (this volume), note 5 and passim. Gill (1996) discusses a variety of scholarly argu-ments about what Aristotelean altruism means; he argues that ". . . other-concern intelligibly develops (though it does so in an ethical framework not centered on the egoism-altruism contrast)" (347).

well being when there was no police force, fire department, social service agencies, or welfare state. Similarly, feuds between powerful citizen-aristocrats continued, sometimes to toxic effect, right down into the world of the fourth-century Athenian orators. It was an important part of your arsenal as a citizen male not only that you return favors to friends but that you reciprocate for injuries and insults both to yourself and to your friends. The military foundation of citizenship continued, I think, to be significant here; even in the classical period, your right to call yourself a citizen was assured by your acceptance into your father's tribe or fighting unit within the city, and your capacity vigorously to defend yourself in word as well as in deed continued to be an important index of your civic standing. Regularly in fourth-century Attic oratory, your preexisting enmity against someone provided your explicit justification to the jury for bringing him to trial, even on an explicitly unrelated issue.[18]

Roughly the same rules prevailed among most Greek *poleis* or city-states as among individual citizens. Ties of *xenia*, or reciprocity among guest-friends from other cities, could be of long-standing consequence: the archaic and classical history of Sparta shows how firmly Spartan leaders conceived of their politics as a continuing exercise in helping their aristocratic friends in other cities assume or maintain an oligarchic control over their own fellow citizens. Xenophon, the fourth-century Athenian historian, was an admirer of Spartan values and Spartan ways; nonetheless, he makes it clear that one of his great heroes, Agesilaos, obeyed the injunction to help one's friends and harm one's enemies even when the friend was committing an outrageous, criminal injustice.[19] As Plutarch much later put it: "[Agesilaos] would not injure his enemies without just cause, but joined his friends even in their unjust practices. And whereas he was ashamed not to honor his enemies when they did well, he could not bring himself to censure his friends when they did amiss, but actually prided himself on aiding them and sharing in their misdeeds. For he thought no aid disgraceful that was given to a friend" (*Agesilaos* 5.1).

It would take too long here to consider in detail the developments from this archaic pattern that took place in fifth-century Athens, but I want to end by noting that in Athens, the city that gave birth to philosophy, things began to change. I would put the first significant signs of change with Solon, the sixth-century Athenian poet and politician who contributed one of the quotations about helping friends and harming enemies at the head of this paper. Many of Solon's poems go beyond the reciprocity/retribution model, however, and articulate instead a loyalty to the city and its laws that would transcend the archaic notions of reciprocity that we have been contemplating here:

This lesson I desire to teach the Athenians:/Lawlessness brings the city countless ills, while Lawfulness sets all in order as is due . . ./The commons I have

---

[18] E.g., Aeschines, *Against Timarchus* 2; see Konstan (2006), pp. 193–4 and notes 18 and 19.
[19] Missiou (1998), pp. 192–93.

granted privilege enough,/not lessening their estate nor giving more;/the influential, who were envied for their wealth,/I have saved them from all mistreatment too./I took my stand with strong shield covering both sides,/ allowing neither unjust dominance. (frr. 4–5, Lattimore)

It was in Athens that loyalty to the city's laws and to a concern for the well-being of all one's fellow citizens were broadly articulated as civic virtues—to the point that ties of aristocratic *xenia* or guest-friendship were discouraged and gifts between citizens were looked on with suspicion as signs of an attempt to exert a generalized reciprocity that meant one was trying to claim too much power over one's democratic fellow citizens and peers.[20]

Athens' attempts to articulate a democratic citizen solidarity were not perfect illustrations of the Golden Rule, as any city oppressed by her fifth-century empire would testify.[21] They were, nonetheless, an important step toward the concept of a world where everyone, friend or foe, fellow citizen or foreigner would receive some of the benefits of the ethical principle that we call the Golden Rule. As Pericles articulated it in Thucydides' Funeral Oration:

> We make friends by doing good to others, not by receiving good from them. This makes our friendship all the more reliable, since we want to keep alive the gratitude of those who are in our debt by showing continued goodwill to them: whereas the feelings of one who owes us something lack the same enthusiasm, since he knows that, when he repays our kindness, it will be more like paying back a debt than giving something spontaneously. We are unique in this. When we do kindnesses to others, we do not do them out of any calculations of profit or loss: we do them without afterthought, relying on our free liberality. Taking everything together then, I declare that our city is an education to Greece. (*Thucydides* 2.40).

As Prof. Berchman shows us, it is out of this city and the philosophical education it provided, that a philosophical ethics emerged that made thinkable a genuine, universal altruism extended to other human beings because they are human. But that is a longer, more complex story.

Acknowledgement

I would like to dedicate this paper to the memory of Walter Donlan, who over many years helped me understand the themes developed here; he is

---

[20] Missiou (1998), pp. 194–97. The basic study of *xenia*, guest-friendship, remains that of Herman (1987).

[21] The Mytileneans put it this way to the Spartans in 428, arguing that they were right to revolt from Athens' dominance: "In wartime they did their best to be on good terms with us because they were frightened of us; we, for the same reason, tried to keep on good terms with them in peace-time. . . in our case fear was the bond, and it was more through terror than through friendship that we were held together in alliance" (Thucydides 3.12).

much missed. His writings underlie every opinion I have on these issues, although he would argue with my articulation of some of them; see esp. Donlan (1999). Other fundamental works that form a general background to the ideas about reciprocity and altruism expressed here include Pearson (1962), Dover (1974), Herman (1987), Konstan (1997) and (2006), and Gill, Postlethwaite, and Seaford (1998). The articles in this last volume in particular have provided much of the stimulus for the current essay's arguments throughout; I also thank Nancy Felson for her acute observations on an earlier draft.

Chapter 4

The Golden Rule in Greco-Roman Religion and Philosophy

Robert M. Berchman
Dowling College

Introduction

The goal of this inquiry is first to throw some light on the classical origins of the Golden rule; secondly to offer examples illustrating its practice; and thirdly, to map the emergence of an ethics of reciprocity in the late Roman period. Initially, focus is upon the reciprocal virtues as they appear in Plato and Aristotle. This is followed by a study of reciprocity in selected Neoplatonists.

Two problems immediately face us. The first is that there are no words in Greek and Latin that translate into English as reciprocity.[1] Moreover the earliest Greek and Latin terms used for "reciprocity" arise out of a notion of economic exchange. Only later does there emerge in Latin the notion of ethical exchange as reciprocity.[2] The second is that the general definition of the Golden Rule offered by Professor Green "that instructs us to treat others as we want, and would want, others to treat us," is lacking in Archaic, Classical, and Greco-Roman sources.[3] Indeed, an emotivist theory of reciprocity does not exist in Greco-Roman writings until late Pagan Antiquity and here only implicitly.[4]

---

[1] The English reciprocity derives from the French—reciprocite which has the meaning of reciprocal obligation, action, or relation. Here reciprocate refers to a trade relation or policy. cf. *Britannica World Language Dictionary*, (Encyclopedia Britannica, 1958), p. 1053.

[2] Greek offers no specific word that translates into English as reciprocity or the Golden Rule. The closest term to reciprocity in Greek is the verb, *prodaneizo*—to lend before, or first; to advance money for public objects. *Orientis Graeci Inscriptiones Selectae*, ed. W. Dittenberger (Leipzig: S. Hirzel, 1903–05), 46.5. Here the word has a narrow economic meaning. See Lidell-Scott-Jones-McKenzie, *Greek-English Lexicon* (Oxford: Oxford University Press, 1972), p. 1473. Latin offers better possibilities for our study: *Mutuus, a, um* has two meanings; the first ethical; the second economic. Ethically it means equal return: *mutuum in amicitia* (equal return in friendship); Cicero: *pedibus per mutua nexis* (fastened on each other); Vergil: *inter se mutual vivunt* (by mutual exchange); Lucretius: *abl.* as adv. *Mutuo; mutuum*—mutually, reciprocally. *Mutuus, a, um* also means—borrowed, lent; Cicero: *pecuniam dare mutuam* and as the substantive it designates a loan. See A. Walde und J. B. Hoffmann, *Lateinisches Etymologisches Woeterbuch*, 2er Band (Heidelberg: Carl Winter Universitaets Verlag, 1956), p. 140.

[3] W. S. Green, "Parsing Reciprocity," p. 1.

However, out of such etymological and definitional incoherence, clarity eventually emerges. It is with Aristotle and his definition of the friend as another self that the concept of ethical, and not merely economic, reciprocity is proposed.[5] Now reciprocity or exchange has its foundation in a rationally justified obligation to enhance the virtue of others. Thus, in reciprocal doing, one enhances one's own moral excellence and the virtue of the community. Here Aristotle's claim, that we have obligations to the other as "another self," reinforces earlier Homeric, Socratic, and Platonic as well as Neoplatonic claims that reciprocity is inclusive of moral, social, and political obligations.[6]

Protagoras said opposing arguments may be found on every topic.[7] This observation underscores Wattles' insight that "the Golden Rule has more than a single sense."[8] Not surprisingly then, the ethics of reciprocity in Greek, Hellenistic, and Roman religion and philosophy has more than one sense. Reciprocity is characterized by five main types: honor, virtue, pleasure, duty, and grace.[9] Moreover, if reciprocity is foundational to the Golden Rule then reciprocal obligations: (1) are essentially ethical and social in their aim and reference; (2) are independent of the desires, aims, and preferences of this or that particular individual; and (3) are autonomous of the desires and feelings of the agent. In brief, reciprocity refers to specific virtues and actions to be taken by a rational agent which are deemed "fine" or "admirable" (*kalon*, also translated "beautiful"). Moreover, reciprocal actions are taken to benefit others but they are not taken to be necessarily beneficial to either the desires of the agent or others. Contradiction and reconciliation explain why the Golden Rule has polyvalent meaning in Greco-Roman philosophy and religion.

The Golden Rule in Ancient Greece

The Sophists and Socrates: The incoherence of virtue

If the Golden Rule appears in Socrates and Plato it would approximate: "The Good always benefits, it does not harm. Be good unto others."

---

[4] Emotivism is a reductionist theory encompassing the doctrine that all evaluative and ethical judgements are reducible to a preference or expression of desire and feeling. Such a theory is initially contextualized by Plotinus through images of grace, light, and love. A. H. Armstrong (trans.), *Plotinus, Enneads* (Cambridge Mass.: Harvard University Press, 1984), cf. *Enneads (En.)*, V.5.12.33–35.

[5] Aristotle introduces the term another self—*allos autos; heteros autos* in *Nicomachean Ethics (NE)*,1166a1–b29. It appears that this term is based on the proverbial phrase "another Heracles." cf. Aristotle, *Eudemian Ethics (EE)*, 1245a30.

[6] Only the Epicureans deny political reciprocity.

[7] H. Diels and W. Kranz (eds.), *Die Fragmente der Vorsokratiker* (Zurich: Weidmann, 1985), Protagoras, D80 B6a

[8] J. Wattles, *The Golden Rule* (Oxford: Oxford University Press, 1996), p. 5.

[9] Pleasure in Epicurean sources is nonemotivist. It is the result of a rational pursuit of virtue. cf. Epicurus, *Ep. Moen*, 131b–132a.

Socrates' and Plato's accounts of the virtues explain how happiness includes virtuous action as a self-directed and other-directed end in itself, not simply as a means to an end.[10] Virtuous action rests upon the nature of a human being as a rational agent. Virtuous action also refers to a person's wisdom, bravery, temperance, justice, or piety. Significantly, all virtues are essentially concerned with the good of others. Here reciprocity emerges. It refers to a person's virtue as a member of a community. The self-directed and other-directed aspects of virtue are especially clear for Socrates and Plato in their examinations of piety and justice.

The Homeric virtues provided a central part of the ethic of reciprocity in Classical Greek society. In Plato's aporertic dialogues, Socrates questions his fellow Athenians on the nature of some virtue, piety in the *Euthrypho,* courage in the *Laches,* and justice in *Republic* I. The intent of such questioning is to judge the other of inconsistency. What this suggests is a general state of incoherence in the use of evaluative language in Athenian culture. It is from the difficulties of relating earlier virtues to contemporary practice that many of the key ethical characteristics of the Golden Rule arise. It is also from the difficulties of relating earlier virtues to contemporary practice that many of the key ethical characteristics of later Greek and Roman understandings of reciprocity arise.

For our purposes, it is useful to contrast what A. W. H. Adkins calls the competitive Homeric virtues and the cooperative virtues extolled in the social world of Athenian democracy.[11] It is also helpful, following MacIntyre, to note that moral disagreement at this level leads to rival conceptions of virtue itself at another.[12] It is when rival conceptions of one and the same virtue coexist that conflict ensues. To illustrate the incoherent state of evaluative language in Athenian culture, we shall examine the *Euthrypho.* The goal is to sketch out the ethics of reciprocity that emerged in Classical Athens and how this resulted in a novel understanding of the Golden Rule. Reciprocity is based on justice.

The Homeric virtues provided a central part of the ethic of reciprocity in Classical Greek society. In Plato's aporertic dialogues Socrates questions his fellow Athenians on the nature of some virtue, piety in the *Euthrypho,* courage in the *Laches,* and justice in *Republic* I. The intent of such questioning is to judge the other of inconsistency. What this suggests is a general state of incoherence in the use of evaluative language in Athenian culture. What follows this is an attempt by Plato in the middle and later dialogues to produce a coherent

---

[10] Three texts are helpful in making sense of reciprocity in Socrates, Plato, and Aristotle. For undergraduates: cf. T. Irwin (ed.), *Classical Philosophy,* (Oxford: Oxford University Press, 2001); N. Melchert, *The Great Conversation Volume I: Pre-Socratics Through Descartes,* (California: Mayfield, 1999). Also see P. Schollmeirer, *Other Selves Aristotle on Personal and Political Friendship,* (Albany: SUNY, 1994).

[11] See A. W. H. Adkins, *Merit and Responsibility* (Oxford: Clarendon Press, 1960).

[12] A. MacIntyre, After Virtue, Notre Dame. University of Notre Dame Press, 1981. op. cit., pp. 131–45.

account of the virtues. Part of Plato's strategy includes a dismissal of the Homeric understanding of the virtues from the *polis*.

What is of note here are first *Euthrypho*'s particularistic *understanding* of piety and Socrates' search for a universal *definition* of the term piety. Socrates speaks of the one Form, presented by all the actions called pious (5d). Secondly, he claims that the gods love what is pious because it is pious; it is not pious because the gods love it (11e). The contrast is between Euthrypho's particular and competitive Homeric understanding of piety and Socrates' universal and cooperative one. Socrates argues as we apply the word pious to different actions or things, these must have a common characteristic and offer a common appearance or form to justify the use of the same term. He says: (1) a satisfactory definition will pick out some feature that is the same in every pious action; (2) this feature will not be shared by any impious action; and (3) it will be that feature (or lack of it) that makes an action pious or impious.

Socratic reciprocity is logo-centric; Homer's is sociocentric. For Homer there are no standards external to those embedded in the structure of community. In Homer evaluative questions were questions of social fact. The foundations of any *arete* (excellence, virtue) were predetermined by one's particular place in society. Owing and oughting were determined by kinship and household obligations. Thus morality and social structure were identical. For Socrates the issue is more complex. He claims that a particular *understanding* of virtue is a necessary but insufficient condition for defining virtue. What Socrates attempts to offer is a universal *definition* of piety, or holiness.

This is a thought beyond the ken of Homer's Archaic Age. Socrates' revolutionary insight is the product of the Greek Enlightenment, and it turns as it were "the world upside down." Homer's physical particularity of reciprocity—as kinship and household obligations; is challenged by Socrates' intellectual universality of reciprocity—as rational and political obligations (11e). Here Socrates makes the novel and radical suggestion that piety and justice are somehow related. Consequently, morality and social structure are separate. Significantly, *arete* (excellence, virtue) is no longer singularly connected to *ethos* as habit or custom. Rather *ethos* is a matter of character.[13] Thus to use a Hesiodic metaphor—a *chaos* (gap) emerges and complexity enters. Moral disagreement in the fifth and fourth centuries not only arises because one set of virtues clashes with another. It is because rival conceptions of the same virtue coexist.[14]

Plato asks the Socratic question: What is justice? For Plato, this is asking the question—what is the Form of Justice? Moreover he asks, is the Form of Justice related to the Form of the Good? And if so how? Here Plato reminds us of that passage where Socrates tells Euthrypho that even the gods dispute with each

---

[13] Plato is not the first to propose this redefinition of *ethos*. See Heraclitus, fr. 119. (Diels-Kranz, Die Fragmente der Vorsokratiker): "Man's character is his fate."

[14] A. MacIntyre, op. cit., pp. 133–34.

other, not about numbers, weights, and lengths but about the just and the unjust, the beautiful and the ugly, and good and evil.[15] Moreover, can we know justice is good? Are there ethical objects that rational persons can come to agreement on or as Herodotus quotes from Pindar—is custom (*nomos*) king of all?[16] Here Plato shifts ground from Socrates' critique of the Homeric understanding of virtue to a rebuttal of the Sophistic claim that *nomos* rules entirely, that justice is merely a matter of social convention. What this underscores is a continuing incoherence in the use of evaluative language and whether the virtues are competitive or cooperative, particular or universal.

Plato: The reciprocity of virtue

Plato wants to argue that justice is the fundamental reciprocal virtue for a community. He begins by raising the question, is the Form of Justice related to the Form of the Good? If so how? What Plato wants to do is offer a dialectic that illustrates Justice participates in Goodness and that all reasonable people would concur with this. Here our focus shifts to the debate in the *Republic* between Socrates and Thrasymachus on justice.

Adkins has noted there is a resemblance between Thrasymachus and the more venal versions of the Homeric hero. "Scratch Thrasymachus and you find Agamemnon," a man who only wants victory and its spoils for himself. Everyone and everything is to be used and abused in the pursuit of power. Thus, Socrates' protagonist is a "Thrasymachus" who argues that the rules of justice are merely conventional and are crafted by those with the power to make them. Moreover, it is not to the advantage of an individual to be just. Rather: "Socrates, injustice, if it is on a large enough scale, is stronger, freer, and more masterly than justice. And, as I said from the first, justice is what is advantageous to the stronger, while injustice is to one's own profit and advantage."[17] What Thrasymachus proposes is the inversion of the Golden Rule: Might makes right and being unjust is good judgment.[18] So the Sophist, of whom Plato's Thrasymachus is the type, makes success the only goal of action and makes the acquisition of power to do and to get whatever one wants the content of success. Furthermore, and this is the dagger at the throat of Plato's definition of the Golden Rule, there is no such thing as universal justice-as-such but only a particular justice as understood by the individual when reflecting in his own self-interest.

This relativism, combined with the claim that a virtue is a quality whose only reciprocity is success, threatens to derail Plato's project altogether. As Parfit notes, Thrasymachus is arguing the Self-Interest Theory of Rationality which

[15] Plato, *Euthrypho,* 7d.
[16] Herodotus, *Histories,* 3.38.
[17] Plato, *Republic,* 344c.
[18] Ibid., 348cd.

argues that a course of action can be rational only if it is in one's self-interest.[19] The competitive virtues are elevated above the cooperative ones and Plato's claim—that the virtues are not only compatible with each other but the presence of each requires the presence of all—is under trial. Reflection on the etymology Justice (*dike*) may help grasp what Plato is claiming. *Dike* basically means the order of the universe. The just man (*dikaios*) is one who respects and does not violate cosmic order. Moreover, Justice requires reference to or belief in a moral order (*harmonia*) in the universe. If there is moral order or justice in the universe or world soul, then there is moral order in the individual soul and in the state. For Plato, Thrasymachus' mistake is he uses the word just without any reference to or belief in the moral order of cosmos, soul, and state.

The general state of incoherence of evaluative language escalates as the fifth century B.C.E. comes to a close at Athens. It is possible for Sophists like Thrasymachus to ask if it is or is not justice to do what the established order requires. Here we have moved beyond the Homeric notion held by Euthrypho that to be just (*dikaios*) is not to transgress that social order. Here moral thinking and action about the Golden Rule takes on an increasing ethical rather than social hue as well. The argument of Plato's Golden Rule is dialectically complex but reciprocally straightforward. Plato's theory of the reciprocity of cooperative virtue is based on the dual notions of Self-Interest and Mutual Interest Rationality which combines justice in the soul (*psuche*) to justice within a state (*polis*). The dialectic of his argument unfolds in this way: (1) Just actions follow from a soul in harmony; (2) since a harmonious soul is a happy soul; (3) it follows that happiness is a natural good; (4) since this is so, justice is a natural good; (5) which means justice is not good for its consequences but is good in itself; (6) because justice participates in goodness. At the core of Plato's view of reciprocity is the virtue justice. Justice radiates out like the spokes of a wheel to kindred virtues such as piety, prudence, courage, and wisdom. The rub is being a good person and being a good citizen is central, but without knowledge of the variety of possible practices of virtue, reciprocity would be impossible. Thus in order for the Golden Rule to work evaluative rationality is necessary. It is also important to view the virtues as cooperative rather than competitive. Otherwise the reciprocity of justice and its kindred virtues would not be possible.

Aristotle: The reciprocal virtues

If there is a Golden Rule in Aristotle it would approximate: "Love the other as another self." Some of Aristotle's most important passages develop from the

---

[19] D. Parfit, *Reasons and Persons* (Oxford: Oxford University Press, 1984).

aphorism that the friend or loved one is "another" self (*allos autos* or *heteros autos*). [20] He brings in this notion in order to characterize a broad range of attitudes that are typical of what we in this study call the Golden Rule. What they have in common is that they all seem to derive from virtuous attitudes an individual has to him/herself which reciprocally are given to the other.

Aristotle inherits Plato's belief in the unity and harmony of both the individual soul and the city-state. He also claims that society, the state, or city-state (*polis*) exists by nature (*phusei*) not by custom (*nomos*). The final cause (*telos*) of its genesis is to provide the conditions necessary for human existence. Also considering that man is by nature a social animal what results is that society is prior in nature to each of us. Indeed, society is prior to understanding any particular person; it came into being for the sake of living well and its function is to serve human welfare. Thus, Aristotle views conflict as something to be avoided or managed. The means to this end (*telos*) is accomplished through the practice of reciprocity and its kindred virtues which include friendship, justice, good wishes and actions, lawfulness, and fairness. He adds to this the argument that one cannot possess any of these virtues of character without possessing all the others.[21] Reciprocity involves the ability to choose "another self" in acts of friendship, justice, good wishes and actions, lawfulness, and fairness. If one is able to do this then the most cooperative of virtues are set in place rendering conflict nugatory thereby preserving the state.

The key to understanding Aristotle here is that excellence of character and intelligence cannot be separated and that there is a connection between practical intelligence and the virtues of character. He claims that human beings, like all other species, have a specific nature with certain aims and goals. Thus humans move by nature toward a specific end (*telos*). For Aristotle, every activity, inquiry, and practice aims at some good. Thus, he sets himself the task of giving an account of the good: one local and particular in society, state, the city-state (*polis*); the other universal in the cosmos (*kosmos*). What then does the good turn out to be? Aristotle calls it *eudaimonia*—variously translated as happiness, blessedness, prosperity, and flourishing. Happiness is a kind of existence where the good is a complete human life lived optimally. To acquire this state of soul (*hexis*), a person has to place the virtues at the center of life. The virtues are the possession of qualities which enable a person to attain happiness. If one lacks these virtues movement toward happiness is thwarted. Why? For Aristotle, the outcome of the exercise of right virtue is a choice which results in right action.

[20] *NE*, 1166a1–b29. It is clear from the *EE* that `the friend is another self' is based on the proverbial phrase "another Heracles," which was presumably said by the hero himself in some story. cf. *EE*, 1245a30.
[21] *NE*, 1145a.

Reciprocity, the self, and others

Aristotle distinguishes three kinds of friendship concerned with advantage, pleasure, and goodness. The first two kinds are easy to understand from a purely self-interested point of view. Often we can advance our own interests more efficiently if we can rely on help from others for mutual advantage. We might also take an interest in other people because we enjoy their company. Here our concern depends on what we enjoy, not on any concern for the other person. The third kind of friendship involves concern for the other because of herself and for her own sake, not as a source of advantage or pleasure. Aristotle also argues that this concern for others promotes one's own good.

He argues that we can see how love of self requires concern for the good of others, once we understand what is meant by self-love and self-interest. What we think is in our self-interest depends on what we think the self is, and what sorts of desires need to be satisfied in order to achieve its interests. Here Aristotle argues that the self is naturally social, so that something is missing from our good if all our concerns are merely self-interested.[22] In a concern for other people, we become interested in aims and activities that would otherwise not interest us and become capable of activities that would otherwise be beyond us. This what Aristotle means when he says that for the virtuous person a friend of the best sort is "another self."[23] If we are virtuous, we care about the friend in the way we care about ourselves. In doing so we take an interest that we would not otherwise take in what the friend does. Thus, concern for others does not interfere with our interests but expands them.

The type of friendship which Aristotle has in mind is that which embodies a shared recognition of and pursuit of several goods. It is this sharing which is essential and primary to the constitution of any form of self and community, whether household (*oikos*) or city (*polis*). The social nature of human beings is the basis of justice. Justice is another's good.[24] In this sense justice is not a separable virtue, but the whole of virtue insofar as it is practiced toward other people. Since virtuous people value the good of other people for the sake of the other people themselves, they also choose virtuous actions for their own sakes. Aristotle describes this attitude to virtuous actions by saying that virtuous people choose them "because they are fine," or "for the sake of the fine." Charles Kahn has taken passages from *Nicomachean Ethics* 8 and 9 to develop a theory of Aristotelian altruism.[25] He argues that the basis for the friendship of human

[22] Ibid., 1097a28–b21; Aristotle, *Politics* (Cambridge, Mass.: Harvard University Press, 1969), 1252a1–1253a39.

[23] Ibid., 1170b3–19.

[24] Ibid., 1129b11–1130a5.

[25] Charles Kahn, "Aristotle and Altruism" in *Mind*, vol. 90 (Cambridge, Mass.: Cambridge University Press, 1981), pp. 20–40.

beings with one another is dependent upon the presence in each rational human being of the principle of the active intellect (*nous poietikos*). The joint presence of intelligence is the basis of human friendship; that the other person is another self because my true self and your true self are identical—which is the *nous poietikos* shared by a rational community.[26]

Thus the performance of the Golden Rule is the basis for a happy life (*eudaimon*) for each human being. Here Aristotle asserts that freedom is a necessary condition for achieving one's *telos*. Slaves, unlike free persons, have their tasks less determined for them because they have less an understanding of what they ought to be doing. [27] Free persons as rational agents, however, are more likely to have their activities determined by their concepts of the good life and their commitment to it. Thus, it is appropriate for each of us to maximize the good life.[28]

These passages convey the sequence of events in the development of reciprocity-affection, good will, and friendship. They also suggest a distinction between essential and accidental friendship based upon the loves exhibited in them. Such loves are distinguished by their objects.[29] Some friends bear goodwill for others reciprocally, while some friends offer good wishes to others self-referentially. The first acts for others essentially, advancing the good for others as an end; while second acts accidentally, advancing the good of another as a means to some other end. This is because it is essentially "a doing unto others what you would done unto you"—that is to say, goodwill and good wishes, reciprocated and recognized, for the sake of the goodness of another, is the Golden Rule.

> Perfect friendship is the friendship of good men and of men who are similar according to their virtue. For they wish things that are good similarly to each other as good men they are essentially good.[30]

Hence, the distinction between good friends and useful and pleasant friends is made. It is only with good friends that one friend loves the other for the sake of the other.

> Those who wish the good to their friends for the sake of them are the most friends, for they do this for their sake and not accidentally.[31]

---

[26] For a critique of altruism in Aristotle see R. M. Berchman, "Altruism in Greco-Roman Philosophy," in J. Neusner and B. Chilton (eds.), *Altruism in World Religions* (Washington, D.C.: Georgetown University Press, 2005), pp. 4–13.

[27] Aristotle, *Metaphysics (Met.)* (Cambridge, Mass.: Harvard University Press, 1969), 12.10. 1075a20–23.

[28] *Politics*, 1280b39.

[29] Ibid., 1156a6–10.

[30] Ibid., 1156b7–9.

[31] Ibid., 1156b9–11.

Aristotle further proposes that friendship is a habit (*hexis*) or activity of the soul, in accordance with a mean and that it concerns an emotion. But here he is careful to make the point that practical wisdom (*phronesis*) determines this emotional mean. This is why friendship as a habit is virtuous. If friendship were merely based on emotions, it would lack requisite rationality, or rational choice (*prohairesis*), and thus would not be virtuous.[32] Now since love is a passion and friendship is a habit, it follows that loves divides into two species—a passion and a habit.[33] Of the two, only love that is reciprocal and for the sake of another qualifies as a habit. This is so because friends love what is lovable in each other.[34] Here the quality of being for the sake of another is the crucial one because it relies on rational choice (*prohairesis*):

> Friends love each other reciprocally from choice and their choice springs from a habit (*hexis*).[35]

What we have here is Aristotle's Golden Rule in cameo, in miniature.

Reciprocity and the other

Why does someone enter into a good friendship and acquire virtue? This answer to this question takes us into the center of Aristotle's theory of reciprocity. The marks of a good friendship begin with a good friendship with oneself.[36]

The reason for this is that it is a short step from being a friend to oneself to being a friend for others. Significantly, in being a friend for others one acquires, what one becomes, is another self (*allos autos* or *heteros autos*). What one comes to acquire as another self are the rational marks of good or excellent friendship, which include the reflective, controlling, discriminating center of his considered attitudes, thoughts, actions, and decisions. It is appropriate to love not only that self in us but that self in others for it is admirable and wise. It is reasoned love not a love driven by vulgar opinion.[37] Such an end is only optimally possible in reciprocity with another, in reciprocity with another self. Thus the desirability of a good person, of a good friend's existence, and being aware of it through intellectual activity is a virtue. If one lacks good friends one forfeits happiness. This is why we need friends if we are to be happy.[38] The question is what sort of self is it that you love? Here the mother finds her interest in the welfare of her child as a friend, or as the friend as another self.

---

[32] Ibid., 1106b36–1107a2; 1105b25–28.
[33] Ibid., 1157b28–29.
[34] Ibid., 1155b17–19; 1156a3–5.
[35] Ibid., 1157b30–31.
[36] Ibid., 1166a1–2.
[37] Ibid., 166a16–17; 1169a2; 1178a2–6.
[38] Ibid., 1170a13–b19.

Anyone who is to be happy, then, must have excellent friends.[39]

This sort of concern for others not only promotes one's own good, but the good of others—as another self.

Neoplatonism: Reciprocity divine

If there is a Golden Rule among Neoplatonists it would read: "Do unto others what by God's grace and love is done unto you."

Plato and Aristotle have produced their own coherent and well-integrated account of reciprocity and its virtues in an attempt clean up the state of incoherence in the use of evaluative language in Ancient Greek culture. At the close of Roman antiquity another reading of reciprocity emerges in the Neoplatonists to muddy the waters further. On the basis of distinction made between state and community, a theology develops to support a new understanding of reciprocity. Reciprocity is divine. The source and activity of reciprocity is grounded in divine will, not human reason. What we encounter here is a novel return to the virtue ethics of Plato and Aristotle with a "divine twist." To understand this return, we need to address changes in the sociology of institutions between Classical Greece and Imperial Rome.

The later Platonists make a distinction between a state and society on the one hand and *a* community on the other. This distinction might appear vapid but bear with me. The political unity of the Roman Empire is clear and precise, and it includes all individuals however unequally. The state also includes institutions, laws, norms, associations, even folkways. At its widest, a state or society may be taken to include all or any dealing among individuals, whether these are direct or indirect, organized or unorganized, conscious or unconscious, cooperative or antagonistic.[40] This generic use of the term is an organizing abstraction which covers all instances of the adjective "social." However, society maybe distinguished from *a* society. Society in this more precise meaning is a more promising candidate to explain later Platonic understandings of reciprocity.

There is Neoplatonic nostalgia that a city of man would be succeeded by a city of god. To facilitate these ends members of *a* divine society withdraw from civil society. The real theological question, in Neoplatonic terms, is whether the social order, imposed by the state and expressed in its laws, actually serves our needs. It does not. Thus, it is the aim of neo-Platonists like Plotinus, Iamblichus, and Proclus to make *a* society into a single, noetic organization.

Plotinus' theology shows an understanding of the neo-Platonic conception of a theo-noetic society: a divine community grounded in the virtues of

---

[39] Ibid., 1170b3–19.
[40] See M. Ginsberg, *Sociology* (Oxford: Oxford University Press, 1955), p. 40.

intellectual contemplation. He describes the One as will, and as love, of itself.[41] And divine grace is seen as the product of divine will or "undiminished giving," which is the nature of divine activity.[42] Within the Intelligible World will, giving and order imply one another. Plotinus is cautious when he addresses what is in all intelligible beings and makes them good?[43] He says it is not sufficient to answer that all humans are intelligible and thus good. It is, however, sufficient and necessary to claim that:

> if they also seek life and everlasting existence and activity what they desire is not intellect insofar as it is intellect, but this is good insofar as it is from the Good and directed to the Good. [44]

The form, order, the goodness of life are given a wider extension than merely intellection, (*noesis*) by Plotinus. Life in all its diverse forms is not only preintellectual in origin but divinely voluntaristic and original. What is novel in Plotinus is a subtle shift from a God, whose activity is purely one of Intellect, to a God who is both Intellect and Will. There is a divine light, both rational and volitional, that the One gives by an act of love and grace to all things.[45]

Here Providence permeates the cosmos in varying degrees, as creatures varying in receptivity react to her. This divine giving is a kind of *natura medicatrix*, where even the evil done by free agents, like the wounds and the broken bones of an organism, may be healed by Providence.[46] Divine reciprocity, the justice of inevitable retribution (*adrasteia*), is a principle that operates in the least details of the organic world:

> [L]eaf and bloom and fruit, and still more, men testify to the care of Providence.[47]

Any consideration of virtue in Plotinus requires some discussion of the reciprocity of divine Providence. Providence helps those who live according to divine law.[48] This law provides a good life, here and hereafter, and for the bad there is the reverse. This is where divine grace comes into play.

---

[41] *En.*, VI. 8.13.5–6; 15.1.
[42] The source of this doctrine is Plato's account in *Timaeus* 29e–30a of the divine motive for creation.
[43] See. K. Corrigan, "Essence and Existence in the Enneads," in L. Gerson (ed.), *The Cambridge Companion to Plotinus*, (Cambridge: Cambridge University Press, 1996), pp. 116–23.
[44] *En.*, VI. 20.22–24.
[45] Ibid., VI. 7.35.30–34.
[46] Ibid., II. 2.5.
[47] Ibid., II. 2.13–14.
[48] Ibid., III. 2.8.

Iamblichus and Proclus argue that both exist under an appropriate mode on successive levels of reality.[49] However, union between the divine and human only occurs through appropriate ritual actions. The rituals that invoke the gods are a voluntary bestowal of divine power.[50] The human soul blessed by such power gains salvation. This claim resulted in the claims by Iamblichus and his heirs that theurgy, not philosophy, leads to divine union.[51] Hence, there is an emphasis in later Neoplatonism of the need for divine grace, combined with a new human receptiveness toward such grace. Without grace the salvation of the soul is impossible. Here, we encounter for the first time the notion of a divine, nonreflective, selfless reciprocity, of giving as a form of charity.

The reciprocity and patronage of the sage

Platonists of the Roman period concentrated their attention on a portrait of reciprocity as it might be, represented by the ideal of the *sapiens* or sage. The anonymity and loneliness of life in the great new cities, where one was a cipher reinforced the need for a community of divine friends and helpers. These foci replaced the inherited local community of the old closed society. They also formed the basis for a new notion of reciprocity in late antiquity friendship (*philia*) is complemented by the cooperative virtue *par excellence*—philanthropy (*philanthropia*). In this context, reciprocity and friendship take on the aura of a divine unity (*henosis*) rather than a human constellation of kinship, familial, and civic obligations.[52] Central to this notion of friendship as divine unity is the concept of a detachable theurgic self. Once activated the soul escapes this world of darkness and penance to arrive in another realm of light and salvation where the soul becomes one with the divine.

In quest of divine unity, Neoplatonists became increasingly preoccupied with the techniques of individual salvation through holy books, prophetic inspiration, and revelation; or by oracles, dreams, and waking visions. Others found salvation in ritual by initiation in esoteric *musteria*. Here we encounter the starting point for a new and entirely different kind of *philosophia* and *religio*. In the words of Justin Martyr:

The aim of Platonism is to see God face to face.[53]

---

[49] Proclus, *PT* (*Platonic Theology*), 1.19, p. 91.16–21.
[50] Iamblichus, *On the Mysteries*, 1.12; 1.14; 3.16–18.
[51] Ibid., 2.11.
[52] See R. M. Berchman, "Rationality and Ritual in Neoplatonism," in P. M. Gregorios (ed.), *Neoplatonism and Indian Thought* (Albany: SUNY Press, 2002), pp. 229–68.
[53] Dial., 2.6. cf. Porphyry, *Ep. ad Marc.*, 16.

Welcome the world of the philosopher-theurgist.[54] Deities, daemons, and the sage as patrons bestow a reciprocity of grace and charity upon their clients.

By the mid-fourth century C.E. the Platonic philosopher and theurgist are indistinguishable. As the knower of divine wisdom and the doer of the hieratic arts, this figure becomes a supernatural extension of divine power (*dunamis*) and love (*eros*) in the universe. Thriving on the tenacious bond of divine friendship (*philia*), their knowledge and activity offered a mantel of divine patronage (*prostateia*) and the possibility of divine salvation (*sotereia*) to all who fell within their orbit. Indeed, the philosophers use and transfer of divine power to their clients rendered accessible the proprietary relationship with the gods thought lost because of the fall of the soul.[55] A divinely grounded reciprocity of love and grace permeates this Neoplatonic understanding of the Golden Rule. Reciprocity was not directed to members of society in general but to members of a specific religious-philosophical community, an *ecclesia Neoplatonica* or Neoplatonic church.

Porphyry nicely illustrates the shifts occurring. Interested in the habits of the Egyptian priesthood, he noted how it had created a caste apart.[56] Quoting Chaeremon, its members lived in highly regulated communities and chastised the impiety of those who traveled outside of Egypt because they exposed themselves to alien ways. Nonetheless, these priests were also dedicated to philosophy and theology. As such, this group becomes a model for Porphyry of a Neoplatonic community, a pagan "church" of the saved who would receive the grace, light, and love of the gods.

Eunapius reports that Maximus assembled a large number of friends in the temple of Hecate and burned a grain of incense, reciting to himself the text of a hymn. The goddesses smiled, then laughed, and finally the torches she held burst into flames, into a blaze of light.[57] Wise men and women, therefore, brought a divine presence into the world and the divine power embraced their human community reintegrating each human soul with her divine source.

Later Platonic hagiographers such as Philostratus, Damascius, Marinus, Eunapius, Sozomen, and Zosimus present the lives of wise men and women who effectively brokered this reciprocal relationship. We are told that Asclepiodorus and Heraiscus spent long periods of their lives in temples while Damascius resided in a cave under a temple devoted to Cybele near Hierapolis.[58] Each communed

---

[54] See P. Brown, "The Rise and Function of the Holy Man in Late Antiquity," *Journal of Roman Studies* LXI (1971): 80–101.

[55] For a study on this phenomenon see E. V. Gallagher, *Divine Man or Magician? Celsus and Origen on Jesus* (California: Scholars Press, 1982).

[56] Porphyry, *de Abst.*, 4.6–8.

[57] *Lives of the Sophists*, 475 (Boiss).

[58] Zosimus, *Epistulae or Letters*, 5.46.3.

with the gods and goddesses who appeared at such places. Venturing forth they became privileged agents and administrators of divine power, love, patronage, and salvation to a wider Roman world. Two women philosophers, Hypatia of Alexandria and Sosipatra of Pergamon, were higher souls protected and guided by blessed daemons and heroes.[59] Using a statue Hypatia telestically cured a man who fell in love with her while Sosipatra victim of a love-spell cast on her by Philometer had it reversed by Maximus, the pupil of Aedesius and teacher of the Emperor Julian.[60] Other women like Asclepigenia and Anthusa of Cilicia joined men like Plutarch and Hermias to contact, fathom, and translate the divine presence and hallowing in statues to aristocratic clients in city, town, and country throughout the Empire.[61]

---

[59] Sozomen, *Historiae or Histories*, 9.8.
[60] Ibid.
[61] A portrait of this mood is nicely sketched by Augustine, *Civ, dei*, 5.23.235.28–29.

Chapter 5

The Golden Rule in Classical Judaism

Jacob Neusner
Bard College

Comparing religions requires identifying points in common, so as to highlight the contrasts between and among them. Without shared traits religions subject to comparison yield observations lacking consequence. If all religions concur that the sun rises in the east, what generalization do we learn about all of those religions that clarify their shared character? And what follows for the particular characterization of any one of those religions? For religions bear distinctive traits. What they share by definition is commonplace, outweighed by what distinguishes them from one another. The more widespread a shared trait among religions, the more it lacks consequence for any particular context.

I propose that a proposition common to a number of religions bears no consequence for the description, analysis, and interpretation of any one of those religions in particular: what is common produces the commonplace. That proposition requires the analysis of a set of religions that share a proposition. It demands an estimate of the importance of the shared proposition in those religions, respectively. But how are we to demonstrate that a trait shared by numerous religions does not play a differentiating role in any given religion? That intuitive proposition requires a test, which I shall carry out here.

The test requires describing the encompassing traits of a religion and its propositions. These propositions are to be shown to form a system of ideas—not random and episodic observations about this and that but a coherent composition. Then the role of the Golden Rule in the articulation of the system is to be assessed by appeal to the logic that sustains the system.

A religious system will appeal to a particular logic. Hypothetically reconstructing that logic will permit us to predict what the religion will say about a topic that is not articulately expounded. Such a system will generate solutions to problems not addressed in the formative writings of the religion: if we know this, what else do we know? Thus from the proposition, "two apples plus two apples equal four apples," the system invites the hypothesis, "two" (anythings) plus "two" (anythings) equal four (anythings). That illustrates what I mean by a religious *system*. It is a mode of thought or logic characteristic of a set of religious ideas that generates new truth, accommodates fresh data, permits us to make predictions concerning what must follow from a given proposition.

The logic of the system then is brought to bear upon the new truth and self-evidence enters in.

That returns us to the task of comparing religions through what is alike and what is different. What is common among several religious traditions does not fit well with what is particular to any one of them. The distinctive logic of a given religion will be obscured by what can just as well fit a competing system. Religions cannot affirm everything and its opposite. So if religious systems coincide, that upon which they concur cannot maintain a consequential, differentiating proposition but only a commonplace in both senses of the word: what is common to a number of systems, what makes slight difference in any of those systems. And my thesis here is as follows:

A proposition that is shared among several religious systems will not play a major role in the construction of any particular religious system.

Religions by their nature differ. They conflict. When they agree, therefore, it is because the point of congruence is systemically neutral to the systems that concur—episodic, not systematic, and commonplace, not consequential.

To test that proposition, I take the Golden Rule, which represents what is common to a variety of religious systems, and I invoke classical Judaism and its canon, which here stands for a coherent religious system. A review of the representation of the Golden Rule in the formative canon will allow us to assess the importance attached to it. We consider its position in the Judaic religious system and measure its generative power. What I shall show is that the Golden Rule is parachuted down into classical Judaism and plays no systemic role in the construction of that system.

The Golden Rule is called the encompassing principle of the Torah, but when the system undertakes to generalize, it ignores the Golden Rule. The faithful are admonished to go, study the generative data of the Golden Rule, but when the system invokes the Golden Rule, it does not elaborate and extend it, analyzing its implications for fresh problems. To state the proposition simply: in classical Judaism the Golden Rule is inert, not active, inconsequential in an exact sense of the word, not weighty in secondary development. It yields nothing beyond itself and does not invite new questions or stimulate speculation about new problems. The Golden Rule emerges as a commonplace that the system invokes without extension and elaboration.

We turn to the case at hand, the Golden Rule in Classical Judaism, the Judaic religious system set forth in the Israelite Scriptures as interpreted by the Rabbinic sages of the first six centuries C.E. The canon of that Judaism contains an explicit expression of the Golden Rule. It is framed in both moral and ethical terms, the moral referring to good or bad, the ethical to right or wrong. Scripture's formulation in terms of morality occurs in the commandment of love: "You shall love your neighbor as yourself" (Lev. 19.18). At issue is attitude, with action implicit. The first-century sage, Hillel, is cited as stating the Golden Rule in ethical terms, "What is hateful to you to your fellow don't do." That negative formulation of the Golden Rule applies to concrete relationships among ordinary people. And what is noteworthy is that classical Judaism maintains that the biblical commandment, "You shall love your neighbor as yourself" (Lev. 19.18), defines the heart of the Torah, which is to say, what we should call the essence of Judaism: its ethics and its theology.

That judgment is set forth in the Talmud, the extension and amplification of the Torah, in a famous story about the sage, Hillel. Hillel reformulated Lev. 19.18, the rule of reciprocal love, in terms of action (don't do) rather than attitude (love your neighbor):

A. [In Hebrew:] There was another case of a gentile who came before Shammai. He said to him, "Convert me on the stipulation that you teach me the entire Torah while I am standing on one foot." He drove him off with the building cubit that he had in his hand.

B. He came before Hillel: "Convert me."

C. He said to him [in Aramaic], "'*What is hateful to you, to your fellow don't do.*' That's the entirety of the Torah; *everything else is elaboration. So go, study.*"

Bavli Shabbat 31a/I.12[1]

The concluding counsel, "Go, study," points to the task of elaborating the Golden Rule to cover a variety of specific ethical cases. Notice how the formulation shifts from the positive, love, to the negative, "what is hateful to you to your fellow don't do." But in both positive and negative formulations, the focus is on "your fellow," and in context that excludes the stranger. A second glance, however, shows that the lacuna in the Judaic formulation of the Golden Rule was filled. It dealt with the question, who is my neighbor? To find the answer for classical Judaism, we turn to the reading in ethical terms of the theological teaching of Lev. 19.18. That reading invokes Hillel's formulation, "That's the entirety of the Torah; *everything else is elaboration. So go, study.*" The issue emerges in a dispute on the encompassing principle of the Torah:

7. A. "[B]ut you shall love your neighbor as yourself: [I am the Lord]:"

B. R. Aqiba says, "This is the encompassing principle of the Torah."

C. Ben Azzai says, "'This is the book of the generations of Adam' (Gen. 5.1) is a still more encompassing principle."

Sifra CC:III

---

[1] Italics signify Aramaic in the original. The Talmud is a bilingual document, in Hebrew and in Aramaic. The Golden Rule is formulated in Aramaic for its ethical version, in Hebrew for its theological statement.

Aqiba, who flourished a century after Hillel, recapitulates the judgment that the Golden Rule of reciprocity as stated at Lev. 19.18 lies at the heart of the Torah. But in that setting the issue of who is my neighbor figures. The dispute between Aqiba and Ben Azzai makes clear that in Aqiba's judgment by "my neighbor" *not* everyone is meant. That emerges in what is implicit as the opposite of Ben Azzai's position. While Aqiba, like Hillel before him, identifies the commandment to love one's neighbor as oneself as the encompassing principle of the Torah, Ben Azzai invokes the universal definition of one's neighbor. One's fellow is any other person.

Ben Azzai accordingly chooses a still more compendious principle, "This is the book of the generations of Adam," which encompasses not only "your neighbor" but all humanity. For the "book of the generations of Adam" covers all the known peoples. By showing how all nations derive genealogically from Adam and Eve the Torah establishes that humanity forms a common family. One's fellow is one's cousin, however many times removed. In the context of Genesis, which sets forth the theory that "Israel" is constituted by the extended family of Abraham and Sarah, the metaphor of a family covering all of the nations of the world carries a weighty message. So at issue is the governing metaphor. Ben Azzai sees humanity as united in its common genealogy beginning with Adam and Eve, and it is in that context that Ben Azzai's reading of "Love your neighbor as yourself" rejects the Golden Rule as too limited in its application.

By his contrary choice of a relevant Scripture as the heart of the matter, Ben Azzai implies the negative judgment that loving one's neighbor limits the commandment of love to one's own group. This he does when he selects a statement that transcends the limits of a particular group. Lev. 19.17–18 establishes a context for his criticism. For it states: "You shall not hate your brother in your heart, but reasoning, you shall reason with your neighbor, lest you bear sin because of him. You shall not take vengeance or bear any grudge against the sons of your own people, but you shall love your neighbor as yourself: I am the Lord" (Lev. 19.17–18). The clear intent is to frame matters in terms of your brother and your own people. No wonder, then, that to oppose that position Ben Azzai has chosen a verse that refers to all humanity.

But that is not the end of the story. Leviticus 19.31–32 explicitly extends the rule of love to the stranger or outsider:

1. A. ["When a stranger sojourns with you in your land, you shall not do him wrong. The stranger who sojourns with you shall be to you as the native among you, and you shall love him as yourself, for you were strangers in the land of Egypt: I am the Lord your God" (Lev. 19.31–32).]

4. A. ". . . you shall not do him wrong:"
   B. You should not say to him, "Yesterday you were worshipping idols and now you have come under the wings of the Presence of God."

5. A. ". . . as a native among you:"
   B. Just as a native is one who has accepted responsibility for all the teachings of the Torah, so a proselyte is to be one who has accepted responsibility for all the words of the Torah.

6. A. ". . . shall be to you as the native among you, and you shall love him as yourself:"
   B. Just as it is said to Israel, "You will love your neighbor as yourself" (Lev. 19.18),
   C. so it is said with regard to proselytes, "You shall love him as yourself."

7. A. ". . . for you were strangers in the land of Egypt:"
   B. Know the soul of strangers, for you were strangers in the land of Egypt.

Sifra CCV: I

Here is an explicit definition of the commandment to love the outsider, and Lev. 19.18 is cited to apply to the stranger. So much for the representation of the Golden Rule in Classical Judaism, a fundamental teaching stated with economy. A negative judgment is in order: the Golden Rule is designated as the fundamental principle of the Torah, but we look in vain for elaborations of the matter, that promise of an elaborate commentary for Lev. 19.18 that Hillel invoked.

What does the Golden Rule say?

The Golden Rule emphasizes reciprocity, in Hillel's formulation stating that one must not do to one's fellow what he would not have him do to himself. But the setting for that teaching hardly intersects with the ethical or moral teaching itself. The story about Hillel makes a point that has nothing to do with the Golden Rule. The contrast with Shammai yields the model of the patient sage as against the captious one. The narrative emphasizes that lesson: "He drove him off with the building cubit that he had in his hand." In the Rabbinic formulation of the Golden Rule, Lev. 19.18 and Hillel's reformulation of it into ethical categories do not define the point of the setting that contains the ethical rule. The Golden Rule takes a subordinated position to the editorial purpose of the story that is told. The composite aims to contrast Rabbinic patience with Rabbinic arrogance.

To answer the first question: In Judaism the Golden Rule is framed positively in the Scripture to deal with moral reciprocity and negatively in the Rabbinic composite to deal with ethical reciprocity. It is formulated in a narrative setting but the narrative does not center upon the Golden Rule. The Golden Rule is hardly integral to the narrative. It serves as merely one among several narratives to illustrate the primacy of patience. So the Golden Rule is formulated within a narrative but not as an integral and extenuating component of a narrative.

What does the Golden Rule mean?

The climactic point of the narrative involving Hillel and the Golden Rule is that the entire Torah can be extracted from the Golden Rule—a formidable claim. The Golden Rule in its theological formulation is represented as the recapitulation of the entire Torah. Judaism's negative formulation of the ethical version of the Golden Rule by Hillel complements the Scripture's affirmative theological version. Given the remarkable claim on behalf of the Golden Rule as the encompassing rule that takes account of the entire Torah, we come to a surprising fact. The Golden Rule is nowhere elaborated. I find in the classical canon of Judaism no attempt to amplify the proposition that the entire Torah is embodied in the Golden Rule. Hillel's mandate, "Now go study," bears no instructions on what one should study, no guidance in how we are to discern the principle of reciprocity in the law and in the ethics of Judaism.

Literature

That free-standing position accorded to the Golden Rule is signaled by the literary context for the Golden Rule. As the extensive composite indicates, the Golden Rule is parachuted down, whole and complete, into the composite that preserves it. It is interchangeable with other narratives. But it does not connect to them and is not represented in dialogue with them. It is interchangeable with other narratives that praise patience over impatience and its particular message—the Golden Rule—does not contribute a message integral to the propositional context that sustains the composite. The Talmud's routine analytical inquiry plays no role, and the dialectical argument that animates Talmudic discourse contributes nothing. The narrative of Hillel is not naturalized into the Talmud or subjected to the Talmud's usual processes of criticism and testing.

We do not know what in that context provokes the appearance of the Golden Rule in particular, and the variety of the propositions that find a place alongside the Golden Rule underscore the autonomy of the proposition. We do not have in the composite a proposition provoked by the Golden Rule. More to the point, the other compositions, also free standing, do not intersect with the Golden Rule—even though it is designated as the comprehensive proposition of the Torah—but make their own points. The literary context does not constrain the Golden Rule's meaning by glossing it or embedding it in a highly particular setting or circumstance.

Interpretation

How important is the Golden Rule in the interpretive tradition of classical Judaism? To answer that question we take up the challenge of Hillel: "Go, study." Specifically, we ask where in the Rabbinic system the principle of reciprocity governs. Then if we generalize matters, the Golden Rule does form the comprehensive principle of the Torah. If I had to specify how the Golden Rule permeates the Judaic law and theology, I would point to the Rabbinic doctrine of justice: measure for measure. Then even though the Golden Rule as formally expressed presents an enigma and a paradox, the Golden Rule does register. Its principle of reciprocity indeed permeates the Rabbinic system of law and theology alike. What imparts to the Golden Rule the power of self-evidence? It is the articulation of the principle of justice or fairness: it is only fair that what one does not want done to himself one should not do to his fellow. In law the Golden Rule in Judaism forms a variation on the theme of justice and fairness.

How does the Golden Rule work?

Social consequence

To which segments of society is the Golden Rule directed? The "you" of Scripture and of Hillel's formulation does not differentiate by class or caste. Women and men are treated equally under the law. The Golden Rule applies uniformly across genders and social classes. The story about Hillel presupposes the opposite of literacy and a certain level of education is not assumed. "Go, study" invites the hearer to follow the exposition of probative cases of Scripture. God in the Torah is the author of or authority behind the Golden Rule, which applies all the time and not only in particular circumstances.

Actor and recipient

The model for the actor of the Golden Rule is God, and the record of his actions is in the Scripture. God acts with justice and responds to virtue with reciprocity. The Golden Rule assumes that the actor is an autonomous moral agent. His subjective and individual desires are the basis for the actions taken toward the other. That is why the actor bears responsibility for his action. And it is because he bears responsibility that the actor is admonished to treat the other as he wishes himself to be treated. What defines ethical conduct is moral attitude, and right and wrong, good and bad, are conveyed by the Torah, hence "go, study." That imposes limits on the moral attitude: "what is hateful to you to your fellow do not do." That is not an invitation to subjectivity because the Torah intervenes.

Reflexivity and reciprocity

Does the Golden Rule include reflexivity as a component of reciprocity, i.e., the notion of treating others as you would treat yourself? The expositions we have reviewed of the Golden Rule and its extension in the principle of measure for measure leave no doubt. It is taken for granted that one treats oneself with dignity and respect. The Golden Rule's basic reference point is the actor not the recipient of the action, the self not the other. Empathy is not at issue in the exposition of justice, and there is no hint of subjective judgment.

How does the Golden Rule matter?

Systemic significance

How important is the Golden Rule in the system of Judaism? The declaration that the Golden Rule encompasses the Torah and all the rest is commentary assigns to the Rule a critical position. But as we have seen, to define the central- ity of the Golden Rule we have to leave the narrow limits of "loving one's neigh- bor as oneself" and introduce the rule of reciprocity in a generic framework of jurisprudence. So is it central or peripheral? That is a question that can be answered only episodically. When the Rabbinic documents attempt to state the heart of the matter, do they invoke the Golden Rule outside of the context in which it is introduced and made explicit? The answer is simple. We do not find the Golden Rule invoked where we should anticipate locating it. Take the case of an explicit exercise in reduction of the laws to the heart of the matter. I indent the supplementary insertions that amplify the primary statement:

> B. R. Simelai expounded, "Six hundred and thirteen commandments were given to Moses, three hundred and sixty-five negative ones, corresponding to the number of the days of the solar year, and two hundred forty-eight positive commandments, corresponding to the parts of man's body."
> D. [Simelai continues:] "David came and reduced them to eleven: 'A Psalm of David: Lord, who shall sojourn in thy tabernacle, and who shall dwell in thy holy mountain? (i) He who walks uprightly and (ii) works righ- teousness and (iii) speaks truth in his heart and (iv) has no slander on his tongue and (v) does no evil to his fellow and (vi) does not take up a reproach against his neighbor, (vii) in whose eyes a vile person is despised but (viii) honors those who fear the Lord. (ix) He swears to his own hurt and changes not. (x) He does not lend on interest. (xi) He does not take a bribe against the innocent'" (Ps. 15).

We have the opportunity to invoke the Golden Rule and to amplify the list of virtues by appeal to the principle of reciprocity. But reciprocity does not enter in.

> V. [Simelai continues:] "Isaiah came and reduced them to six: '(i) He who walks righteously and (ii) speaks uprightly, (iii) he who despises the gain of oppressions, (iv) shakes his hand from holding bribes, (v) stops his ear

from hearing of blood (vi) and shuts his eyes from looking upon evil, he shall dwell on high'" (Isa. 33.25–26).

Once more we have the opportunity to invoke the Golden Rule. It comes close to the surface at X: "one who does not belittle his fellow in public." But there is no appeal to the Golden Rule, though one may claim that it is implicit.

FF.   [Simelai continues:] "Micah came and reduced them to three: 'It has been told you, man, what is good, and what the Lord demands from you, (i) only to do justly and (ii) to love mercy, and (iii) to walk humbly before God'" (Mic. 6.8).

GG.   "only to do justly:" this refers to justice.

HH.   "to love mercy:" this refers to doing acts of loving kindness.

II.   "to walk humbly before God:" this refers to accompanying a corpse to the grave.

JJ.   And does this not yield a conclusion a fortiori: if matters that are not ordinarily done in private are referred to by the Torah as "walking humbly before God," all the more so matters that ordinarily are done in private.

KK.   [Simelai continues:] "Isaiah again came and reduced them to two: 'Thus says the Lord, (i) Keep justice and (ii) do righteousness'" (Isa. 56.1).

LL.   "Amos came and reduced them to a single one, as it is said, 'For thus says the Lord to the house of Israel. Seek Me and live.'"

MM.   Objected R. Nahman bar Isaac, "Maybe the sense is, 'seek me' through the whole of the Torah?"

NN.   Rather, [Simelai continues:] "Habakkuk further came and based them on one, as it is said, 'But the righteous shall live by his faith'" (Hab. 2.4).

Bavli Makkot 3:12 II:1/23B–24A

"The righteous shall live by his faith" treats right attitude toward God as the generative principle of the Torah—and not the ethical rule of reciprocity. One's trust in God defines the heart of the matter, and in the exposition of that matter loving one's neighbor as oneself does not register. Here we have an occasion for appeal to the Golden Rule, but there is no hint that the matter makes an impact. Faith and trust in God, now form the heart of the matter. There is no hint that the Golden Rule is the ultimate generative rule of the Torah.

How does the Golden Rule work with the religion's other component parts—myths, beliefs, rituals, ethics—to produce coherence? The answer is, for the Golden Rule to interact with the theological principles of Judaism, we must invoke the principle of God's justice, which man emulates. Then the Golden Rule requires translation into the principle of divine justice. On its own it does not register. It is, as I said, parachuted down into a composite to the details of which the Golden Rule is irrelevant. Other teachings and practices hardly depend on the Golden Rule. We cannot identify specific teachings or actions as particular applications of the Golden Rule. But I can identify no major alternatives or challenges to the Golden Rule. It is inert.

Conclusion

Classical Judaism is defined by generative propositions and invites judgment concerning systemic traits. But the Golden Rule in its articulated form is not one of these. Hillel is given another aphorism, one that competes with the Golden Rule:

> He [Hillel] would say,
>   (1) "If I am not for myself, who is for me?"
>   (2) "And when I am for myself, what am I?"
>   (3) "And if not now, when?"
>   Abot 1:14 A

That forms the corollary to the Golden Rule. One must preserve one's own dignity. But in doing so, one must accommodate the dignity of others. And the occasion is always the present. Reciprocity requires self-esteem, but also regard for the other, and urgency pervades. If the Golden Rule stands solitary in the Rabbinic system, its corollary stands in splendid isolation even from the Golden Rule, the paradox on which it is built forming an enigmatic variation. What of Hillel's mandate, "go, study?" The legal system and its rules await the analysis of how the Golden Rule pervades the whole. The theological-narrative system and its exegesis of Scripture wait the extenuation of the conflict captured in the clauses, "If I am not for myself, who is for me? And when I am for myself, what am I?" When descriptive and analytical work has produced for other religious systems a comparable description of the systemic consequence of the Golden Rule, we shall find it possible to compare the role of the Golden Rule in two or more systems. Then we may generalize about the role of commonplace propositions in religions.

Chapter 6

The Golden Rule in Zoroastrianism

Mahnaz Moazami
Columbia University

The Golden Rule is a well-entrenched concept in Zoroastrian ethics. It has been advocated and practiced throughout the history of its moral philosophy, a history imbued with remarkable verve and vigor, and conveying a sense of realism and high seriousness to moral life. The very idea of a radical distinction between the good and the bad is an essential source of this vigor. The goal of Zoroastrian ethics is summed up in the triad of "good thought, good word, good action," and constitutes the foundation for faith. These virtues imply thinking and speaking about the world as an ordered cosmos created by the Good Spirit, performing the acts required to maintain this sense of equilibrium, and conducting a virtuous life by implementing truth, purity, the right measure, and god-given order.

In order to bring out the significance of the Golden Rule within the context of the history of Zoroastrianism, some preliminary general remarks may be helpful: Zoroastrianism, the religion of the ancient Iranians, named after prophet Zarathustra (Zoroastres in Greek sources) is one of the oldest religions in the world. It flourished in the long era of the Sasanian dynasty (224–651 C.E.) when it was the state religion of the Persian Empire. Zoroastrian sources are principally the Avesta and the Middle Persian (Pahlavi) texts. These constitute a considerable corpus of liturgies, hymns, commentaries, and theological works, much of it orally transmitted and covering an immense time-span from Zarathustra himself to the late Sasanian period and beyond.

The Avesta contains the sacred texts in Avestan language. It is a collection of texts of different dates and various contents that were orally transmitted for centuries and exposed to the changing views and perceptions of different times, before they were finally written down in about 500 C.E. It was organized into twenty-one sections, but much was lost.

From 520 B.C.E. on we have the inscriptions in Old Persian on the order of Achaemenid kings who worshipped Ahura Mazda and followed the religion of the Avesta. From that time to the seventh century C.E. Arab-Islamic conquest of Iran, Zoroastrianism was the religion of the Iranian kings. The religion survived foreign invasion and the challenge of new faiths, but in the ninth century many Zoroastrians migrated to India to escape oppression in Iran. It was at that time that Zoroastrian theologians began writing down their knowledge about the religion, producing new compilations in Middle Persian.[1]

One of the defining features of Zoroastrian religion, as delineated in the Gathas and in other parts of the Avesta, is the doctrine of dualism. The world is imagined as a field of conflict in which Order and Chaos, good and bad, truth and falsehood, are constantly locked in a struggle for supremacy. God (Ahura Mazda, the Good Spirit, Ohrmazd) and the Devil (Angra Manyu, the Evil Spirit, Ahreman) were both involved in the creation process and the world naturally contains both good and evil elements. The struggle is intense, but the Good will ultimately triumph over the Evil.

This idea of a choice between good and evil has been at the heart of Zoroastrianism throughout its entire history. Freedom of the will forms the basis and foundation of the Zoroastrian ethos. A human being is a creature of the Good Spirit and belongs to the realm of good, but is created as a free agent and has a right to choose. In fact, all living beings have to make a choice between the constructive and destructive values represented by the two spirits. Those who choose the just become the most precious allies of the Good Spirit in his struggle with the Evil Spirit and will prepare the world for salvation.

At the end of the world, each person is required to pass over the bridge of the Compiler,[2] before which the register of one's thoughts, words, and deeds is made, accompanied by the *Daena*. The *Daena/Den* represents the totality of a person's thoughts, words, and acts in life. In the Pahlavi commentary on *Yasna* 26.6 *Daena* is glossed by *kunishn* "acts." In the *Hadokht nask* (10–11) and the later Zoroastrian texts, the *Daena* is identical with the soul's good thought, speech, and deeds. The first Zoroastrian teachers considered *Daena* to be "that which one always does";[3] for in relation to thoughts and words, it is one's deeds that can effectively be counted and verified (on the day of reckoning), for words are unreliable, thoughts unascertainable, but deeds are palpable, and (it is) by deeds that human beings are judged.[4]

The Zoroastrian religion puts a great emphasis on morals and ethics. A Zoroastrian is expected to be capable of making a conscious effort every moment of his life, to reject all forms of evil and lies in thought, word, and deed and strive at all times to walk on the path of Asha, the Cosmic Law of Order and Harmony on which the entire Universe is based. It is through Order that Ohrmazd created the universe and it is through Order that mankind will achieve perfection and become one with his creator. In the Avesta it is stated repeatedly that Zarathustra was the first to worship Ahura Mazda's Order and this became the duty of every good Zoroastrian, as expressed in the *Fravarane*, the Zoroastrian "profession of faith."[5]

[1] See H. W. Bailey, *Zoroastrian Problems in the Ninth-Century Books*, Oxford, 1971, pp. 151–53.
[2] *Vidēvdād*, chap. 19.29, ed. Darmesteter, 1960, vol. II, p. 270.
[3] *Dēnkard Book VI*, ed. Madan, 1911, p. 479.21; ed. Shaked, 1979, 34, p. 15.
[4] Kanga, 1960, p. 24.
[5] That is, "statement of one's choice"; *Yasna* 11.16, ed. Darmesteter, 1960, vol. I, p. 116.

Acts that are in accordance with Order are meritorious and productive activities with respect to land and herds of animals, establishing secure and peaceful settlements and promoting the welfare and the well-being of others. But beyond these general utilitarian considerations there are other fundamental issues in the ethical conception: The value of freedom, the right and responsibility of an individual to make his or her own choice is of utmost importance.

The Middle Persian texts constitute the largest corpus of Zoroastrian writings. These texts were mainly collected, edited and codified in the ninth century, but based on earlier traditions. A popular branch of Middle Persian literature consists of *Andarz* or wisdom literature,[6] and it is particularly in this corpus of literature that the Zoroastrian Golden Rule appears, although no specific term for it seems to exist in these texts.

It is possible that the Golden Rule in its first general formulation entered Zoroastrian literature from Mesopotamia. Apart from fragments of the Aramaic version of the trilingual Bisotun inscription found in the Jewish community of Elephantine (mostly from the fifth century B.C.E.), there were also fragments of the writing known by the name of "the Wisdom of Ahiqar."[7] But summaries of Avestan passages in Middle Persian are also found in the wisdom literature, which testify to the existence of this literature in Iran as early as the period when the late Avestan literature was composed.[8] This was the time when Zoroastrian religion found itself at close quarters with Judaism and Christianity in the Sasanian period and Zoroastrians had to encounter all kinds of "irreligious" peoples.[9]

The wisdom literature covers mainly three essential topics: instruction on the Zoroastrian code of behavior and morals, advice regarding suitable thought and action in everyday life, and rules of etiquette. The main theme of this literature is wisdom, obtained through experience and for the benefit of the person himself, not for any other purpose.

Zoroastrians, by following the advices and counsels of the sages, itself the legacy of the experience of several seasoned and knowledgeable generations, can avoid making mistakes and suffering through their own inexperience. They would all as a result live better lives in the more secure, friendly, and harmonious society that this principle would generate, and cooperate with each other more willingly.

The Zoroastrian wisdom literature cannot be ascribed to a single author, even though several well-known religious personalities, men of authority, kings and counselors, have been named as authors of the most popular ones. These collections are often in the form of questions asked by a disciple or a son with

---

[6] For a survey of this literary genre see Shaked, 1987a, pp. 11–16.
[7] Ahiqar was an Assyrian sage celebrated in the ancient Near East for his wisdom.
[8] See de Menasce, 1958, pp. 38–39.
[9] It must be noted that the extant manuscripts that contain wisdom literature in Middle Persian are of much later period, mostly from the fourteenth century onwards.

answers provided by the sage in short and pithy sentences that emphasize the moral and spiritual aspects of faith. As Mary Boyce puts it, many of them are simply the surviving representatives of a popular type of oral composition, which have become associated with religious works, and have thus had the chance to survive.[10]

The aim of the redactor of these texts was to provide the Zoroastrians with an interpretation of their religion that would encourage them to remain steadfast in their faith. The emphasis is on the virtues of generosity, truthfulness, wisdom, and kindness: "People have seven things which are best. Good fame, righteousness, nobility, lordship, authority, health and satisfaction. Nobility is this: a man who gives presents to the good and the worthy."[11] The majority of the wisdom literature seems to have belonged to the type of compositions that could be used as catechetical instructions. As Shaul Shaked has attempted to demonstrate with regard to Book VI of the *Denkard* (deeds of the *Den*/religion), in spite of relative sophistication of thought, scholastic moralizing, and allegorizing, *andarz* are not a departure from orthodox religion but rather another means of urging the laity toward religion.[12]

The most complete extant record of wisdom literature replete with religious and ethical precepts is Book VI of the *Denkard*,[13] which recounts the sayings of the first teachers of Zoroastrian religion as well as some precepts of the Zoroastrian high priests. The book is introduced as presenting what has been done and held by the pious and the word of the Zoroastrian religion, that is the Avesta. Mary Boyce has pointed out that, of the series of wisdom literature that constitutes Book VI of the *Denkard*, the first and longest set of these probably derives from the Middle Persian translation of the *Barish nask*,[14] a lost book of the Avesta on religious ethics.[15] It is also possible that these may be late gnomic sayings attributed pseudepigraphically to the Sasanian sages.[16]

It is in the opening section of Book VI of the *Denkard* that we find the most quoted Zoroastrian Golden Rule: "that character is best, one who does not do to another that which is not good for himself."[17] Among the five rules of conduct or virtues the first one is: "not to do to others all that which is not good to one's self."[18]

---

[10] Boyce, 1968, p. 53.
[11] *Denkard Book VI*, ed. Shaked, 1979, 113, p. 45; see also *The Pahlavi Rivāyat*, chap. 62, ed. Williams, 1990, in which several of the sayings correspond to passages in *Denkard VI*.
[12] Shaked, 1969, p. 199.
[13] The *Denkard* is an encyclopedia of Zoroastrian religious knowledge; it consists of nine books, of which the first, second and part of the third book are no longer extant. The contents of the book, which is essentially a compilation, belong to different periods, but the final redaction took place in the ninth century.
[14] Boyce, 1968, p. 52.
[15] *Denkard Book VIII*, ed. Madan, 1911, p. 685, 11.
[16] See Shaked, 1979, p. xviii.

Book III of the *Denkard* is another source for the Zoroastrian Golden Rule. In this book the record of moral qualities and faults is laid out more strictly. Among the ten supreme advices of Zarathustra to humans, the fourth is: "In order that to each person comes not misfortune, but happiness, desire for everybody not misfortune, but happiness."[19] The passage is followed by the admonitions of Akht, a sorcerer and, according to Zoroastrian tradition, a fiery early opponent of the Zoroastrian religion. The book attributes to Akht "of evil knowledge" ten admonitions against the Religion. He is portrayed as taking up the opposite of Zarathustra's commands: hostility to the gods, friendship with the demons, and the practice of evil works, sorcery, and harm to people. His fourth admonition is: "one must desire for each person not happiness, but misfortune."[20] These objections mainly function as an introduction to the establishment of the proper Zoroastrian point of view and reflect a situation where Zoroastrianism found itself competing with a number of religions that attempted to convert Iranians to their message. They were also used for instructing and educating Zoroastrians and perhaps for preparing them for actual debates with other beliefs.

The dominant theme of the wisdom literature in Zoroastrianism emphasizes the important significance of the good deed. The life of good thought, word, and deed is the logical and determined enactment of Order that brings progress, harmony, and happiness. Good thought and good words lead humans to good intentions, to bring order into action, and reinstate happiness and harmony. This conception is in accord with free will, the need for choice, and shouldering responsibility for the consequences of one's choices. The duty of improving the world is viewed by Zarathustra as a religious obligation, and people who live by it gain salvation. The main thrust of wisdom literature is on the demand for an active effort in the service of religion and the glorification of the deed as merit. "Religion is that, namely: one who causes comfort to every creature."[21]

The good deed is its own reward,[22] for which reason people are strongly warned against the sinful deed,[23] while the honorable deed is of such a character that it can speed up the eschatological transformation.[24] The deed paves the way for faith, for "it has been said that thousand men cannot by speaking make one man to believe to the same degree (in such a way) as one man by a deed can make thousand do so."[25] A good deed in a proper sense, that is,

---

[17] *Denkard Book VI*, ed. Shaked, 1979, §2, p. 5.
[18] See *The Supplementary Texts to the Šāyest nē-Šāyest*, ed. Kotwal, 1969, chap. 13.29.
[19] *Denkard Book III*, ed. de Menasce, 1973, chap. 195, p. 203.
[20] Ed. Madan, I, pp. 210–12; ed. de Menasce, 1973, 196, pp. 203–05.
[21] *Denkard Book VI*, ed. Shaked, 1979, 36, p. 17.
[22] *Denkard Book IX*, ed. Madan, 1911, p. 875, 14.
[23] For example, *The Pahlavi Texts II*, ed. Jamasp-Asana, 1913, p. 98, 180.
[24] *The Pahlavi Texts II*, ed. Jamasp-Asana, 1913, p. 99, 195.
[25] *Denkard Book VI*, ed. Madan, 1911, p. 577, 2–4; ed. Shaked, 1979, E15, p. 191.

without considering its function in the religious system of compensation and
the ethical ideals altogether, is easily determined, positively and negatively, by
means of the lists of vices and virtues. According to the *Denkard* the five best
things in religion are: "truthfulness, generosity, being possessed of virtue, dili-
gence and advocacy. This truthfulness is best: one who acts (in such a manner)
to the creatures of Ohmarzd that the recipient of his action has so much more
benefit when he acts like that to him."[26]

During the Sasanian period several religious movements competed for adher-
ents with one another and with the official religion. This can be seen from the
inscriptions of the Sasanian kings and notably from those of Kerdir,[27] the high
priest, who states that thanks to his efforts under king Bahram II (276–293),
Zoroastrianism was promoted in the empire and other religious communities
were persecuted. Kerdir's religious policy is clearly an ideal program, a literary
construct, based upon the requirements of the religion. In Sasanian Iran, religion played a central role in the life of society, regulating the entire range of
social and political life and official standards of behavior. Religious authorities
were present everywhere from the local places of worship to the royal court to
watch over the preservation of religious tradition in all aspect of people's life,
and Sasanian kings acted as promoters of the Zoroastrian creed. And it was
during the Sasanian period that the first written recording of the Avesta was
undertaken to follow and compete with such models as the Torah, the Bible,
and the Manichaean books, thereby including the Zoroastrians in the category
"people of books." The establishment of a written scripture was to have a great
significance for the later history of the Zoroastrian community, particularly
those in Islamic lands.

Similar to many other scriptural traditions, Zoroastrians commentators have
come forward to encounter this intellectual and spiritual challenge in order to
reconcile the powerful and simple message of the Golden Rule with finer points
of doctrine. Adurbad, son of Mahraspand, the high priest of Shapur II (309–379)
and a key figure in Zoroastrian history is supposed to have been the author of
a number of works of wisdom literature.[28] According to the Zoroastrian tradition, Adurbad successfully underwent the ordeal of molten bronze in order to
prove the truth of the Zoroastrian faith.[29] Adurbad played an important role

[26] *Dēnkard Book VI,* ed. Shaked, 1979, 23, p. 11.
[27] The high priest Kerdir served under five consecutive Sasanian kings in the second half of
the third century and left four great inscriptions in Fars, all written in Middle Persian.
Three of the inscriptions are at Naqsh-e Rajab and Naqsh-e Rostam near Persepolis, the
fourth at Sar Mashad on an ancient highway between Susa and Persepolis, in which he
records the deeds of a powerful career and the multitude of titles he received. See Skjaervø,
1997.
[28] Five Pahlavi *andarz* works and at least another one in an Arabic translation (The *Mawa'z
Adhurbadh* in Ebn Meskawayh's *Al-Hekmat al-Khaleda: jawidan kherad,* ed. A. Badawi, Cairo
1952, pp. 26–30; see Shaked 1979, p. 283) are assigned to him.
[29] See *Škand-Gumānīk Vičār,* ed. de Menasce, 1945, 10.71, p. 119; also the Book of *Ardā Wīrāz,*
1.1–17, for the translation of the passage see Bailey, 1971, pp. 151–52.

in the definition of the Zoroastrian doctrine[30] and his ordeal might be related to matters of scriptural disagreement.[31]

. In fulfilling his religious fervor, Adurbad was instrumental in directing and implementing of decrees against non-Zoroastrians. Book III of the *Denkard* attributes ten precepts to Adurbad,[32] which follow a set of evil counsels supposedly pronounced by the prophet Mani (d. ca. 276 C. E.) to contradict the good sayings of Adurbad. This may well reflect an actual participation of the high priest in the persecution of Manicheans. Mani appeared at a time when the Sasanian kings were striving to establish a firm spiritual basis for their rule by strengthening the clergy and defining the religion. Adurbad's composition is a lucid and vigorous declaration of faith designed to encourage Iranians to hold on to their faith against alien temptations. In one of his sayings, Adurbad addresses his son: "Do not do unto others what would not be good for yourself."[33]

A collection of questions addressed to Adurbad by a disciple, and Adurbad's answers to these, is found in *The Pahlavi Rivāyat Accompanying the Dādestān i Dēnīg*. And it is in this collection that he says: "love for people is that he for whom the benefit and well-being of all good men is just as necessary as his own; that which does not seem good for himself he does not do to anyone (else).[34] In another he says: "that one disposition (is) good when one does not do unto others (that) which (is) not goodness unto himself."[35]

Parallels between the admonitions attributed to Adurbad and the sayings of Ahiqar in both the frame story and the precepts strengthen the hypothesis that the latter was one of the main sources used by the compiler of Adurbad's wisdom.[36]

Zoroastrian theologians were also familiar with the Aristotelian system of thought and used it extensively. Greek ideas were adopted in the Pahlavi writings and had an important role in the formation of late Zoroastrian thinking in the Sasanian period. The influence of Greek thought on Iranian ideas can be seen specifically in the area of ethics.[37] The main concept of the Aristotelian

---

[30] According to tradition, he divided the Avesta in 21 sections, and compiled the Zoroastrian book of common prayer, the *Khordeh Avesta* (the "Little Avesta"), and composed in Middle Persian works of moral and theological instruction. His son, Zardusht, carried on the work, authoring a book of catechism, *The Čidag andarz ī Pōryōtkēšān* ("Select Counsels of the Ancient Sages").

[31] It must be noted that the final version of the scripture seems to have been established during the reign of Khosrow I, A.D. 531–79; see Bailey 1943, p. 173.

[32] Ed. de Menasce, 1973, chap. 199, pp. 208–10.

[33] *The Pahlavi Texts II*, ed. Jamasp-Asana, 1913, p. 58, 5.

[34] *The Pahlavi Rivāyat*, chap. 62.25, ed. Williams, 1990, p. 109; cf. also *Dēnkard VI*, ed. Madan, 1911, pp. 588.22, 589.2; ed. Shaked, 1979, E45e, p. 215.

[35] JamaspAsa, 1970, p. 208; Cf. *Pahlavi Texts II*, ed. Jamasp-Asana, p. 58, 13–59.

[36] See de Blois' collection of 24 parallel sayings of Adurbad and Ahiqar, 1984, pp. 41–53.

[37] J. de Menasce was the first to point out the similarity between the Zoroastrian discussions of virtues and vices and the schemes that emerge from Aristotle's *Nicomachean Ethics*; de Menasce, 1945, p. 30–32; 1958, 39–40.

theory of ethics, the idea of the Mean, finds its echo in the Zoroastrian concept of *payman,* the right measure. This concept of right measure is discussed at length in the Middle Persian texts and is central to its wisdom literature. The right measure is the middle way, doing as much as one ought to, neither too much nor too little.

In the Book VII of *Denkard,* it is said that it was by the strength of the right measure that Jam, the king of Golden Age of mankind, maintained the creation immortal.[38] Once the right measure was lost, immortality also became impossible. In two chapters about "right measure" and "too much and too little" in the Book III of *Denkard,* a myth is related that people in Jam's perfect world were lured by the demons and corrupted to the point that they could no longer be immortal. Jam called the demons and asked them who created the world, to which they answered that they created it and would now destroy it. Jam told them that it is not possible to be both a creator and a destroyer, thus revealing the lie of the demons and ensuring the immortality of humans.[39] According to this story, the *Asn khrad,* the wisdom one is born with, had been stolen by the demons, but brought back to humans together with the right measure by Jam, who spent thirteen years in Hell in the disguise of a demon, finally overcoming them and returning to human beings their "desire and profit."[40]

Moderation, entrenched in justice in law and moral behavior in ethics, is the touchstone in Zoroastrian religious philosophy: "moderate is he who plans everything according to the (right) measure, so that more and less should not be therein, for the (right) measure (is) the completeness of everything, except those things in which there is no need for moderation: knowledge, love, and good deeds."[41] This concept appears to be in conflict with the dualistic system of Zoroastrianism. Nevertheless, the Aristotelian ethical theory was grafted to the traditional Zoroastrian notions of ethics. The authors of Zoroastrian texts mixed the Greek idea with their own worldview while providing the Aristotelian theory with a strong Zoroastrian flavor.[42] The notion is even presented as a purely Iranian one,[43] and indeed it has old Iranian roots, for example, in the grading and taxonomy of characters not only as good or as extreme or moderate, but also as forward-inclined and backward-inclined. The former type indicates qualities of energy, initiative, and activity, both good and bad, and the latter groups together qualities of restraint and withdrawal. A wise man has virtues of both types in the right measure, allotted to him by the Creator.[44]

---

[38] *Dēnkard Book VII,* 1.20, ed. Molé, 1967, p. 7.
[39] *Dēnkard Book III,* 227, ed. de Menasce 1973, pp. 239–40, 281–83.
[40] Ibid, 286; for the full translation of the passage see Zaehner, 1955, pp. 250–51; ed. de Menasce 1973, pp. 281–83.
[41] *The Pahlavi Rivāyat,* chap. 62.18, ed. Williams, 1990, p. 108.
[42] See Shaked, 1987b, p. 219.
[43] *Dēnkard Book IV,* ed. Madan, 1911, p. 429, 11–12.
[44] See Shaked, 1979, pp. xl–xli and 1987b, p. 220.

Since, as indicated above, the concept of the right measure is an integral part of Zoroastrian wisdom literature, it follows that in the Zoroastrian Golden Rule the emphasis is always placed on moderation and the avoidance of extremes. But what is demanded first and foremost of man is common sense. The common sense view of life is that humans should enjoy the good things of this world while at the same time preparing themselves, through right and reasonable conduct, for eternal life in the other world.

The high ethical implications of the Golden Rule are explicit in Book IX of *Denkard,* which recapitulates passages on ethics from the lost Avesta: "Those are beneficial who increase for the developer,[45] that is, they shall make goodness for him who would make that goodness which is for others."[46] Here the Golden Rule is associated with desiring goodness for all humankind. And "The best prosperity is produced for whoever produces for anyone else what is suitable/good for him."[47]

The sense of responsibility toward just people is one of the strongest characteristics of Zoroastrian religion as "every just man is the counterpart of the Lord Ohrmazd."[48] According to *The Dādestān ī Mēnōg ī Xrad* (the judgments of the divine wisdom), "the greatest deed is to be grateful in the world and to desire good fortune unto all."[49] The wise man asked the divine wisdom: "Through how many ways and means of righteousness can people reach the paradise? The divine wisdom replied: Through charity, truth, gratitude, contentment, goodness toward the victorious and friendliness toward all."[50]

In Zoroastrianism the Golden Rule evolved from and remained bound to the concept of justice. But what would promote contentment and be just to all? It is the responsibility of the believer to stand for what is regarded as essentially right: "Do not do anything for others which is not good for yourself."[51] One should do good rather than evil because it is in one's own self-interest to do so. He who does good deeds will be rewarded, and he who sins will be punished.[52] All that the body has done, the soul will see.[53] Human beings are bodily and spiritually creatures of the Good Spirit and by their actions have a strong potential for what is good. After they have chosen their side, they expect divine beings to be on their side. The relation between the divine and human is part of a system of reciprocity and both participants have their assigned tasks and are dependent on each other.

---

[45] Lit. provider of much growth.
[46] *Denkard Book IX,* ed. Madan, 1911, p. 936, 11–13.
[47] Ibid, p. 876, 14–15.
[48] *The Supplementary Texts to the Šāyest nē-Šāyest,* ed. Kotwal, 1969, chap. 15.8, p. 59.
[49] Ed. Sanjana, 1895, chap. 63.
[50] Ed. Sanjana, 1895, chap. 37.1–8, p. 54.
[51] *The Pahlavi Texts II,* ed. Jamasp-Asana, 1913, p. 58, 5.
[52] Ibid, p. 67, 108.
[53] Ibid, p. 77, 32.

Wisdom and righteousness, piety and justice, are the virtues most prominently associated with a Zoroastrian Golden Rule that is revered as the central pillar of an entire moral edifice. It requires a correct attitude toward one's fellow humans. It is presented as an indispensable point of doctrine: "If you desire that anybody may not insult you, do not insult anybody,"[54] and "Anybody who digs a well for an enemy will himself fall into it."[55] It governs the way the righteous individual treats each and every other person. In other words, the ethical precept in Zoroastrianism is a means for cultivating virtue.

In the Zoroastrian religion negatively stated rules are more frequent, delineating boundaries that must not be transgressed. Rules become a principle of justice requiring the virtue of self-restraint in all human beings, while the positively stated expressions of the Golden Rule invite people to be morally active and prescribe generosity. "These two instruments are best for men: to be oneself good and do good to others."[56]

Religious beliefs provide a way of looking at the world, and suggest a meaning to one's existence. The religious vision gives significance and value to human life and some direction toward salvation. The believer chooses to look at the world in this way and dedicates himself to a worthy way of life.

The original religious inspiration and the interpretation, perhaps even the additions and variations introduced at various times from which one can extract the fundamental core of the religious doctrine, must be taken into account. It should provide a vision of the world to which one can dedicate oneself and thereby find the relevance of one's existence and effort in the total scheme of things. One accepts a faith with all its contradictions and relies on an authority and standard used in judging beyond oneself or others. Faith is the keyword, defined above all as a compliance with the moral imperative. A religious tradition, its beliefs, practices, and its social structure, lives in the consciousness of its believers. In a world in which two opposing forces of good and bad constantly strive for domination, a human being is perpetually prone to being misguided as to what constitutes right behavior. The ethical qualities instilled by Zarathustra's teachings have enabled the religion to survive countless ups and downs, persecutions, and hardship. Zoroastrians equate morality with justice, rights, and the welfare of the individual. For Zoroastrians loyalty, respect for authority, and sanctity are moral concepts.

The commitment of Zarathustra to the moral precept is found in the following passage: "Apart from the salvation of one's soul, it is best to strive for saving other people's souls,"[57] which suggests that the Golden Rule is given not only to

---

[54] Ibid, p. 66, 92.
[55] Ibid, p. 67, 109.
[56] *Dēnkard Book VI*, ed. Shaked, 1979, 117, p. 49.
[57] Ibid, 127, p. 51.

the individual but also to the community. To act thus is to bring order into operation and restore wellbeing and harmony. It is a simple and open attitude toward one's happiness in conjunction with that of others.

However, in Zoroastrian morality there are no extremes of self-sacrifice: "One should take goodness from every one; one should not take evil from any one."[58] The Golden Rule mode of thinking in Zoroastrianism expresses a logic of fairness and consideration based on the recognition that others are like oneself. It gives guidance on practical issues to the community of the faithful. It protects individuals, prevents harm to the person with reciprocity and fairness, and applies to all members of the community, men and women. Each individual human being must take up the responsibility consciously to fight the forces of evil for good to win, for this created world, that is fundamentally good, to be purged and transformed, to be made immortal.

[58] Ibid, 22, p. 11.

Chapter 7

Jesus, the Golden Rule, and Its Application

Bruce Chilton
Bard College

Jesus insisted that we should love, not only our neighbors (Mt. 22.34–40; Mk 12.38–34; Lk. 10.27–28), but also our enemies (Mt. 5.43–48; Lk. 6.27–36), doing to them all as we would be done by (Mt. 7.12; Lk. 6.31).

His principle is simple; the complex relationship among the Gospel texts that state the principle shows that early disciples internalized Jesus' teaching and interpreted his words in ways that comported with their understandings of Jesus' significance.[1] Both New Testament and Patristic thinkers came to terms with his challenge, trying to define what the love by Jesus demanded is, and—often confronted by hostility, sometimes by lethal threats—to see whether at least some neighbors, or some enemies, might be excluded some of the time.

That attempt to deflect the force of Jesus' instruction grew as Christianity came to power, and the counterpoint between Jesus' plain imperative and theological maneuvers designed to reshape his teaching provides a lesson in the unease of intellect in the face of revelation. The tendency to think oneself out of an evident moral obligation is by no means unique to Christian discourse, but interpreters in the tradition of the Church have identified the problem in their own heritage in a way that might be productive within comparative study, as well as within Christian theology. The intellectual evasion of moral and/or revealed values is obviously too broad a topic for a short essay, but we can at least analyze this tendency by considering how the Golden Rule has been handled (1) in Christian interpretation; (2) in the most influential of the Gospels, the Gospel according to Matthew; and (3) in recent public discussion.

The Golden Rule in Christian interpretation

Even when the Fathers of the Church attempted to evade the call to universal love that is implicit in the Golden Rule, they understood it was an ethical

---

[1] A topic I have taken up elsewhere; see Chilton, "Altruism in Christianity," *Altruism in World Religions* edited with Jacob Neusner (Washington: Georgetown University Press, 2005), pp. 53–66. In this essay, I wish to extend some of the interpretative principles set out in the earlier, more exegetical publication, in terms of history and hermeneutics.

principle that was to be enacted. Recent studies have revealed the Rule's sim-
plicity within the diverse Gospel and Patristic texts, demonstrating that Jesus
taught the Rule and that his disciples have grappled with its significance from
the outset of the process of transmitting his words. Similarly, the questions
in regard to what love is and to whom it is owed are thoroughly investigated
within Patristic literature.[2] The outcome of a rich discussion is straightforward:
ethically, love is for the good that draws one's actions and one's being, and—if
Jesus is one's standard—there can be no exclusions in love's application. Patristic exegesis, following the precedent of the Gospel according to Matthew that
will be discussed below, deflected the force of Jesus' teaching by restricting its
application, not by denying its meaning.

Yet post-Enlightenment discussion of the Rule has taken a different turn in
critical circles, as compared to ancient interpretation. Instead of asking, "What
is love, and to whom is it directed?" the issue has become, "How did teaching
the Golden Rule make Jesus different from other teachers?"

In the attempt to argue that Jesus was unique, modern interpreters have
claimed that, while he insisted upon a Golden Rule of doing to others what you
wish them to do to you, other teachers "only" required their followers *not* to do
to others what they didn't want done to them. Examples are frequently cited
from sources as diverse as the Torah, Tobit 4.16, the Mahabharata, Confucius,
and the Talmud.

The language that modern interpreters have used to refer to all teachings
other than Jesus' is instructive. Two expressions are especially striking. Some
scholars call teachings other than Jesus' "the Silver Rule," making it valuable
indeed, but not quite up to the gold standard. The justification, as offered for
example by Ethelbert Stauffer,[3] is that the guidance of not doing what you dis-
like is a prohibition of bad action rather than an incentive toward good action.
As compared to this relegation to silver in relation to Jesus' gold, a current
dismissal more abruptly writes off the teachings of others as "The Negative
Form of the Golden Rule," or even as "The Negative Golden Rule."[4] This curious wording presents Jesus' teaching as if the switch from incentive to prohibition somehow reversed the force of the imperative.

The relegation and dismissal of expressions of the Rule unlike Jesus', along
with their equivalents, prove bankrupt in exegetical terms. After all, the base
text that Jesus cites from Leviticus (19.18)—to love your neighbor as yourself—
renders the Rule in its positive form, so Jesus can by no means be claimed as
the originator of the mandate as an incentive. Once the basic principle of the

---

[2] See *Lux in lumine: Essays to honor W. Norman Pittenger* edited by R. A. Norris, Jr. (New York: Sea-
bury Press, 1966).
[3] *Die Botschaft Jesu, Damals und Heute* (Bern: Francke, 1959).
[4] The fallacy was exposed long ago in an article by George Brockwell King that unfortunately
has not been accorded the attention it deserves: "The 'Negative' Golden Rule," *The Journal
of Religion* 8.2 (1928), 268-79.

affective life is stated, as in Leviticus, it is obviously applicable to negative affects of avoiding what is hurtful, as well as to positive affects of seeking what is beneficial.

For that reason, the *Letter of Aristeas* (207), which functions as an introduction to the Septuagint, refers *both* to avoiding evil on behalf of others as well as to seeking their good (see also Eccl. 31.15). This combination of prohibition and incentive, good and bad affect, has been shown to be part and parcel of several interpretive traditions, so that it is implausible to claim that Jesus is unique is framing the Golden Rule in positive terms.

The attempt to make a global contrast between Jesus and other teachers has produced a countertendency in New Testament exegesis. When Jesus was asked about the first commandment of all, he replied in the words of the *Shema' Yisrael*, that you are to love God with all your heart, all your soul, and all your mind (Deut. 6.4–5; Mk 12.29–30). That is the basic confession of Judaism that Jesus embraced, even if some rabbis today might legitimately question Jesus' orthodoxy on other grounds.[5] The second injunction Jesus cited (Mk 12.31), to love one's neighbor as oneself, also draws from the Torah (as we have already seen). When Jesus' teaching is described atomistically, in terms of its literal content point by point, it all but disappears against the background of contemporary ideas.

The two modern approaches, the one to contrast Jesus as much as possible with other teachers, and the other to equate him as much as possible with his environment, correspond to opposing claims about Jesus since the Enlightenment. One insists he is unique, and only understandable by faith, in the manner of John Henry Newman during the nineteenth century and Pope Benedict XVI today.[6] The other insists he is fully understandable as a product of his time, in the manner of Thomas Jefferson, who is named as the equivalent of its patron saint by "the Jesus Seminar" in its principal publication.[7]

In the case of the Golden Rule, neither view of Jesus in history proves viable. The Rule articulates a principle of the Torah, its interpretation, and of wider Near Eastern culture that existed for centuries prior to Jesus. Yet at the same time the Rule as expressed by Jesus is not a simple repetition of earlier statements. In between "unique" and "routine," we discover Jesus in history in the same way that we discover other historical figures—neither completely unprecedented nor banal, but distinctive and influential.

Love of God and love of neighbor were basic principles embedded in the Torah. Jesus' innovation lay in his claim that the two were indivisible. Love of

---

[5] See Jacob Neusner, *A Rabbi Talks with Jesus* (Montreal: McGill-Queen's University Press, 2000).

[6] Joseph Ratzinger (Pope Benedict XVI), *Jesus of Nazareth. From the Baptism in the Jordan to the Transfiguration* translated by Adrian J. Walker (New York: Doubleday, 2007).

[7] *The Five Gospels. The Search for the Authentic Words of Jesus: New Translation and Commentary* edited by Robert W. Funk and Roy W. Hoover (New York: Macmillan, 1993).

God *was* love of neighbor, and vice versa. Because, according to Jesus, God's love was transforming the world—thereby manifesting "the kingdom of God" (*malkhutha' d'Elaha'*) in Jesus' Aramaic language—and every person, friendly or not, needs to be seen in the context of God's presence. That is the basis of Jesus' distinctive and challenging ethic of love in the midst of persecution.[8] He linked the Rule to the transformed society the prophets had predicted. He promised that suffering could achieve transcendence, provided people are seen neither as threatening strangers, nor even as allies of convenience, but as mirrors of God's presence in the world. Because the neighbor reflects divine presence among us, loving that neighbor was tantamount to loving God in Jesus' teaching.

Jesus' vision of God in the midst of humanity marks his articulation of the Rule as distinctive. He believed he saw God at work changing the world, and he conveyed what he saw to his followers in the words and the practices that secured his reputation as a sage, a rabbi in the language of his time.[9] Seeing transformation involves willingness to be transformed, so that the kingdom of God in Jesus' teaching is an ethical imperative as well as an assurance of faith. The Golden Rule conveys that ethical imperative, putting it into words.

The promise of God's kingdom was that it should come, Jesus said, "in strength" (Mk 9.1)—that is both with the force of revelation and as a matter of action. The term for "strength" in Greek is *dunamis*, which appears over a hundred times in the New Testament, with surprising frequency in a work written by groups well away from political power or influence. That brings us to the Aramaic word *taqpha*, used before, during, and after Jesus' time to speak of the effective strength of revelation. He used that word to claim that love of neighbor effects the love of God and transforms the world. The disciples of Jesus, whose interpretations are embodied in the New Testament, as well as the Fathers of the Church, appreciated that ethics and revelation were indistinguishable, and that a dedication to the kingdom of God committed them to transformation. In the end they realized, as Jesus himself barely intuited, that the kingdom relativized even the Torah.

When we place Jesus within the context of his time and of the movement that derived from him, he does not disappear into his background. Neither does he appear alien within that setting. Rather, properly comparative and historical attention reveals him as a principal figure in generating a new religious vision, which saw God and humanity reflected in one another and as transforming the world with the strength of that revelation.

---

[8] See Chilton, *Rabbi Jesus. An Intimate Biography* (New York: Doubleday, 2000).
[9] See Chilton, *God in Strength. Jesus' Announcement of the Kingdom:* Studien zum Neuen Testament und seiner Umwelt 1 (Freistadt: Plöchl, 1979); *Pure Kingdom. Jesus' Vision of God: Studying the Historical Jesus* (Eerdmans: Grand Rapids and London: SPCK, 1996).

The Golden Rule in the Gospel according to Matthew

The Gospel "according to Matthew" (its title in antiquity) owes its position as the first book in the New Testament to its widespread usage in the ancient Church, as is shown by frequent references to this Gospel among the Fathers and within Gnostic writings. Understanding its perspective on Jesus' significance and its presentation of the Golden Rule will therefore help to explain how the early Church interpreted the Rule.[10]

This Gospel seems to owe its title to its identification of a tax agent and disciple by that name, Mathew (9.9), although he is called Levi in Mark (2.14) and Luke (5.27). Yet the name "Matthew" does appear in all three Synoptic Gospels as among the Twelve (Mt. 10.3; Mk 3.18; Lk. 6.15): the first Gospel's innovation lies not in the name, but in its association of that name with the disciple who was or had been a tax agent.

The first Gospel shows a keen interest in how Jesus' life and work fulfills prophecies in the Scriptures of Israel, in the final judgment which is to accompany the end of the world, in Jesus' teaching of angelology, and in the emerging custom of celibacy among believers (see, for example, Mt. 19.1–12, a passage with uniquely Matthean additions as compared to Mark, the earlier text). All of these features suggest a Syrian provenience, and particularly an origin in Damascus (although Antioch has also been suggested), where there were disciples of Jesus from shortly after the resurrection, and where Jewish communities thrived. Among them, the Essenes also featured prominently and some distinguishing characteristics of Matthew's Gospel echo features of the Dead Sea Scrolls. Chapter 23 of the Gospel nonetheless reflects the growing tension with many Jewish communities that did not recognize Jesus as son of God and messiah, as well as the growing importance of the institution of the synagogue in the period after 70 C.E., when the Romans destroyed the Temple. The Roman arson finds its allusion in Mt. 22.7. That reference, together with the evidence of the growing power of the Pharisees and the influence of synagogues, has suggested to scholars that the Gospel should be dated around 80 C.E.

Considerable overlap with the Gospel according to Mark has led many scholars to suppose that Mark constituted a source for Matthew, but the shared material need not all have been in written form, since oral instruction was vital within the primitive Church. Similarly, the presence of some 200 verses, for the most part sayings of Jesus, in both Matthew and Luke has prompted the hypothesis of a written document called "Q," named after the German term *Quelle*

---

[10] For recent discussion of Matthew in literary and theological terms, see Raymond E. Brown, *The Birth of the Messiah: A Commentary on the Birth Narratives in Matthew and Luke.* (New York: Doubleday, 1977); W. D. Davies and Dale C. Allison, *A Critical and Exegetical Commentary on the Gospel According to Saint Matthew* (Edinburgh: T. & T. Clark, 1997); A. H. McNeile, *The Gospel According to St. Matthew* (New York: St. Martin's, 1955); Daniel Patte, *The Gospel According to Matthew: A Structural Commentary on Matthew's faith* (Philadelphia: Fortress, 1987).

("source"), but sayings need have been no more formalized in writing than the teachings of Peter, James (the brother of Jesus), and Barnabas, which also seem to have influenced the composition of Matthew.

But the first Gospel is no mere patchwork of sources. Its structure is clearly marked through its preface, a unique presentation of Jesus' birth from the perspective of Scriptural fulfillment (chapters 1–2), and through five clearly marked sections that tie together narrative and discourse (including the famous and uniquely Matthean Sermon on the Mount) as Jesus progresses from his baptism and preaching in Galilee (section one, chapters 3–7), through his healings, both personally and by means of the Twelve (section two, chapters 8–10), into an emphasis upon his own persona (section three, chapters 11–13), until he explicitly proclaims his authority to his followers (section four, chapters 14–17), and clashes with the authorities in Jerusalem (section five, chapters 19–25). Jesus' passage through death to resurrection (chapters 26–28) is the capstone of the Gospel, which is more strongly marked by narrative than by discourse, as in the five central sections.

The fivefold structure of the middle section recalls the five books of Moses. This impression is strengthened by the explicit contrast between Jesus' rules for his people and those given by Moses in the first discourse (Mt. 5.21, 27, 31, 33, 38, 43). Just as Moses went up on the mountain to give instruction to God's people (Dt. 8.1–2), so Jesus repeatedly in Matthew ascends a mountain to instruct God's people and to manifest his divine authority (Mt. 4.8; 5.1; 14.23; 15.29, 39; 17.1; 28.19–20). In Jesus' sketch of this people's responsibility to God in the first Gospel there is a distinctive emphasis on true righteousness, in contrast to that of the Pharisaic tradition (Mt. 3.15; 5.6, 10, 20; 6.1, 33). That theme is most fully developed in a discourse section that does not fit the pattern sketched above in our outline, and seems to have been added to earlier traditions of the Gospel as the hostility between Matthew's community and the Pharisees (or Rabbis) intensified (Mt. 23). This hostility comes to its most radical expression when the Jewish people willingly call down responsibility for shedding Jesus' blood on themselves *and their children*, and this after Pilate—the only person with authority to order the execution—has washed his hands of guilt (Mt. 27.24–25). The climax of the Gospel is reached at the close, when the eleven disciples (after Judas delivered Jesus to the authorities and then killed himself) are commanded to make disciples of all nations by baptism "in the name of the father and of the son and of the holy spirit," and by teaching them to keep Jesus' commandments (Mt. 28.19–20).

Matthew's structure reflects a fraught relationship with Judaism, and therefore with Jews, who are all but formally excluded from the horizon of the love expressed in the Golden Rule.[11] References within the Gospels as a whole to

---

[11] See Bruce Chilton and Jacob Neusner, *Judaism in the New Testament. Practices and Beliefs* (London and New York: Routledge, 1995; electronically published, London: Taylor & Francis,

groups and movements within Judaism typically become sensible within the context of the social history of Christianity. Priests appear locally, in adjudications of purity (Mt. 8.1–4; Mk 1.40–45; Lk. 5.12–14 cf., 10.31, 17.14; see the exceptional role of Zechariah in 1.5–23), where Jesus challenges their role. He claims that he can declare clean in a matter that Leviticus expressly assigns to priests (cf. Lev. 14.1–9). Evidently, Jesus understood purity in a way that brought him into conflict with a straightforward, priestly interpretation of scripture, and the issue of purity also set him at odds with some Pharisees. References to high priests in the Gospels portray their power as essentially circumscribed by the boundaries of Jerusalem, or they use Jerusalem as a base of power (cf. Mt. 2.4; 16.21; 20.18; 21.15, 23, 45; 26.1–28.15/Mk 8.31; 10.33; 11.18, 27; 14.1–15.32/Lk. 3.2; 9.22. 19.47; 20.1–24.20/John 1.19; 7.32, 45; 11.47, 49, 51, 57; 12.10; 18.3–19.22). Their close association with the execution of Jesus makes it plain that his activity in the Temple figured centrally in his condemnation before Pilate.

In the Gospels Jesus enters into disputes with the Pharisees (Mt. 9.10–13, 14–17; 12.1–8, 9–14; 15.1–20; 16.1–12; 19.3–12; 22.15–22/Mk 2.15–17, 18–22, 23–28; 3.1–6; 7.1–23; 8.11–21; 10.2–12; 12.13–17/Lk. 5.29–32, 33–39; 6.1–5, 6–11; 11.37–12.12; 15.1, 2), and finally teaches in the Temple itself and occupies the holy precincts (Mt. 21–25; Mk 11–13; Lk. 19.28–21.38), where the high priests, particularly Sadducees, find him guilty of blasphemy and denounce him to the council of Jerusalem, which makes its recommendation to Pilate (Mt. 26.1–27.2; Mk 14.1–15.1; Lk. 22.1–23.5). Jesus' disputes with the Pharisees typically center upon issues of purity (Mt. 9.10–13/Mk 2.15–17/Lk. 5.29–32; Mt. 15.1–20/Mk 7.1–23; Mt. 16.5–12/Mk 8.14–21/Lk. 12.1; 15.1, 2), fasting (Mt. 9.14–17/Mk 2.18–22/Lk. 5.33–39), keeping the sabbath (Mt. 12.1–8, 9–14/Mk 2.23–28; 3.1–6/Lk. 6.1–5, 6–11), tithing (Mt. 23.23/Lk. 11.42, cf. Mt. 17.24–27; 22.15–22/Mk 12.13–17/Lk. 20.20–26), and the interpretation of scriptures (Mt. 19.3–12/Mk 10.2–12/Lk. 16.18), all of which are characteristic of Pharisaic concerns. The Pharisees engage in vigorous debate with Jesus, because he is also interested in developing teaching in respect of purity. He is called "rabbi" (meaning, "my master," cf. Mt. 26.25, 49/Mk 9.5; 10.51; 11.21; 14.45/John 1.38, 49; 3.2; 4.31; 6.25; 9.2; 11.8), has close followers, deliberately

2002); W. D. Davis and Louis Finkelstein (eds), *The Cambridge History of Judaism. Volume One: Introduction; the Persian Period* (London and New York: Cambridge University Press, 1984); Robert A. Kraft and George W. E. Nickelsburg, *Early Judaism and Its Modern Interpreters*, The Bible and Its Modern Interpreters 2 (Atlanta: Scholars Press, 1986); A. R. C. Leany, *The Jewish and Christian World 200 B.C. to A.D. 200*, Cambridge Commentaries on Writings of the Jewish and Christian World 200 B.C. to A.D. 2007 (Cambridge and New York: Cambridge University Press, 1984); Martin McNamara, *Palestinian Judaism and the New Testament*, Good News Studies 4 (Wilmington: Glazier, 1983); Jacob Neusner, "Josephus' Pharisees: A Complete Repertoire," in L. H. Feldman and G. Hata (eds) *Josephus, Judaism, and Christianity* (Wayne State University Press: Detroit, 1987), pp. 274—292; *The Pharisees. Rabbinic Perspectives*, Studies in Ancient Judaism (Hoboken: Ktav, 1984).

promulgates his teaching by travel and sending his disciples to teach, and attempts to influence the conduct of worship in the Temple. In all of those aspects, Jesus' portrait in the Gospels comports well with a recognized pattern of teaching concerning purity in early Judaism, although the substance of his teaching was distinctive (and, for many, controversial).

Scribes appear both in a local context (Mt. 5.20; 7.29; 9.3; 12.38; 15.1; 17.10/ Mk 1.22; 2.6, 16; 7.5/Lk. 5.21, 30; 6.7), even as a part of Jesus' movement (Mt. 8.19; 13.52; Mk 12.32, 34; Lk. 20.39), and during the final confrontation in Jerusalem (Mt. 16.21; 20.18; 21.15; [26.3,] 57; 27.41/Mk 8.31; 10.33; 11.18, 27; 12.35, 38; 14.1, 43, 53; 15.1, 31/Lk. 9.22; 19.47; 20.1, 19, 39, 46; 22.2, 66; 23.10). They are probably to be identified with references to "lawyers" in the Gospels (Mt. 22.35/ Lk. 7.30; 10.25; 11.45, 46, 52; 14.3), and the presence of "scribes" among both local and high-priestly elites reinforces the impression that the category concerns more a function than a distinctive teaching (as in the case of the Essenes or the Pharisees) or a special interest (as in the case of the Sadducees).

The social history of Christianity tended to cast scribes, Pharisees, and lawyers into a single category of persecutors and hypocrites, like the "Jews" themselves, and that influence is evident in the present text of the Gospels (cf. Mt. 15.1; 23.2, 13, 15, 23, 25, 27, 29/Mk 3.6, 22; 7.1, 5/ Lk. 6.7; 11.45, 46, 52, 53, 54; 15.2). The Matthean Jews in particular are liars in respect of the resurrection (28.15), and willful murderers who implicate their own children in the crucifixion (27.25). That is the most prejudicial charge in all of the Gospels, but it is not unlike Mark's condescending and unique claim that "all the Jews" hold to practices of washing "cups and pots and copper vessels" (7.3, 4), or Luke's unique scene of Jesus' rejection at Nazareth by his own people (4.16–30), or John's uniquely anachronistic claim that "the Jews" excluded the followers of Jesus from synagogues during his lifetime (9.22; 12.42, cf. 16.2). *The Gospel according to Thomas* has Jesus himself ironically asking the disciples whether they have become as obtuse as the Jews, in that they must ask concerning Jesus' identity, when they ought simply to recognize it (*l.* 43). Within all five sources, which are of primary importance in the study of Jesus, Judaism and the Jews appear more as a foil for Jesus than as the matrix of his movement. But the realities of a radically pluralized Judaism in which Jesus was a vigorous participant also shine through the texts as they may be read today.

In order to understand the portrayal of Jews within the New Testament, the perspective on Judaism within the documents needs to be appreciated. Paul believed that the example of Abraham showed that a completely new definition of Israel had emerged with the coming of Jesus. He says that when believers hear with faith, they are "just as Abraham, who believed in God, and it was reckoned to him as righteousness" (Gal. 3.6). Paul attributes to Abraham the role of the principal patriarch of Judaism, but he argues that Abraham's faith, not his obedience to the law, made him righteous in the sight of God (Gal. 3.7).

Descent from Abraham, therefore, was a matter of belief, not a matter of genealogy. Paul therefore argued that the Scripture attests a radically new definition of Israel, which challenges the received understanding of both Judaism and the Greco-Roman world. Although this new definition did not deny the role of Judaism within Israel (see Romans 9–11, above all), for Paul "the Israel of God" (Gal. 6.16) signaled a departure from conventional understandings of Judaism.

Although Paul was radical, and more often than not isolated, in his new definition of Israel, even documents within the New Testament that do not formally share his theology, as he formulated it, nonetheless agree with his theological evaluation of Israel. In Matthews's Gospel, although scribes, Pharisees, and the Jewish people are severely (and even racially, as we have seen) criticized for complicity in the death of Jesus, Jesus commands his followers to do what Jewish leaders command, because they "sit on Moses' seat" (Mt. 23.2–3). This apparent paradox is resolved when it is kept in mind that, for Matthew, the Torah remains a regulative principle—but as interpreted according to Torah's fulfillment in Christ. The ambivalence between Judaism as it was designed to be and Judaism as it had become reaches deep into the characterization of Jesus' in this Gospel.

The Sermon on the Mount, unique to Matthew's Gospel, lies on the fault line of Matthean ambivalence toward Judaism, and this is just where the Golden Rule appears (7.12), near the close of the Sermon (at the end of chapter 7). By the time Jesus pronounces the Golden Rule in Matthew, he has already characterized Judaism as teaching its opposite, hatred (Mt. 5.43–48):

> You have heard that it was said, "You shall love your neighbor and you shall hate your enemy." Yet I say to you, "Love your enemies, and pray for those who persecute you, so you might become sons of your father in heavens. Because he makes his sun dawn upon evil people and good people, and makes rain upon just and unjust. For if you love those who love you, what reward have you? Do not even the customs-agents do the same? And if you greet only your fellows, what do you do that goes beyond? Do not even the Gentiles do the same? You, then, shall be perfect, as your heavenly father is perfect."

The pattern of antithesis ("You have heard that it was said. . . Yet I say to you") has been well established early in the Sermon on the Mount (from Mt. 5.21). Ordinarily, antithetical contrast relates a statement in the Hebrew Bible to Jesus' teaching. In this case, however, no biblical passage corresponds to the commandment to hate one's enemies. Perhaps the imperative in the Community Rule from Qumran, a foundational document among the Dead Sea Scrolls, to "hate all the sons of darkness" (1QS 1.10), is in mind; in that case, the environment of Damascus, with which the Dead Sea covenanters cultivated ties, would help explain the expression in Matthew. But whatever the understanding of exactly why this position is attributed to Judaism, the fact remains that a global imperative of hatred is projected on to the religion from which Christianity was in the process of separating at the time.

Matthew brings to clearest expression a conviction that emerges both in the New Testament and in Patristic literature: that the distinction of Christianity from Judaism reveals that only Christian faith, and not its Judaic prototype, conforms to the divine imperative to love. Yet it would be artificial to imagine that this claim, often associated with Christian supersessionism, is a mere artifact of Matthean theology. As a matter of fact, all the essentials of the assertion in Matthew are present in the counterpart in Luke to the Matthean passage (Lk. 6.27–36, an earlier form of "Q," albeit in a Gospel from about a decade later than Matthew):

> But I say to you who hear, Love your enemies, act well with those who hate you, bless those who accurse you, pray concerning those who revile you. To the one who hits you on the cheek, furnish the other also. And from the one who takes your garment, do not forbid the tunic! Give to the one who asks you, and do not demand from the one who takes what is yours. And just as you want men to do to you, do to them similarly. And if you love those who love you, what sort of grace is that for you? Because even the sinners love those who love them. And if you do good to those who do you good, what sort of grace is that to you? Even the sinners do the same. And if you lend to those from whom you hope to receive, what sort of grace is that to you? Even sinners lend so that they receive the equivalent back. Except: love your enemies and do good and lend—anticipating nothing—and your reward will be great, and you will be sons of the most high, because he is fine to the ungrateful and evil. Become compassionate, just as your father is also compassionate.

Here, in a passage that overlaps with Matthew in a way that suggests we are dealing with "Q," source that reaches back to 35 C.E., the contrast is set up between those who accept the ambit of the Golden Rule, and "sinners" whose attitude puts them outside the circle of grace established by the Rule. Although the Sermon on the Mount within its Matthean context is probably the clearest expression of the hermeneutic of exclusion in the New Testament, it expresses a tendency with ample resonance both within Christianity and outside it.

The Golden Rule in recent public discussion

Since 1976, when Jimmy Carter's Evangelical faith became a campaign issue, candidates' religious orientations have factored in political debate. When George W. Bush cited Jesus Christ as his favorite political philosopher during the campaign of 2000, his statement represented a crescendo of devout rhetoric, but by no means an aberration. The relationship between Jesus and politics

has been taken up again in 2008, and Democratic politicians have been adver-
tising faith-based credentials that they once kept lit under a bushel —if they
had been ignited at all. In this environment, it is helpful to have the careful,
close reading offered by Tod Lindberg—not a theologian but a Hoover Institution research fellow.[12]

Mercifully, Lindberg avoids equating Jesus with progressive *or* conservative
policies, recognizing the anachronism involved in such claims. But he does
identify Jesus not as a progressive, but as "*the progressive*" (italics his): the force
in Western politics who made progress possible by asserting the full equality of
men and women. The closest and most effective of Lindberg's readings involves
the Sermon on the Mount in Matthew. Through the careful, literal attention
Lindberg pays to the text, he is able clearly to identity two related principles
that are often missing from popular conversation and even from scholarly
discussion of the Gospels' political perspective.

The first of these insights is that the Sermon on the Mount, beginning
with the Beatitudes (in Mt. 5.3–11), is built around a strict injunction to righteousness. In speaking of the persecution his disciples should expect, Jesus does
not endorse that outcome, but he does accommodate to it. To be persecuted
should be accepted as a badge of honor, he teaches, if it comes for righteousness' sake (Mt. 5.10–12). The second of Lindberg's central observations is that
the way in which Jesus commends the Law of Moses, the Torah, involves a key
qualification of the conventional reading: in Matthew, Jesus says the Law will
not pass until all is accomplished (Mt. 5.18). Though that has been taken to
suggest that the Law is fixed in its content, Jesus truly believed in a prophetic
fulfillment that would bring all the peoples of the world to recognize the God
of Israel. That fulfillment necessitated a radical transformation of the Law in
Jesus' mind, as in the minds of Prophets before him, so that it enabled people
entirely unrelated by genealogy or custom to Abraham, Isaac, and Jacob to
inherit all the promises of the covenant with the patriarchs.

Both principles—the preeminent importance of righteousness and the transcendence of Law—are inherent in Jesus' overall religious vision of the significance of human life, and correspond evocatively to current concerns for justice,
especially as they deal with economic repression and racism. But a basic correction needs to be introduced into Lindberg's careful reading. Although he works
closely with the texts involved, he lacks proper attention to context. He acknowledges that Jesus approach is not political at base, and yet he lists "equality"
among Jesus' concerns, as though Jesus lived in the eighteenth-century Europe
rather than first-century Palestine. Though political in consequence, the basis
of Jesus' position was not an Enlightenment concern with the nature of political authority, but the vision of Israel's prophets promising a superpolitical

---

[12] *The Political Teachings of Jesus* (New York: HarperCollins, 2007).

malkhutha' d'Elaha', in which divine justice would "roll down like waters and righteousness like an ever-flowing stream" (Amos 5.24).

The tendency to short-circuit the cultural development between Jesus' time and later periods also appears in Lindberg's repeated treatment of the text of Matthew's Gospel as a direct statement of Jesus' political position, rather than one mediated by the community of Matthew some fifty years after Jesus' death. The unfortunate result is that the disagreements between Matthew's community and its surrounding Jewish community are flattened into a superficial reading of Jesus' teaching. At one point, Mr. Lindberg finds himself saying, on the basis of Mt. 5.43, that the Hebrew Scriptures explicitly instructed people to hate their enemies. Of course that is not the case, as has been explicitly recognized by scholars for more than half a century, especially as a result of the detailed contributions of Krister Stendahl.[13]

Although this deficiency in attending to context mars the book, it also signals an underlying problem in the wider contemporary debate concerning the relationship between politics and religion. If even careful, close readers are going to take their terms of reference from the broad-spectrum handbooks that Lindberg cites—*Vine's Complete Expository Dictionary*, based upon a work published in 1939, and the more recent but still recycled *Backgrounds of Early Christianity*[14]—without reference to specific scholarship, we are surely in trouble. Whether you see Jesus' political influence as positive or negative, a flat reading of the Gospels will take you as far from a historically accurate assessment of Christianity as the assumption of a flat earth would take you from drawing an accurate map of the earth. In the world we live in, the religious maps we use are every bit as important as our geographical ones. And in the case of the Golden Rule, the belief that a spiritual chasm separates Christianity from all other religions is as deceptive as the medieval belief that a physical abyss prevented Europe from exploration westward. Where the study of religion is concerned, the only abyss to fear is the one in which practitioners isolate themselves in a refusal to consider the faith and the ethical motivations of others.

---

[13] See *The School of St. Matthew and its Use of the Old Testament* (Lund: CWK Gleerup, 1968).

[14] W. E. Vine, *Vine's Complete Expository Dictionary* (London: Thomas Nelson, 1996); *Backgrounds of Early Christianity* edited by Everett Ferguson (Grand Rapids: W. B. Eerdmans, 2003).

Chapter 8

The Golden Rule as the Law of Nature, from Origen to Martin Luther

Olivier du Roy
Paris

This paper seeks to explain how Origen was the first to comment on Rom. 2.14 (these, having not the law, are a law unto themselves. . .) in relation to Mt. 7.12 (all things whatsoever ye would that men . . .), thereby suggesting that the Golden Rule is Natural Law. All the Church Fathers adopted this perspective (St. Augustine, St. John Chrysostom, etc.). Likewise, all the theologians of the Middle Ages, up to Albert the Great and St. Thomas Aquinas—for them, it was the synderesis (bonum est faciendum) that was the first Natural Law. Martin Luther was the key figure who later gave renewed impulse to the Golden Rule, which explains why it spread so dramatically throughout the sixteenth and seventeenth centuries in all the countries where the Reform took root, and especially in England.

This paper is part of a larger study into the Golden Rule in all religions and especially into the history of morals in the West.

The first researcher to highlight this patristic doctrine, which makes the Golden Rule the very substance of Natural Law, was Hans Reiner in 1948, followed by two articles in 1955. He also saw clearly that it was the connection attested by Justin (second century) and Origen (beginning of the third century) between Mt. 7.12 and Rom. 2.14–15[1] which was to structure this doctrine and make it one that would be bequeathed to the whole patristic tradition, and thence to medieval theology.

History

The doctrine, explicating Natural Law by means of the Golden Rule, is widespread throughout the whole Christian tradition. However, its precise origins

---

[1] Rom. 2.14: For when the Gentiles, which have not the law, do by nature the things contained in the law, these, having not the law, are a law unto themselves; 2.15: Which shew the work of the law written in their hearts, their conscience also bearing witness, and their thoughts the mean while accusing or else excusing one another.

are not always conscious: the authority of Augustine in the West and of Basil
and John Chrysostom in the East, who are the most cited in the late patristic
period or Middle Ages, obscures older sources. The direct influence of Origen
may perhaps only be seen during the twelfth century in Abelard (1133–37) and
Peter Lombard (1140), in their *Commentaries of the Epistle of the Romans*: Abelard's
makes reference to Origen, and Peter Lombard's is considered to be largely
a gloss of Origen's.

The story begins very early in the Christian tradition: as early as the second
century. The first manifestation of this doctrine is to be found in Justin the
apologist,[2] around 150, in Rome. It is next found in Irenaeus of Lyon[3] between
180 and 200. And, around 230, there is a very elaborate account in Origen of
Alexandria:

It is certain that the Gentiles who do not have the law are not being said to
do naturally the things of the law in respect of the Sabbath days, the new
moon celebrations, or the sacrifices written about in the law. For it was not
that law which is said to be written in the heart of the Gentiles. The reference

[2] Justin, *Dialogue with Tryphon*, 93: "For [God] sets before every race of mankind that which is
always and universally just, as well as all righteousness; and every race knows that adultery,
and fornication, and such like, are sinful; and though they all homicide and commit such
practices, yet they do not escape from the knowledge that they act unrighteously whenever
they so do, with the exception of those who are possessed with an unclean spirit, and who
have been debased by education, by wicked customs, and by sinful institutions, and who have
lost, or rather quenched and put under, their natural ideas. For we may see that such persons are unwilling to submit to the same things which they inflict upon others, **and reproach
each other with hostile consciences** for the acts which they perpetrate. And hence I think
that our Lord and Saviour Jesus Christ spoke well when He summed up all righteousness
and piety in two commandments. They are these: "Thou shalt love the Lord thy God with all
thy heart, and with all thy strength, and thy neighbour as thyself. . . And the man who loves
his neighbour as himself will **wish for him the same good things that he wishes for himself,
and no man will wish evil things for himself.** Accordingly, he who loves his neighbour would
pray and labour that his neighbour may be possessed of the same benefits as himself. Now
nothing else is neighbour to man than that similarly- affectioned and reasonable
being-man."
[3] Irenaeus, *Adversus Haereses*, Book 4, XIII, 1: "And that the Lord **did not abrogate the natural**
[precepts] of the law, by which man is justified, which also those who were justified by faith,
and who pleased God, did observe previous to the giving of the law, but that He extended
and fulfilled them, . . ."
Book 4, XV, 1: "They (the Jews) had therefore a law, a course of discipline, and a prophecy
of future things. For God at the first, indeed, warning them by means of **natural precepts**,
which from the beginning He had implanted in mankind, that is, by means of the Decalogue
(which, if any one does not observe, he has no salvation), did then demand nothing more of
them."
Book 4, XIII, 3: "But the righteous fathers had **the meaning of the Decalogue written in their
hearts and souls**, that is, they loved the God who made them, and did no injury to their
neighbour. There was therefore no occasion that they should be cautioned by prohibitory
mandates (*correptoriis literis*), because **they had the righteousness of the law in themselves**.
But when this righteousness and love to God had passed into oblivion, and became extinct
in Egypt, God did necessarily, because of His great goodwill to men, reveal Himself by
a voice, . . ."

is instead to what they are able to perceive by nature (*quod sentire naturaliter possunt*), for instance that they should not commit murder or adultery, they ought not steal, they should not speak falsely, they should honour father and mother, and the like . . . And yet it seems to me that the things which are said to be written in their heart agree with the evangelical laws, where everything is ascribed to natural justice (*ad naturalem aequitatem*). For what could be nearer to the natural moral senses (*naturalibus sensibus*) than **that those things men do not want done to themselves, they should not do to others** (*quae nolunt sibi fieri homines, haec ne faciant aliis*). **Natural law** (*lex naturalis*) is able to agree with the law of Moses according to the spirit but not according to the letter.[4]

In under 80 years, this doctrine became the common good of the Christian tradition, from the Gauls to Alexandria. Nothing of the type is announced in the Gospels, nor directly in the apostolic writings: it appears out of the connection between Mt. 7.12 and Luke 6.31 (the Golden Rule) and a passage from the Epistle to the Romans (Rom. 2.14). This means that, faced with pervasive paganism and with the desire to affirm Christian moral value, Christian thinking very quickly made the connection between the gospel maxim of the Golden Rule and this law which Paul declares was not absent among the pagans. What is this law which the pagans have for themselves? "What men do not want done to themselves, they should not do to others." For Justin, for Irenaeus as for Origen, this is the natural law of which Saint Paul speaks.

From that point on, this doctrine of natural law, the content of which is expressed by the Golden Rule, would spread throughout the whole of the patristic period. It can be traced in the Pseudo-Clementines[5] probably of Ebionite origin (end of the second or beginning of the third century) then in Ephrem the Syrian in the fourth century. In Lactantius,[6] in Africa, in the fourth century, then in Basil in Cappadocia and in John Chrysostom in Constantinople at the

---

[4] Origen, *Commentarius in Epistulam ad Romanos*, II, 9, *Migne, Patrologia series graeca (P.G.)*, Paris, 14, 892; English translation: by Thomas Scheck, Washington D.C, Catholic University of America Press, 2001, vol. I, p. 131.

[5] *Recognitiones Clementi*, VIII, 56, *P.G.* I, 1397; *Pseudo-clementines Homilies*, VII, 4, *G.C.S.* 42, 118; R. H. Connolly, *Didascalia Apostolorum. The Syriac version*, Oxford, Clarendon Press, 1929, pp. 2–4.

[6] Lactantius, *Epitome*, 55, 3: "It 'tis bitter unto thee to bear an injury and he that does it seems unjust in thy account; remove that by way of supposition to another person which thou feelest in thy self, and that to thy own person which thou judgest of another, and you wilt presently understand that thou thyself dost as much unjustly in injuring of another, as another hurting thee." And also: *Epitome*, C.S.E.L., 19, p. 737 and *Divinae Institutiones, Corpus Scriptorum Ecclesiasticorum Latinorum (C.S.E.L.)*, 19, p. 568–69: "We should therefore think of our selves in other men, and others in ourselves. Because the all justice is: **not to do unto others what we would not have done unto us.**"

same time. In the words of this great preacher, who, well before Kant, announced the autonomy of moral law in man:

Wherefore Christ, for the purpose of declaring this, and shewing that He was not introducing a strange law, or one which surpassed our nature, but that which He had of old deposited beforehand in our conscience, after pronouncing those numerous Beatitudes, thus speaks; "*All things whatsoever ye would that men should do to you, do ye even so to them.*" (Mt. 7, 12) "Many words," saith He, "are not necessary, nor laws of great length, nor a diversity of instruction. **Let thine own will be the law**. Dost thou wish to receive kindness? Be kind to another. Dost thou wish to receive mercy? Show mercy to thy neighbour. Dost thou wish to be applauded? Applaud another. Dost thou wish to be beloved? Exercise love. Dost thou wish to enjoy the first rank? First concede that place to another. Become thyself the judge, thyself the lawgiver of thine own life. And again; "*Do not to another what thou hatest.*" (Tob. 4, 16). By the latter precept, he would induce to a departure from iniquity; by the former, to the exercise of virtue. "Do not do to another," he saith, "what thou hatest." Dost thou hate to be insulted? Do not insult another. Dost thou hate to be envied? Envy not another. Dost thou hate to be deceived? Do not deceive another. And, in a word, in all things, if we hold fast these two precepts, we shall not need any other instruction. For the knowledge of virtue He hath **implanted in our nature**; but the practice of it and the correction He hath entrusted to our moral choice."[7]

It reappears in Jerome and in Procop of Gaza in Palestine in the fourth and fifth centuries. In Italy in Ambrosiaster, in Saint Ambrose of Milan,[8] and Gaudentius of Brescia in the fourth and fifth centuries. In Africa in Saint Augustine, then in Aquitaine in Prosper in the fifth century. In Rome, popes Gregory the Great (sixth century) and Nicholas I[st] (ninth century) adopted the same doctrine. Augustine's amazing sermon reveals his eloquence, and the Christian people can be seen to applaud and respond to his exhortations:

Anyone at all when questioned about what is just can easily give the right answer, as long as he or she is not an interested party!

And this is not surprising, for by **the hand of our Fashioner truth has written in our very hearts the precept**, *Do not do to another what you would not want anyone to do to you* (Tob. 4, 16). **Even before the law was given no one was allowed to be ignorant of it, for even those to whom the law had not been**

---

[7] *Ad populum Antiochenum*, Homily, 13, §3, *Patrologia Graeca*, vol 49, col. 139–40. And again *Commentary on Job*, 31,6 in *Sources Chrétiennes*, vol. 348, Paris, Cerf, 1988, pp. 134–35.
[8] Ambrose of Milan, *De fuga saeculi*, 3, 15, *C.S.E.L.*, vol. 32, 2, p. 175.

revealed were held liable to judgment by this standard. . . Because men and women were so avid for external things that they had become estranged from themselves, a written law was given. This did not imply that its provisions were not already inscribed in human hearts; but you, mortal, were a deserter from your heart, and so you are arrested by him who is present everywhere, and you are called back within yourself. . .

After all, who taught you to resent it if another man makes approaches to your wife?

Who taught you to hope that you will not be robbed?

Who taught you to be indignant if you suffer some injury?

Plenty of other examples can be given, relating to public or private issues. There are many such points on which, if people are questioned, they will unhesitatingly reply that they do not want to suffer such treatment.

Come now, tell me: if you do not want to be treated like that, do you think you are the only person who matters? . . . Well then, *do not do to another what you would not want anyone to do to you.* You judge something to be bad from the fact that you do not want to have it done to you; and it is the secret inner law, written in your very heart, that has taught you to view it so.

When you behaved toward someone else like that, he or she cried out under your ill-treatment; and when you endure the same at the hands of another, are you not driven back to your own heart?

Is theft a good thing? No? I ask you: is adultery a good thing? Everyone shouts, "No!" Is homicide good? They all shout their detestation of it. Is it good to covet your neighbour's property? The unanimous reply is, "No!" If you are not yet persuaded on this subject, imagine that someone comes trying to get his hands on your things. I hope you enjoy it! Then come back and give me your answer. Clearly, then, everyone questioned about such actions will attest that they are not good.

. . . suppose a traveller arrives in your region. He has no roof over his head, yet no one takes him in. He protests that this is an inhuman city, that he could more easily have found a place to stay among savages. He is keenly aware of the injustice, because he is the victim of it. You perhaps are insensitive to it; **but you should imagine yourself in the same situation**, on a journey, and ask yourself how you would resent it if someone refused to give you what you are unwilling to give to that traveller in your own country.

I put it to you, all of you: are these things true? "Yes, they are true," you say. Is this a just appraisal? "Yes," you say, "just it is."[9]

Later, following somewhat of an eclipse in the sixth and seventh centuries, Western tradition takes up the baton again with the Carolingian empire and the

[9] Augustin, *Enarr.in Psalm.* 57, 1, in *The Works of Saint Augustine: A Translation For the 21st Century*, New York City Press, 2001, Part III, vol.17, p. 120–21.

development of theology in the monastic and episcopal schools. In the ninth and tenth centuries, this assimilation of the Golden Rule to natural law can be rediscovered in Smaragde, Strabo, Haymo of Auxerre and Atto of Vercelli. In the eleventh century, in Anselm of Canterbury. The twelfth century is the richest with Anselm of Laon, Bernard of Clairvaux, William of Champeaux, Hugh of Saint-Victor, Abelard, Pierre Lombard, Odo of Ourscamp, Pierre of Poitiers, and finally the great jurist Gratian along with all his commentators, who places the evangelical Golden Rule at the beginning of his *Decretum* as the first principle of natural law.

The twelfth century and the beginnings of scholasticism maintain this tradition with William of Auxerre, Alexander of Hales, John of la Rochelle, Saint Bonaventure, Robert Grosseteste, and Mt. of Aquasparta. After suffering at the hands of Albert the Great and Thomas Aquinus, who vigorously disparaged this interpersonal conception of natural law in favour of a philosophy of Good, it makes a reappearance in the fourteenth and fifteenth centuries, in Duns Scotus, Nicholas of Lyra, John Gerson, Henry Herp, and Marcilio Ficino. Erasmus still holds to it in the sixteenth century, where it would be taken up by Luther and all the great reformers (Calvin, Melanchton, Bucer, Zwingli, John Cameron, amongst others). In Luther, we have found more than 40 texts, in all periods in his life and preaching.[10] His first known sermon (1510–12) is devoted to it.[11] The following is an extract from his *Lectures on Romans* (1514–15):

> This law is impressed upon all, Jews as well as Gentiles; and all are therefore bound to obey it. In this sense our Lord says in Mt. 7, 12: *'All things therefore whatsoever you would that men should do to you, do you also unto them; for this is the law and the prophets.'* The whole law handed down to us is, therefore, **nothing else than this natural law** which everyone knows and on account of which no one is without excuse.[12]

From that point on, seventeenth-century England extends this tradition with the Reverend Thomas Jackson,[13] the first to call our maxim the "Golden Rule"

---

[10] Martin Luther, *Treatise on Good Works* (1520), Seventh Commandment, "And it fights not only against theft and robbery, but against all stinting in temporal goods which men may practice toward one another: such as greed, usury, overcharging and plating wares that sell as solid, counterfeit wares, short measures and weights, and who could tell all the ready, novel, clever tricks, which multiply daily in every trade, by which every one seeks his own gain through the other's loss, and forgets the rule which says: "*What ye wish that others do to you, that do ye also to them.*" If every one kept this rule before his eyes in his trade, business, and dealings with his neighbour, he would readily find how he ought to buy and sell, take and give, lend and give for nothing, promise and keep his promise, and the like."

[11] Weimarer Ausgabe, *Sermo ex autographo Lutheri quod reperiebatur in Monasterio Augustinen: Erffurdiae*, vol. 4, p. 591, 11–22.

[12] Martin Luther, *Lectures on Romans*, 2, 10, in *The Library of Christian Classics*, vol. XV, London, SCM Press, p. 46.

[13] "**The Law of Nature** is *Do as thou wouldst be done to* . . ." (Thomas Jackson, *First sermon upon Matthew 7.12*, Book XI, chap. 32, in *The Works*, vol. 3, p. 612).

in 1615; Benjamin Camfield[14] in the first treatise ever written on the Golden Rule in 1671; Cumberland,[15] one of the Cambridge Platonists in 1672; George Boraston,[16] in 1684; John Goodman (the author of the second treatise known on the Golden Rule); and John Tillotson, Archbishop of Canterbury. In France, Bossuet calls it the *Loi de l'équité naturelle* (the law of natural equity).

As long as we remain within the Christian tradition, and without interrogating it too closely, the Golden Rule unquestionably remains the first principle of natural law, except in the interlude represented by the Aristotelian critique of Albert the Great and Saint Thomas, who replace it with the *synderesis*. But then there came the time of secularization and independence of thinking regarding the foundations of rights and the law. For Grotius and Pufendorf, the Golden Rule retains a major role, but it is no longer the ultimate basis of natural law and social life. However, Thomasius and Wolff in the eighteenth century restore its status.

Locke and Leibniz (in a more nuanced fashion) challenge the possibility of the rule's being a primary, self-evident principle. But the problematic has clearly changed and the shift is now toward an attempt at an epistemic basis of natural law. Which takes us straight to Kant and to his well-known devaluation of the maxim: this trivial maxim that, according to him, cannot be compared to his categorical imperative. On this point he would be contradicted by Schopenhauer and Feuerbach. In addition, Voltaire, drawing on the writings of Confucius brought back from China by the Jesuits, would return the Golden Rule to the heart of Natural Law:

> Only the author of nature may have made **the eternal laws of nature. The single fundamental and immutable law** for men is the following: "**Treat others as you would be treated.**" **This law is from nature itself**: it cannot be torn from the heart of man.[17]

[14] For, to say the truth of it, this precept of our Blessed Saviour is no more than a plain **Law of Nature**, obliterated by evil habits and custom, revived and brought to light again by Christ. **A Law of Nature**, I say, it is undoubtedly, whereof we may find clear foot-steps among the Heathens, and which takes hold immediately on the conscience of every one that duly considereth of it (Benjamin Camfield, *The Comprehensive Rule of Righteousness*, sect. II, p. 19, William Leach, 1671).

[15] Richard Cumberland, *De legibus naturae*, 5, 14, London, 1672, p. 212; French transl. of Barbeyrac, p. 233. The English translation by John Maxwell would be published in 1727, *A Treatise Of The Laws Of Nature*, London, 1727, p. 216.

[16] A Law which is deduced from that **common natural inclination** implanted in every one by God himself; from whence it is, that every Man doth naturally seek his own preservation, and welfare: That then which is naturally, and sufficiently grounded in every Man, is laid there as a pattern for the exercise of Charity and Justice towards all other Men: For by **this Native Law**, we are obliged to deal with others, as if we had exchanged Persons, and Circumstances with them, and they were in ours" (George Boraston, *The Royal Law: Or the Golden Rule of Justice and Charity*, London, 1684, p. 5).

[17] Voltaire, *Remarques pour servir de Supplément à l'Essai sur les mœurs and l'esprit des nations*, 17° Remarque: Des lois, Paris, Garnier, 1963, vol. II, p. 935–36.

Here, it would simply not be feasible to list every example of how thinking has persisted to the present day in regarding the Golden Rule as an expression of Natural law: in everyday religious teaching, in lay catechism, and even in freemasonry. Even in a secularized form, isolated from Christian theology, the Golden Rule remains for many thinkers, even those outside Christianity, the expression of this natural law which offers an autonomous basis for moral exigencies and law, inscribed in the nature of man.

What is the origin of this doctrine?

The genesis of the Natural law=Golden Rule concept is to be found in several places:

1. Judaism and Christianity converge at the time of Christ to proclaim that the Golden Rule on its own encompasses all Law (Mt. 7.12; Hillel in *Shabbat* 31a). But this of course refers to the Law of Moses and not natural law.
2. As early as the first and second centuries A.D., a frequent moral exhortation (or *parainesis*) appeared in Jewish or Judaeo-Christian writing, developing the reasoning behind this condensed formula: the key to understanding the commandments of the Decalogue is to be found in the Golden Rule:

> It happened that one came to Rabbi Akiba and said to him, "Rabbi, teach me the whole Law all at once." He answered, "My son, Moses, our teacher, tarried on the mountain forty days and forty nights before he learned it, and you say, Teach me the all Law all at once! Nevertheless, my son, this is the fundamental principle of the Law: that which you hate respecting yourself, do not to your neighbour. If you desire that no one injure you in respect to what is yours, then do not injure him. If you desire that no one should carry off what is yours, then do not carry off what is your neighbour's ."[18]

In the *Doctrina Apostolorum*, doubtless the version of the *Duae Viae*, also attested by the *Didache*, which appears to be closest to the Jewish source:

I, 2   ***Do not unto others as you would not have them do unto you.***
I, 3   Here is the interpretation of those words:

---

[18] *Aboth from Rabbi Nathan*, 26a, ed. Schlechter, Vienna, 1887, Chap. 16, p. 53. Akiba seems to have the words of Hillel in mind. But both quote probably an even more current maxim. Cf. R. Travers Herford, *Talmud and Apocrypha. A Comparative Study Of The Jewish Ethical Teaching In The Rabbinical And Non-Rabbinical Sources In The Early Centuries*, London, Soucino Press, 1933, p. 148–49.

II, 2 Thou shalt not commit adultery, thou shalt not kill, thou shalt not bear false witness, etc.[19]

The same schema can be found in the Pseudo-Clementines (*Recognitiones, Pseudo-Clementine*)[20] and in the *Didascalia*. Let us just recall the doctrine attested by the first two of those texts:

The Recognitiones Clementi:

For almost the whole rule of our actions is summed up in this, that *what we are unwilling to suffer we should not do to others*.
   For as you would not be killed, you must beware of killing another;
   and as you would not have your own marriage violated, you must not defile another's bed;
   you would not be stolen from, neither must you steal;
   and every matter of men's actions' is comprehended within this rule. [21]

The Pseudo-Clementines Homilies:

   . . . and the rest in one word,—as the God-fearing Jews have heard, do you also hear, and be of one mind in many bodies; let **each man be minded to do to his neighbour those good things he wishes for himself**. And you may all find out what is good, by holding some such conversation as the following with yourselves:
   You would not like to be murdered; do not murder another man:
   you would not like your wife to be seduced by another; do not you commit adultery:
   you would not like any of your things to be stolen from you; steal nothing from another.
   And so understanding by yourselves what is reasonable, and doing it, you will become dear to God, and will obtain healing.[22]

---

[19] *Doctrina Apostolorum*, chap. I §1–chap. II §2. See the Latin text in S. Giet, *L'énigme de la Didachè*, Publications de la Faculté des Lettres de l'Université de Strasbourg, Fasc. 149, Paris, Éd. Ophrys, 1970, p. 41–42: "I, 1. Viae duae sunt in saeculo, uitae and mortis, lucis and tenebrarum. . . 2. Via ergo uitae haec est: primo diliges deum aeternum qui te fecit ; secundo proximum tuum ut te ipsum. **Omnia autem quae tibi fieri non uis alii ne feceris. 3. Interpretatio autem horum uerborum haec est**; II, 2. Non moechaberis, non homicidium facies, non falsum testimonium dices, etc."

[20] Texts probably from an Ebionite source from the late second or third centuries, showing profound Judaeo-Christian characteristics. The origin of this foundational work can be located between 222 and 325, see Pierre Geoltrain, *Introduction au Roman pseudo-clémentin*, in *Écrits Apocryphes chrétiens*, Paris, La Pléiade, 2005, p. 1186–89; and G. Strecker, *Das Judenchristentum in den Pseudoklementinen*, *T.U.*, 70, Berlin, 1981.

[21] *Recognitiones Clementi*, VIII, 56, *P.G.* I, 1397.

[22] *Pseudo-clementines Homilies*, VII, 4, *G.C.S.* 42, 118.

3. In Alexandrian Judaism, in Philo[23] for example, then in Judaism in the first and second centuries C.E., there is a rethinking of the unwritten law practised by the Righteous before Mosaic Law (Abraham, Noah . . .).[24] This is known not as natural law, but as unwritten law, prior to Mosaic law.

4. The major text of the *Epistle to the Romans* was to mark a transition and from the second century was to cause the Church Fathers, as we shall see, to bring together Gentile law and the Golden Rule:

> For when the Gentiles, which have not the law, do by nature the things contained in the law, these, having not the law, are a law unto themselves. Which shew the work of the law written in their hearts, their conscience also bearing witness, and their thoughts the mean while accusing or else excusing one another. (Rom. 2.14–15)

5. With Justin, and later Irenaeus, this idea of the Golden Rule appeared in a context that suggests Rom. 2.14, but it was with Origen that the link between the two neotestament texts (Mt. 7.12 and Rom. 2.14) is clearly and definitively established, as we saw above.

From that point on, all the Greek, Syriac, and Latin Fathers accept and teach this doctrine of the Golden Rule as being the content of natural law, the two most important and influential of whom are Augustine in the West and John Chrysostom in the East. However, as this tradition became established, the fact would be overlooked that it went some way further back, to Origen. It became a common, shared belief.

What does the conception of the Golden Rule as "natural law" mean?

First of all, it is understood as a law inscribed by God in the heart of man, according to a metaphorical expression, borrowed from a law inscribed by God

---

[23] Philo of Alexandria, *On Abraham*, §275, *Philo's Works*, vol.6, Loeb Classical Library, Cambridge (Mass.), Harvard University Press, 1984, p. 133–35: "This man did the divine law and the divine commands (Gen. 26, 5). He did them not taught by written words, but unwritten nature gave him the zeal (*ou grammasin anadidachtheis, all'agraphô tè phusei spoudasas*) to follow where wholesome and untainted impulse led him."

[24] *The Apocalypse of Baruch*, Chap. LVII, §1, Engl. transl. by R. H. Charles, *Translation Of Early Documents*, ser. 1, 9, London, Macmillan, 1918, p. 175: "After these, thou didst see bright waters. This is the fount of Abraham, also his generations and advent of his son, and of his son's son, and of those like them." §2. Because at that time, the unwritten Law was named amongst them, and the works of the commandments were then fulfilled. Text written between 70 and 135 (Pierre Bogaert, Éditions du Cerf, coll. *Sources Chrétiennes*, vol.144, 1969, Introduction, p. 270). In his *Commentary* (vol. 2, *S.C.* 145, p. 110), Pierre Bogaert quotes many rabbinic texts about this distinction between written and unwritten Law, and about the respect in which it was held by Abraham: Eccli. 44,20. See also Strack-Billerbeck,

on the tablet on Mount Sinai. The precept "Do not unto others as you would not have them do unto you" is now taken as a commandment on the same level as those of the Decalogue, which it recapitulates.

But the Fathers were not fooled by this representation: Origen himself demystifies the metaphorical representation:

> Now with respect to the words, "on their hearts," it is not to be thought that the law is said to be written on the bodily organ which is named the heart. For how could the flesh bring forth so much understanding of wisdom or contain such a great reservoir of memory? Rather one should realize that the soul's rational power is normally called the heart.[25]

Their commentary also shows how this "naturalness" means that man may, by himself, recognize what is good or evil based on what horrifies or pleases him when it is done to him. The commentary of the Decalogue through the Golden Rule follows this line: the Golden Rule provides the key to understanding the prohibitions of the Decalogue. It is not an additional precept, but it does permit man on his own to understand what is good or evil by transferring to others what seems to him unjust or painful when he suffers it himself.

Finally, much later and only at the beginning of the seventeenth century, the term "natural law" was coined, the reason being that it is also attested by pagan authors, outside the Christian faith, as would be shown first by La Mothe le Vayer in France in 1642 in *La Vertu des Payens*, then by Benjamin Camfield in England, in 1671, in *The Comprehensive Rule of Righteousness*, and Pufendorf in Germany, in 1672, in *De Iure naturae et Gentium*.

But today this law is recognized as natural for much more fundamental reasons:

1. The recognition of the other is rooted in the animal nature of man, as is demonstrated today by primatologists investigating the empathic behaviour of certain higher animals, such as the anthropoid apes;
2. The recognition of the other as the other, the capacity to "put oneself in other people's shoes"[26] is the basis of social life and language, because human nature is fundamentally interpersonal and relational.

Finally, one may wonder if the Golden Rule is not, anthropologically, a more fundamental and structuring rule than the prohibition on incest.

Kommentar zum Neuen Testament aus Talmud und Midrasch, vol. 3. *Die Briefe des Neuen Testament*, München, Beck, 1926, p. 88–91.

[25] ORIGEN, *Lectures on Romans*, 2, 9, 2; *Commentarius in Epistulam ad Romanos*, II, 9, *Migne, Patrologia series graeca (P.G.)*, Paris, 14, 892; English translation: by Thomas Scheck, Washington D.C, Catholic University of America Press, 2001, vol. I, p. 132.

[26] "To deal with others, as if we had exchanged Persons, and Circumstances with them, and they were in ours (George Borraston); "If I do but change the Scales, and put him in my place and my Self in his" (John Goodman); "Let the Tables be turned" (John Goodman).

Chapter 9

The Golden Rule in Islam

University of Rochester

The religion of Islam arose in Arabia during the sixth and seventh centuries C.E. At this time among the pre-Islamic Pagan Arabs, hospitality and generosity were celebrated virtues, though the Golden Rule was not. Like many other tribal peoples, the pre-Islamic Arabs regarded the survival of the tribe, not the individual, as most essential and to be insured by the ancient rite of blood vengeance.[1] In such a context, the law of the land was not the Golden Rule, but *lex talionis*, payback:

> We forgave the sons of Hind
> and said: "The folk are brothers.
> Perhaps the days will restore
> the tribe as they were."
> But when the evil was plain and clear,
> stripped bare to see,
> And nothing remained but enmity,
> then we paid back as they paid!
> We strode like the stalking lion,
> the furious lion,
> With a devastating, crunching,
> crushing blow,
> And a thrust, gashing, spewing
> like the mouth of a very full wineskin!
> A little restraint when quick action is called for,
> tells of servitude.
> And in evil is salvation
> when goodness cannot save you.[2]

---

[1] Th. Emil Homerin, "Altruism in Islam," in Jacob Neusner and Bruce Chilton (eds), *Altruism in World Religions* (Washington, D.C.: Georgetown University Press, 2005), pp. 67–87, esp. 67–70; and Jeffrey Wattles, *The Golden Rule* (Oxford: Oxford University Press, 1996), pp. 182–83.

[2] Abū Tammām, *Sharh Dīwān al-Hamāsah*, A. A. Amīn and A. Hārūn (eds) (Cairo: Matbaʿah Lajnah lil-Taʾlīf wa-al-Tarjamah wa-al-Nashr, 1951), 1:32–38; all translations are mine unless otherwise noted.

As suggested by this ode by Shahl ibn Shaybān al-Zimmānī (late fifth century C.E.), revenge might protect the clan, but it could also ignite a prolonged vendetta and intratribal warfare between clans, thus destabilizing life and society. As a result, pre-Islamic Arab society became known as the *al-Jāhilīyah*, the "Age of Impetuosity," as the Arab ideals of wisdom and restraint fell victim to quick tempers and rash actions.

The Golden Rule and the Qur'ān

However, in the seventh century, the prophet Muḥammad (c. 570–632) brought a different message and world view with the Qur'ān. As Muḥammad declared in Mecca, God, not the tribe, ruled supreme over humanity, which was to submit to the Lord's will and law. From this point on, the individual believer in community with other Muslims took precedent over the tribe and its obligations.[3] *Lex talionis* was still permitted for redressing murder and physical injuries willfully inflicted upon a victim, but the Qur'ān forbade vendetta, and urged more peaceful forms of settlement, including material compensation and outright forgiveness (Q. 2.178; 4.92).[4]

Forgiveness is a key theme in the Qur'ān, which repeatedly draws attention to God's compassion and mercy for humanity. Every human being has a covenant with God to believe in Him and to do what is right, and God has sent prophets and scripture to guide humanity to correct belief and proper behavior. Therefore, the Qur'ān urges people to be mindful of the fact that while they are free to believe and do as they like, the standards of judgment belong to God:

> Oh, you who believe, be mindful of God. Let each person consider what they have set aside for tomorrow. Be mindful of God, for He knows what you do. The residents of Hell and those of Heaven are not equal, for the residents of Paradise will be the winners! (Q. 59.18–19)

As a result, the Qur'ān underscores individual moral responsibility in its many depictions of the Judgment Day when each person will be called to account for the good and bad deeds that s/he did:[5]

> On that Day, people will come forward separately to be shown their deeds, and, so, whoever did an atom's weight of good will see it, and he who did an atom's weight of evil will see it. (Q. 99.6–7)

---

[3] See Frederick M. Denny, "Ethics and the Qur'ān: Community and World View," in Richard G. Hovannisan (ed.), *Ethics in Islam* (Malibu, CA: Undena Publications, 1985), pp. 103–111.

[4] Fazlur Rahman, "Law and Ethics in Islam," in Hovannisan, *Ethics in Islam*, pp. 3–15.

[5] See Fazlur Rahman, *Major Themes of the Qur'ān* (Minneapolis: Bibliotheca Islamica, 1980), pp. 106–20; and Arzina Lalani, "Judgment," in Jane Dammen McAulffe (ed.) *Encyclopaedia of the Qur'an* (Leiden: E. J. Brill, 2001–2005), 3: 64–68.

Each person, then, must submit (*islām*) to God and His will and strive to cultivate righteousness for success in this world and the next:

> Righteousness is from believing in God, the Last Day, the angels, the scrip-
> tures and the prophets, and from giving, out of love for Him, to one's rela-
> tives, orphans, the wretched, travelers, and beggars, and [righteousness is]
> from freeing slaves, undertaking prayers, giving alms, fulfilling covenants
> that were pledged, and from patience in adversity. (Q. 2.177)

As noted in this verse, a righteous life is based on correct belief and right
actions. Repeatedly the Qur'ān calls to "those who believe and do good works,"
and a major theme of the Qu'rān is the need to work for social justice.
Frequently, the Qur'ān exhorts Muslims to aid the oppressed:[6]

> Those who spend their wealth in the way of God are like a grain that germi-
> nates into seven spikes, each with a hundred grains. Indeed, God will increase
> in abundance whomsoever He will, and God is bounteous, all-knowing. Those
> who spend their wealth in the way of God, and do not follow up their giving
> with reproach or insult, they will have their reward from their Lord. They
> have nothing to fear, nor will they grieve . . . [Spend] on the poor who are
> beleaguered in the way of God, unable to move about the land [to earn a
> living], though the ignorant thinks them rich because [of their] restraint.
> You will recognize them by their mark: they do not beg from people demand-
> ing things. Whatever charity you give, God is aware of it. Those who spend
> of their wealth [on others] night and day, in secret and in public, they will
> have their reward with their Lord; they have nothing to fear, nor will they
> grieve. (Q. 2.261–62; 273–74)

Furthermore, people are to be kind to each other and to be fair in their social
and commercial transactions. They are always to "give full measure," for to do
otherwise is unjust:[7]

> Accursed be those who give short measure, those who, when they receive
> their share among people, they take their full share. Yet when they measure
> or weigh the shares of others, they give less. Do they not imagine that they
> will be resurrected on an awesome day, a day when people will stand before
> the Lord of the Worlds? (Q. 83.1–6)

---

[6] See Rahman, *Major Themes*, pp. 37–49; and Homerin, "Altruism in Islam," pp. 70–74.
[7] Cf., Qur'ān 6.152; 7.56; 11.84–85; 17.35; 26.181–82; 55.7–9. Qur'ān 83.1–6 is also cited by
H. T. D. Rost in his brief remarks about the Golden Rule in Islam in *The Golden Rule* (Oxford:
George Ronald, 1986), pp. 100–101. Rost also cites Qur'ān 59.9 as another example, though
this verse is about giving to others in the name of God, not the Golden Rule; see Homerin,
"Altruism in Islam," p. 74.

According to some Muslim authorities, this revelation came after Muḥammad had immigrated with other persecuted Muslims to Medina in 622; there he found merchants who were not giving fair measure.[8] The philosopher-commentator Fakhr al-Dīn al-Rāzī (d. 1209) noted that the issue of weights and measures was a fundamental function of any society, as the Qur'ān makes clear:

> [God] raised the sky and set the balance that no one could cheat the scales. So give full measure and do not give less on the scales! (Q. 55.7–9)

> Indeed, We sent Our messengers with clear signs, and We sent down with them the book and the scale so that people may practice justice! (Q. 57.25)[9]

Ḥadīth of the Golden Rule

Fakhr al-Dīn al-Razi and several other Qur'ānic commentators have pointed out that Qur'ān 83.1–6 is an implicit statement of the Golden Rule, which is explicitly stated in the tradition:

> Pay, Oh Children of Adam, as you would love to be paid, and be just as you would love to have justice![10]

Similar examples of the Golden Rule are found among the *ḥadīth* of the prophet Muḥammad. The *ḥadīth* recount what Muḥammad is believed to have said and done, and traditionally Muslims regard the *ḥadīth* as second only to the Qur'ān as a guide to correct belief and action. One *ḥadīth* of the Golden Rule is most often quoted in the major *ḥadīth* collections of sound traditions and, subsequently, in other Muslim religious literature. There Muḥammad said:

> None of you believes until he loves for his brother what he loves for himself![11]

---

[8] Maḥmūd al-Zamakhsharī, *al-Kashshāf* (Beirut: Dār al-Maʿrifah, n.d.), 4:194; Fakhr al-Dīn al-Rāzī, *al-Tafsīr al-Kabīr* (Beirut: Dār Iḥyāʾ al-Turāth al-ʿArabī, n.d.) 31:87–88; and Jamāl al-Dīn al-Suyūṭī, *al-Durar al-Manthūr* (Beirut: Dār al-Maʿrifah, n.d.), 6:323–24.

[9] Al-Rāzī, *al-Tafsīr*, 31:89; and also see ʿImād al-Dīn Ibn Kathīr, *Tafsīr al-Qurʾān al-ʿAẓīm* (Beirut: Dār wa-Maktabat al-Hilāl, 1986), 6:365.

[10] Ibid. and al-Zamakhsharī, *al-Kashshāf*, 4:195. Also see the comments of the twentieth-century translator A. Yusuf Ali, *The Holy Quran* (Cambridge, MA: Murry Printing Co., 1946), 2:1703; also quoted in Rost, *Golden Rule*, p. 101.

[11] See Yusūf al-Mizzī, *Tuḥfat al-Ashrāf bi-Maʿrifat al-Atrāf*, ʿAbd al-Samad Sharaf al-Dīn (ed) (Bombay: al-Dār al-Qayyimah, 1965), 1:322, #1239; and also see Dwight M. Donaldson, *Studies in Muslim Ethics* (London: S.P.C.K., 1953), 89, and Rost, *Golden Rule*, pp. 102–04.

Two of the most important collectors of *ḥadīth*, Muḥammad al-Bukhārī (d. 870) and Muslim ibn al-Ḥajjāj (d. 875), cite this *ḥadīth* in their chapters on *īmān*, that is on "faith" or "belief."[12] This relates directly to Qur'ān 49.14:

> The Bedouin say: "We believe." Say [to them, Muḥammad]: "You do not believe. Rather say: 'We submit,' for belief has yet to enter your hearts. Then if you obey God and His messenger, He will not withhold from you any [reward] for your actions. Indeed, God is forgiving, merciful!"

According to Muslim tradition, some Bedouin professed Islam in order to have an alliance with Muḥammad during a time of draught so as to receive charity. The Qur'ān, then, distinguishes between a *muslim*, "one who submits" and professes to be a believer, and a *mu'min*, "one who believes" in God and His revelations deep within his/her heart.[13] This verse implies that there are levels of faith ranging from nominally holding a religion to being held intensely by it.

In this context, the great fifteenth century Muslim *ḥadīth* scholar Ibn Ḥajar al-ʿAsqalānī (d. 1449) asserted that when Muḥmmad said, "None of you believes," he did not mean that one who fails to live the Golden Rule is an infidel but, rather, that one's faith is not complete "until he loves for his brother what he loves for himself." On the other hand, Ibn Ḥajar added, to claim that one who practiced the Golden Rule but not the Five Pillars of Islam, had perfect faith, was absurd.[14] Clearly, for Ibn Ḥajar and other Muslim scholars, the Golden Rule was an ethical principle sanctioned by God, but enmeshed in a larger system of correct beliefs and actions.[15]

Ibn Ḥajar also cited an example of the negative Golden Rule, that "one loath for one's brother what one loathes for oneself of evil," as well as several variations in the transmission of Muḥammad's positive Golden Rule:[16]

> No worshipper (*ʿabd*) believes until he loves for his brother and neighbor what he loves for himself!

> No worshipper believes until he loves for his Muslim brother what he loves for himself of good things!

---

[12] Muḥammad al-Bukhārī, *Saḥīḥ al-Bukhārī*, Muḥammad Muhsin Khān (ed) (Medina: Dār al-Fikr, n.d.), 1:19 (Bk 2, chap. 7, #12); and Muslim ibn al-Hajjāj, *Saḥīḥ Muslim* (Cairo: Dār al-Hadīth, n.d.), 1:67–68 (Bk 1, chap. 17, #71).

[13] ʿAbd Allāh al-Baydāwī, *Anwār al-Tanzīl* (Beirut: Dār al-Jīl, 1992 reprint of the 1329/1911 Egyptian edn.), pp. 685; and al-Suyūtī, *al-Durar*, 6:99–100.

[14] Ibn Hajar al-ʿAsqalānī, *Fatḥ al-Bārī bi-Sharh Saḥīḥ al-Bukhārī* (Beirut: Dār al-Maʿrifah, n.d.), 1:56–58.

[15] See Michael Cook, *Commanding the Right and Forbidding the Wrong in Islam* (Cambridge, MA: Cambridge University Press, 2000), esp. pp. 3–12 and 585–96.

[16] Ibn Hajar al-ʿAsqalānī, *Fatḥ al-Bārī*, 1:56–58.

For Ibn Ḥajar, this last version clarified that Muslims were intended by the word "brother" as those to be loved as oneself. Perhaps, Ibn Ḥajar took comfort in this reading since he lived in Egypt during a time when more conservative Muslim scholars, like him, felt challenged by the Crusaders, Mongols, Turks, and their infidel ways.[17] However, the most common *ḥadīth* of the Golden Rule does not contain the adjective "Muslim," and Ibn Ḥajar's commentary on this *ḥadīth* generally treats the Golden Rule as a moral principle to desire sincerely for others the same exact material and spiritual good that one desires for oneself, and to act humbly. Indeed, humility is the key to the Golden Rule, and Ibn Ḥajar cites in support of this position the scholar and judge al-Qāḍī ʿIyāḍ (d. 1149), and Abū al-Zinād ibn Sarrāj who stated:[18]

> The literal meaning of this *ḥadīth* is the pursuit of equal rights, and its realization necessitates giving preference (to others). Everyone loves to be preferred over others. So, if one can love for his brother as for himself, then he is among the virtuous.

Ibn Ḥajar then concludes his discussion of the *ḥadīth* of the Golden Rule by drawing out its ethical implications and the moral conduct required to put the Golden Rule into practice:

> The upshot of this position is to incite one to humility, so that one does not want to be preferred over others, for it requires equality as supported by His, most high, saying [28.83]: {As to the next abode, We will give that to those who do not desire to be exalted in the world, nor are they corrupt}. One cannot attain that except by eliminating (from oneself) envy, malice, resentment, and deceit, for all of those are base qualities.[19]

The Golden Rule in Muslim tradition

Interpreted in this light, Muḥammad's statement of the Golden Rule is a call to self-examination and religious transformation aimed not at reciprocity so much as humility by acknowledging the humanity of other human beings. Not surprisingly, this interpretation is found in the writings of Muslim mystics who stress the power of selfless love to bring the devotee closer to God.[20] One of the most extensive discussions of the Golden Rule in Islamic mysticism appears in

---

[17] See Jonathan P. Berkey, "The Mamluks as Muslims," in Thomas Philipp and Ulrich Haarman (eds), *The Mamluks in Egyptian Politics and Society* (Cambridge, MA: Cambridge University Press, 1998), pp. 163–73.

[18] Ibn Ḥajar al-ʿAsqalānī, *Fath al-Bārī*, 1:58. Perhaps Abū al-Zinād ibn Sarrāj is the *ḥadīth* scholar ʿAlī ibn Sarrāj (d. 920); see ʿUmar Kahhālah, *Muʿjam al-Muʾallfīn* (Damascus: al-Maktabah al-ʿArabīyah, 1957), 7:98.

[19] Ibid.

the Qur'ānic commentary by the celebrated eleventh-century Sufi scholar Abū al-Qāsim al-Qushayrī (d. 1037) during his discussion of Qur'ān 83.1–6:

{Those who give short measure} are those who cheat when measuring or weighing. What is meant by that are those who do business with people, such that when they take for themselves, they take a full share, but when they wait on their customers, they short change them. This is seen clearly in weights and measures, and applies to finding fault, in making judgments, payments, and restitution. For if one does not want for his Muslim brother what he wants for himself, he is not fair.[21] As for the righteous, whenever they regard Muslims, they regard everyone to be treated the same. Truth is honorable! This is their position regarding friendship and social relations.

As for him who sees faults in people, but does not see the fault in himself, then he is among "those who give short measure." Just as it has been said:

You see the mote in my eye,
but not the log in your own!

So one who demands his right, but does not demand for others what he demands for himself, he is among {those who give short measure}.
The chivalrous man (*fatan*) is he who demands the rights for others, but does not demand from anyone a right for himself.[22]

In his commentary on "those who give short measure," al-Qushayrī extends the Qur'ān's critique of unfair business transactions to other human interactions, including the criticism of others. Similar to Ibn Ḥajar, al-Qushayrī appears to call for the Golden Rule to be applied between Muslims; nothing is said about Muslim interactions with non-Muslims. This is not to deny non-Muslims their humanity, but to acknowledge the Qur'ān's recognition of religious diversity as found in a number of passages that state that various monotheistic religious communities have their own particular scripture and law to follow:

For each of you, We have made a law and a course of action. Had God wished, He would have made you one religious community, but He tests you by what He has given you. So vie with one another in doing good deeds! (5.48)

---

[20] For Sufism, see Annemarie Schimmel, *Mystical Dimensions of Islam* (Chapel Hill: University of North Carolina Press, 1975).
[21] A later Sufi, the famous Persian poet Jalāl al-Dīn Rūmī (d. 1273), put it his way (*Masnavī*, Bk 6, v. 1569):
    That which you don't find agreeable for yourself, O Shaykh of Religion
    How can you find it agreeable for your brother, O trustworthy one?
My thanks to Dr. Frank Lewis, University of Chicago, for this reference and translation.
[22] Abū al-Qāsim al-Qushayrī, *Laṭ'if al-Ishārāt*, Ibrāhīm Basyūnī (ed) (Cairo: al-Hay'at al-Misrīyah al-ʿĀmmah lil-Kitāb, 1983), 3:699–700.

Moreover, the Qur'ān warns Muslims against being overly friendly with Christians, Jews, or others who may wish them harm (e.g., 2.120, 5.51, 5.82). In such cases, the Golden Rule would not be recommended, as other commands of God would take precedence (e.g., 9.29).[23]

Al-Qushayrī then highlights the basic reciprocal nature of the Golden Rule by comparing the righteous with the unrighteous Muslim. The righteous Muslim strives to treat all Muslims as his equal, while the unrighteous Muslim wants only his due; he sees other people's shortcomings while being heedless of his own. Finally, al-Qushayrī adds a third type of person, the *fatan* or "chivalrous man." Within Islamic mysticism such an individual has conquered his selfishness and concupiscence (*nafs*) and so is regarded as a true hero.[24] Discussing such spiritual chivalry known as *al-futuwwah*, al-Qushayrī wrote elsewhere:

> The companions of the cave (Qur'ān 18.13) are called [chivalrous men] because they believed in their Lord without any intermediary. It is said, "The chivalrous man is he who smashes idols, for God Most High says, 'We heard a youth [*fatan*] denounce the idols. He is called Abraham' (21.60), and 'He smashed the idols to pieces'" (21.58). The idol of every man is his own self [*nafs*]. So one who opposes his passions is truly chivalrous.[25]

For such a hero, the ultimate goal of the Golden Rule is altruism and the elimination of selfish desires by putting the needs of others before one's own:

> [The Sufi] Maʿrūf al-Karkhī [d. 815], may God have mercy upon him, said: "One who claims to be chivalrous must have three qualities: fidelity without fear, generosity without thought of praise, the ability to give without being asked."[26]

> Chivalry is when one does not hold himself or his actions in high regard, nor expects a return for his effort.[27]

Another noted Sufi and theologian Muḥammad al-Ghazālī (d. 1111) mentions the Golden Rule in an epistle directed at those who desire to live a pious life:

> [M]ake your relations with God the Exalted such that were a servant of yours to behave thus with you, you would be content with him and not be weary of liking him, nor get angry. Whatever would dissatisfy you for yourself on the

---

[23] See Th. Emil Homerin, "Islam," in Jacob Neusner (ed.), *Religious Foundations of Western Civilization*, (Nashville: Abingdon Press, 2006), pp. 118–21; also see the relevant references to non-Muslims in Cook, *Commanding the Right*.

[24] See "Futuwwa," *EI2* 2:961–65 (Cl. Cahen); Michael Chodkiewicz and Tosun Bayrak al-Jerrahi, "Introduction" to al-Jerrahi, *The Way of Chivalry* (Rochester, VT: Inner Traditions International, 1991), pp. 6–28; and Homerin, "Altruism in Islam," pp. 79–84.

[25] Al-Qushayrī, *The Principles of Sufism*, translated by B. R. Von Schlegell (Berkeley: Mizan Press, 1992), pp. 215.

[26] Muḥammad al-Sulamī, *al-Futuwwah*, Iḥsān Dhunūn Thāmirī and Muḥammad ʿAbd Allāh al-Qadhāt (eds) (ʿAmmān: Dār al-Rāzī, 2002), p. 88.

[27] Ibid., 17.

part of this hypothetical servant of yours, should dissatisfy you also for God the Exalted, and He is actually your Lord!. . . [W]henever you interact with people, deal with them as you would wish yourself to be dealt with by them, for a worshipper's faith is incomplete until he wants for other people what he wants for himself.[28]

Similar to al-Qushayrī, al-Ghazālī paraphrases the *ḥadīth* of the Golden Rule as he clearly states that our interactions with others should mirror our relationship with God. Just as a slave owner would wish his servants to be honest and obedient, so, too, should we be unselfish and obedient toward God, our true Lord.[29] Perhaps building on al-Ghazālī's brief remarks, the great thirteenth century Sufi theologian, Muḥyī al-Dīn Ibn al-ʿArabī (d. 1240) referred to the Golden Rule in his own epistle to those who wish to follow the Sufi path:

Among the things you must posses is [the grace of] avoiding those who are opposed [to your way of life], and people who are not of your sort, without, however, entertaining any thought of wronging them such as may occur to you, but with the intention of choosing the friendship and company of the True One rather than theirs. Also in your relations with animals let there be tenderness and compassion for them, for they are creatures whom the True One has put under constraint for your service. So do not load them more than they can bear, nor ride them carelessly or with abandon. Similarly with regard to slaves who are under your hand, [remember that] they are your brethren, whose forelocks [God] has given you to possess that He may see how you conduct yourself with them. You are His slave—glory be to Him— and you would not like Him to conduct Himself in an evil manner with you. Treat them exactly as He [has treated you], and you will be rewarded for that on a Day when you stand in need of it. If you have a family, treat them with kindness, for all [of us] are children, including yourself. All the commandments are summed up in this, that whatever you would like the True One to do to you, that do to His creatures, step by step.[30]

From this passage, Ibn al-ʿArabī appears to justify the Golden Rule based on God's acts of mercy toward His creation.[31] The Golden Rule, then, becomes a general principle of compassion that also relates to human interactions with

---

[28] Muḥammad al-Ghazālī, *Letter to a Disciple*, Tobias Mayer (ed. and trans.) (Cambridge: The Islamic Text Society, 2005), pp. 54–57.
[29] See Wattles, *Golden Rule*, pp. 33–35, and the very similar argument put forward by Socrates in the *Phaedo*.
[30] Ibn al-ʿArabī, *Kunhi mā lā budhu lil-murīd* in Arthur Jeffery (trans.) *Reader on Islam* (The Hague: Mouton & Co., 1962), p. 647.
[31] Cf., the second century B.C.E. Jewish Ben Sira text and *The Letter of Aristeas* mentioned in Wattles, *Golden Rule*, pp. 44–46.

animals. Since God created the world and made humanity vice-regent over the animals, human beings should care for them with kindness. So, too, a parent is to be kind to his children, while slaves should be treated respectfully for they are humans, like their masters, and all humans are, in fact, God's servants. What is also noteworthy about this passage by Ibn al-ʿArabī, as well as earlier statements by al-Qushayrī, al-Ghazālī, and Ibn Ḥajar is that the Golden Rule does not nullify all difference in a universal equality so much as it operates among groups of similar members. That is to say, within Classical Islam, and I suspect in nearly all premodern religious and philosophical traditions, there are basic social, legal, theological, even ontological, distinctions and hierarchies that constrain the Golden Rule; these include God-humanity, Muslim–non-Muslim, free person-slave, ruler-subject, adult-child, and man-woman. The Qur'ān's statements on male-female relations are instructive here. The Qur'ān declares unequivocally that male and female believers are equal in the eyes of God (33.35):

> Indeed, men who have submitted and women who have submitted, believing men and believing women, pious men and pious women, truthful men and truthful women, patient men and patient women, modest men and modest women, men who give alms and women who give alms, men who fast and women who fast, men and women who guard their private parts and remember God often, God will forgive them and give them a great reward!

Nevertheless, men are still ranked "a degree" above women (2.228) in terms of social relations, particularly within the family which the husband is expected to support financially (e.g., 4.34).[32] The issue then is not so much treating everyone the same, but rather treating each person appropriately, as noted by the Chinese philosopher Confucius:[33]

> What you would require of your son, use in serving your father; . . . what you would require of your subordinate, use in serving your prince . . . what you would require of your younger brother, use in serving your elder brother; . . . what you would require of your friend, first apply in your treatment of him.

Only in the last category of "friend," do we find a notion of equals, and this holds true for Islam as well, particularly in its philosophical tradition. Owing much to Plato and Aristotle, the Persian philosopher and ethicist Aḥmad Miskawayh

---

[32] For a range of positions on this complex issue see Fazlur Rahman, "The Status of Women in Islam: A Modernist Interpretation," in Hanna Papanek and Gail Minault (eds) *Separate Worlds: Studies of Purdah in South Asia* (Delhi: Chanakya Publications, 1982), pp. 285–310; and Seyyed Hossein Nasr, "The *Sharīʿah*: Divine Law—Social and Human Norm," in Neusner (ed.), *Foundations*, pp. 195–208, esp. 205–08.

[33] Quoted by Wattles, *Golden Rule*, p. 18.

(d. 963) noted that love is the key to being fair and just.[34] Yet, social relations must be carefully observed and taken into account:

> [O]ne should know the ranks of the various kinds of love, and what each per-
> son deserves to get from the other so that he will not offer to a foreign chief
> the honor due to a father, nor to a sovereign that due to a friend, nor to kins-
> men that due to a child, nor to a father that due to a mother. For every one
> of these and their like is entitled to a kind of honor and a right of repayment
> which are not appropriate to any other. If one does not discriminate among
> these obligations, confusion and corruption will affect them and reproaches
> will take place, but if he discharges to every one his due and share of love,
> service, and good counsel, he will be acting justly and his love and the justice
> manifest in it will obligate his friends and associates to love him in return.
> The same should be followed in one's fellowship with one's friends, com-
> rades, and companions; he should observe their rights and render to each
> one of them what is due to him.[35]

Miskawayh also stressed that love and its relationships must be based on a mutual respect and for seeking the good, and not for purposes of personal profit or aggrandizement. Such adulterated or counterfeit love will quickly degenerate along with the relationship leading to hypocrisy, discord, and hate:[36]

> Reproach and rebuke may enter even into the love that exists between the
> chief and the subject, or the rich man and the poor, because of the diver-
> gences of the causes, and because each of them expects from the other a
> reward which he does not get. Their mutual intentions become spoiled, they
> find each other slow [to give], and they blame each other. This condition
> ceases when the two parties observe justice, and when each of them is satis-
> fied to get from the other only as much as he has a right to and each of them
> accepts to treat the other with the justice which lies between them. Slaves, in
> particular, are not satisfied unless their masters give them more than what
> they deserve, while the masters find them too slow in the performance of
> their duties and in [showing] solicitude and goodwill, all of which leads to
> reproach and bad conscience.[37] This is the reproachful love of which [one]
> can hardly ever be free unless one follows the stipulation of justice, and seeks

[34] See Constantine K. Zurayk's introduction to Ahmad Miskawayh, *The Refinement of Character* (Beirut: American University of Beirut Press, 1968), p. 135; Lenn E. Goodman "Miskawayh's Courtly Humanism," in Goodman, *Islamic Humanism* (Oxford: Oxford University Press, 2003), pp. 101–12; and Donaldson, *Muslim Ethics*, p. 130.

[35] Ahmad Miskawayh, *The Refinement of Character* (*Tadhīb al-Akhlāq*) in Constantine K. Zurayk (trans.) (Beirut: American University of Beirut Press, 1968), p. 135.

[36] Ibid., 130–34.

[37] Regarding the dilemma of slaves and the Golden Rule, see Wattles, *Golden Rule*, pp. 39–40; and William Scott Green, "Parsing Reciprocity: Questions for the Golden Rule," p. 4.

the mean in what he deems to be his right and is satisfied with it. But this is difficult.

On the other hand, the mutual love of virtuous people is not motivated by any external pleasure or any benefit, but is due to their essential similarity, namely in aiming at what is good and seeking virtue. Thus, when one of them loves another because of his similarity, no difference or dispute takes place between them. They exchange advice and agree to be just and equal in their desire of the good. This equal rendering of advice and desire of the good is what unifies their multiplicity. This is why a friend is defined as another person who is yourself, but is other than your person, and this is why he is so rarely found. The friendship of the young, the common people, and those who are not wise is unreliable because such people love and befriend for the sake of pleasure and benefit. They do not know the good in reality and their motives are not sound.

For Miskawayh, then, true friendship as embodied in the Golden Rule is very rare indeed.[38] Nevertheless, if only as an ideal, the Golden Rule may usefully serve as a basis for a social contract to promote civic virtue and good government:

For a man loves his friend and wishes for him what he wishes for himself; and no confidence, or cooperation, or mutual help can take place except among those who love one another. Thus, if people cooperate and are bound by love, they will attain all the desirable things and will not fail to secure the objects of their search, even though these objects may be hard and difficult. They will then bring forth sound opinions, their minds will collaborate in deducing any right measures which may be obscure, and they will strengthen themselves in order to gain all the goods by cooperation. Aristotle was one of those who supported and confirmed this opinion . . . Indeed this is the noblest end for the people of a city. For if the citizens love one another, they will be in close relation, and each man will wish for his companion what he wishes for himself. Their numerous capacities will become one, and none of them will fail to arrive at a sound opinion or right action. In all that they attempt to do, they will be like a person who wants to move a heavy weight by himself and is not able to do so, but if he is assisted by others he can then set it in motion. Indeed, the manager of the city aims, in all his measures at binding his people by ties of affection. If he succeeds in attaining this aim in particular, he will achieve all the goods which will be difficult for him, or for

---

[38] Miskawayh would probably agree with those thinkers who believe that "the Golden Rule can be accepted unambiguously but applied only after considerable reflection and qualification." See Green, "Parsing Reciprocity," p. 3.

the citizens, to achieve individually. He will then overcome his rivals, build up his country, and live happily with his subjects.[39]

Miskawayh's linking of the Golden Rule to the idea of a just ruler has earlier precedents in Muslim literature, including the "mirrors for princes." This genre gave advice to caliphs, viziers, amirs, and their sons regarding political and ethical norms, statecraft, and justice, whether as *Realpolotik* or righteous ideals.[40] Among the earliest and influential "mirrors" were several works by ʿAbdallāh Ibn al-Muqaffaʿ (d. c. 756) a Persian secretary to the caliph's court in Baghdad. Ibn al-Muqaffaʿ's most popular work, *Kalīlah wa-Dimnah*, is his translation into Arabic of ancient Indian animal fables, which offer advice and political wisdom regarding human relations and governance. The tales are told by a philosopher in response to questions from an Indian king. The story of "The Lioness, the Archer and the Jackal" may ultimately derive from the twelfth book of the Indian epic, the *Mahābhārata*:[41]

The King said to Bidpai, the philosopher: "Strike me a parable about someone who avoids harming others after he had experienced his own tragedy, which served as a warning and a restraint to him regarding perpetuating oppression and aggression toward others."

The philosopher replied: "No one seeks to harm people or act meanly toward them save the ignorant low-lifers and those who are short-sighted regarding the consequences of affairs in this world and the next, and who are dim-witted regarding the resulting punishment and unimaginable effects that will befall them in turn. A few give up harming others after misfortune befalls them, and so they become mindful of what they do. But one who never thinks about the consequences is never safe from misfortunes and, truly, he does not escape from ruin. On occasion, however, an ignorant person is warned and taught a lesson. . . Then as a result, he profits and abstains from hurting others, as was the case in the story of the lioness, the archer, and the jackal."

The King said: "How does that go?"

The philosopher said: "There once was a lioness in the jungle who had two cubs. It happened that she went out to hunt, and she left the two behind in their cave. An archer passed by and came upon the two cubs. He shot and killed them both. Then he skinned off their hides, put the hides in his bag,

[39] Miskawayh, *Refinement of Character*, p. 118.
[40] On this genre see C. E. Bosworth, "Mirrors for Princes," in Julie Scott Meisami and Paul Starkey (eds), *Encyclopedia of Arabic Literature* (London: Routledge, 1998), 2:527–29.
[41] ʿAbdallāh Ibn al-Muqaffaʿ, *Kalīlah wa-Dimnah* (Beirut: Maktabat Lubnān, 1987), pp. 306–10. Also see F. De Blois, "*Kalīlah wa-Dimnah*," in *Encyclopedia of Arabic Literature*, 2:423–25.

and left for home. When the lioness returned, she saw the shocking fate that had occurred to her cubs. She doubled over in grief, screeching and moaning. A jackal was nearby, and when he heard her screeching he said to her:

'What are you doing? What has befallen you? Tell me about it."

The Lioness said: 'My two cubs! An archer passed by and killed them both! He stripped their hides, bagged them, and left my two skinned cubs!'

The jackal said to her: 'Don't cry; pull yourself together! Know that the archer did to you only what you have done to others. For you did similar things to those who found their friends and dear ones, as you have found your cubs. So you must endure the actions of others, as others have endured you actions. As it has been said: "As you pay, so you will be repaid." Every deed, whether great or small, bears the fruit of a like reward or punishment. Like sowing, the reaper harvests as he has sown.'

The lioness replied: 'Explain to me what you have said. Speak plainly its implications'.

The jackal said: 'How old are you?'
The lioness replied: 'One hundred.'
The jackal said: 'What do you eat?'
The lioness replied: 'The meat of wild animals.'
The jackal said: 'Who feeds it to you?'
The lioness replied: 'I hunt wild animals, and I eat them.'
The jackal said: 'Haven't you thought about the wild animals that you have eaten, that they had fathers and mothers?'
The lioness replied: 'Yes.'
The jackal said: 'And me, I have seen and heard those fathers and mothers grieve and mourn just as I saw and heard you. Isn't what has befallen you due to your short-sightedness regarding consequences and your thinking so little about the harm they would return to you?'"

"When the lioness heard these words from the jackal, she realized that she had sinned against herself, that her actions were unjust and oppressive. So she gave up hunting and instead of eating meat, she lived on fruit, ascetic practices, and worship. But when the wild dove, who resided in this jungle and lived on fruit, saw this he said to her:

'I have long thought that this tree we have in common would cease bearing fruit because of scarce water. Then I saw you eating the fruit, though you are a carnivore. But you gave up your sustenance, food, and what God decreed for you, and adapted to the sustenance of others, with whom you now compete and overpower in your consumption. I know that the common tree bore fruit, just as it bore fruit before today. But it gave little fruit relative to your large appetite. So woe to the tree, woe to its fruit, and woe to those who live on it! How quick will be their destruction when one who is not supposed to be a vegetarian competes and overpowers them in eating fruit!'"

"When the lioness heard the words of the wild dove, she gave up eating fruit and turned to living off grass and worship."

"So I have struck this parable for you to show that the ignorant may turn away from harming people after suffering harm themselves, just as the lioness, after what happened to her cubs, gave up eating meat, then fruit after listening to the wild dove, and she turned to ascetic devotions and worship. For it has been said: 'That which you do not want for yourself, do not do to someone else.' In that is justice, and God wishes for justice, and people wish for justice too."

"The Lioness, the Archer, and the Jackal" is ostensibly a tale about actions and their consequences. The Indian law of karma is suggested by the jackal's early remark: "Every deed, whether great or small, bears the fruit of a like reward or punishment." The story may also be read as an argument for nonviolence and, certainly, as a parable of the Golden Rule, the negative version of which ends the story: "That which you do not want for yourself, do not do to someone else." Further, the tale has political implications, since in *Kalīlah wa-Dimnah*, the lion is the king of beasts and so represents a human ruler. On the one hand the message is clear that a ruler should not ignore his subjects and thereby oppress them. However, when the lioness changes her ways, her vegetarianism has the unexpected consequence of depriving others of their vital food source. Ultimately, the lioness gives up fruit to live on grass and acts of worship, and while this rather odd image of a grazing lion might portray an Indian and/or Muslim ascetic ideal, it does go against the animal's God-given nature as the dove points out: "But you gave up your sustenance, food, and what God decreed for you, and adapted to the sustenance of others, with whom you now compete and overpower in your consumption." Once again, the Golden Rule may have been evoked not to counsel equality, but action appropriate to one's station in life.

Reciprocity: retaliation or reconciliation?

Treating people equitably in commercial transactions is a Qur'ānic command for social justice, and the *ḥadīth* of the Golden Rule in its most popular and general form "None of you believes until he loves for his brother what he loves for himself!" may be understood to apply to all humanity, not only a select group. This appears to be the gist of another saying ascribed to the prophet

Muḥammad. One day a certain Muslim man commanded his servant to slaugh-ter a sheep and distribute it to others beginning with his Jewish neighbors. The servant, perplexed that he should give a portion to a Jewish family, let alone the first portion, hesitated until his master told him that he had heard the Prophet say: "One should look after one's neighbors to the extent that one considers them his legal heirs."[42]

As with many examples of the Golden Rule found in Muslim sources, this *ḥadīth*, too, proscribes for the actor that he treat others with kindness, dignity, and respect by placing their needs before his own. For many Muslim scholars, and especially the mystics, the Golden Rule was not primarily a call for recipro-city or retaliation, but a means to cultivate humility, selflessness, and altruistic behavior. By contrast for the Muslim ethicist Miskawayh, the Golden Rule rep-resented a rare, ideal friendship between equals as well as the basis for a social contract leading to the greater good of all. In Ibn al-Muqaffaʿ's advice to rulers, the Golden Rule warned them to treat their subjects with justice or face the consequences, whether in this world or the next.

We see, then, that Muslims have interpreted and applied the Golden Rule in several contrasting ways, and two recent examples underscore dramatically dif-ferent understandings of reciprocity. On the negative side is retaliation as pay-back, the *lex talionis* of old, now championed in the name of Islam by Osama Bin Laden:

There is a lesson in what is happening in occupied Palestine, and what hap-pened on September 11, [2001] and [in Spain] on March 11, [2004] are your goods returned to you. . . In what creed are your dead considered innocent but ours worthless? By what logic does your blood count as real and ours no more than water. Reciprocal treatment is part of justice, and he who com-mences hostilities is the unjust one . . . Therefore stop spilling our blood to save your own . . . For we only killed Russians after they invaded Afghanistan and Chechnya, we only killed Europeans after they invaded Afghanistan and Iraq, and we only killed Americans in New York after they supported the Jews in Palestine and invaded the Arabian peninsula, and we only killed them in Somalia after they invaded it in Operation Rescue Hope. We restored them to hopelessness, thank God.[43]

As we all know too well, Bin Laden's calls for reciprocal violence have been answered by the United States and some of its allies with more violence, as the crisis in the Middle East has escalated and precipitated a civil war in Iraq.

[42] Ibn Abī Dunyā, *Kitāb Makārim al-Akhlāq*, James A. Bellamy (ed.) (Wiesbaden: Franz Steiner, 1973), p. 80.
[43] Osama Bin Laden, *Messages to the World*, translated by James Howarth (New York, 2005), pp. 235–36, also see pp. 173–75.

Daily, clashes between Muslims and non-Muslims result in blood shed and death, often of children and other innocent civilians. In such a situation, invocations of a "war on terror" or "jihād" do not bring justice; they are cynical justifications for crimes against humanity and a new *Jāhilīyah*, a new "Age of Impetuosity."

Yet in contrast to Bin Laden, there is another Muslim call for reciprocity, a positive one of reconciliation. In an attempt to seek world peace and international justice, over 125 Muslim clerics and scholars from around the world sent an open letter to Pope Benedict XVI and other world leaders of Christianity on October 13, 2007. Entitled "A Common Word Between Us" the letter affirms that the common beliefs held by Jews, Christians, and Muslims in "the love of one God, and love of the neighbor" should serve as "a basis for peace and understanding."[44] Central to their message is the Golden Rule in various forms including Lev. 19.17–18, Mt. 22.38–40, Mk 12.31, and the *ḥadīth*: "None of you believes until you love for your brother what you love for yourself!"[45] The letter interprets the Golden Rule as referring to a common human kinship and to compassion for one's fellow human beings.[46] Moreover, the letter accepts religious pluralism and states emphatically "that Muslims, Christians, and Jews should be free to each follow what God commanded them. . . for God says elsewhere in the Holy Qur'ān: *Let there be no compulsion in religion*" [2.256].[47] The letter ends with a call for building a world of peace and harmony on this common ground. Invoking the Golden Rule, these Muslims seek to end the violence in order to promote justice and mutual goodwill, so that, together, we may "vie one with another in good works" (5.48).[48]

[44] http://www.acommonword.com/, p. 3.
[45] Ibid., pp. 11–12.
[46] Similarly, see Wattles, *Golden Rule*, pp. 183–84.
[47] http://www.acommonword.com/, p. 14.
[48] Ibid., p. 16.

Chapter 10

The Formulation and Significance of the Golden Rule in Buddhism [I]

Kristin Scheible
Bard College

In Theravāda Buddhism, the universe depends on the actions of individuals within it. Moral action has an impact on the status of beings in *samsāra*, the "wandering on" cycle of birth, life, death, and rebirth. The goal, both proximate and eventual, of a Theravāda Buddhist is to cultivate oneself as a moral agent. The eventual goal to become an enlightened being who is no longer subject to the bounds of *samsāra* requires the cultivation of ten perfections (*pārami* in Pāli, *pāramitā* in Sanskrit).[1] The rounds of rebirth within *samsāra* occur because of *karma*, literally action, which is an assumed system that operates in the universe of human actions. Through the many rounds of rebirth an individual endures, the individual meets with multiple opportunities to cultivate merit through action. Moral actions are skilful, unskillful, or neutral, and they accrue concomitant weight. Skilful moral actions earn merit, or *puñña*, while negative or unskillful actions result in demerit, *pāpa*. This is the way the world works—one's actions have effects, and one has the ability to exert agency in determining the moral weight of one's effects by intending to do good things. The canonical formulation attributed to the voice of the Buddha himself links moral actions with intention, "It is intention (*cetanā*), O monks, that I call Karma; having willed one acts through body, speech, or mind."[2]

In what follows, the focus will not be on the particular frameworks of thought that arise through and determine the course of the history of Theravādin practice, such as the development of the doctrine of ten perfections. Instead, the focus will be on the underlying sentiment running through Theravāda, namely that individuals are compelled to do good acts and cultivate their own self potential for enlightenment and the eventual snuffing out of *samsāra* that is *nibbāna*, that is of a moral nature, and that is articulated in text. Within the

---

[1] The ten perfections, as they appear in the Buddhavamsa and Jātaka Nidānakatha among other texts, are as follows: *dāna* (generosity), *sila* (morality), *nekkhamma* (renunciation), *paññā* (wisdom), *viriya* (effort), *khanti* (patience), *sacca* (honesty), *aditthāna* (determination), *mettā* (loving-kindness), *upekkhā* (equanimity).

[2] Anguttara Nikāya, iii. 415.

matrix of karmic relationships through time, individuals have repeated opportunities to be each other's mothers or daughters, and so in Buddhist understanding the distinction between the self and an other is less concrete. Moral
agents can be viewed as not necessarily inhabiting conflicting universes. In his
chapter in this volume, William Scott Green asks:

> Are we to conceive the other in terms of ourselves, ourselves in terms of the
> other, some combination of the two? This ambiguity is particularly trouble-
> some if we and the other inhabit conflicting moral universes. To achieve reci-
> procity, does the rule require or imply that we should respect moral positions
> we oppose and shape our actions around them?[3]

In the Theravādin conception, the self and the other do not inhabit conflicting,
but rather conflated moral universes. In other words, when each and every
"other" might have been your mother in a past life or might be your mother in
a future one, what you do in this life that you have now matters. Reflecting on
the Golden Rule as it appears in one particular canonical text affords the opportunity to see another indication of the central importance of the moral life.

What does the Golden Rule say?

There is one canonical passage that is often chosen to represent the Buddhist
take on the Golden Rule. In isolation from its context, the Golden Rule in
Buddhism reads "*one who loves himself should not harm another.*"[4] It is neither
completely positive nor negative, but conditional and relative; moreover, it falls
somewhere between a simple observation and a prescriptive command. If a
person loves himself, he should not harm another because that would violate
the integrity of an other's self. This becomes clearer when more of the context
for the verse is revealed:

> *On traversing all directions with the mind*
> *One finds no one dearer than oneself.*
> *Likewise everyone holds himself most dear,*
> *Hence one who loves himself should not harm another.*[5]

The verse states that throughout the universe there are many individuals,
and yet an individual has the most investment in himself. Self-interest is simply

---

[3] William Scott Green, *Parsing Reciprocity: Questions for the Golden Rule*, p. 1.
[4] John Ireland, *The Udāna: Inspired Utterances of the Buddha* (Kandy, Sri Lanka: Buddhist Publication Society, 1990), p. 68.
[5] Ireland, p. 68.

a fact, and we can deduce that every other individual is similarly self-interested. It is on this basis that one should not harm another, because it would be a violation of an other's self-interest.

To properly assess the gist of the rule, even more of the context should be considered. In fact, the Golden Rule comes in the form of an "inspired utterance" of the most legitimating voice, the Buddha himself. That utterance is contained within a frame narrative, and the frame reveals the catalyst for the proclamation as another story altogether. As we will see, the narrative is integral to the right comprehension of the Golden Rule.[6] "That the basic formulation of the Golden Rule so easily generates and fails to solve basic problems about its practicality suggests that our project should focus less on the rule itself than on the preconditions, contexts, settings, frameworks, stipulations, etc. that give the Golden Rule its concrete and substantive significance."[7] We will follow William Scott Green's suggestion and pay particular attention to the narrative context in which we find Theravāda Buddhism's correlative Golden Rule.

It is no accident that such a universally salient teaching, for the Buddhist tradition, comes filtered through narrative. Narrative literature plays a formative part in the making of a Buddhist moral agent. Narratives are some of the first vehicles employed to teach profound truths, *dhamma*.[8] And narratives are employed throughout all genres of Buddhist texts to illustrate the profundity and applicability of *dhamma*.

What does the Golden Rule mean?

In the *Khuddaka Nikāya* ("Miscellaneous Collection"), a subsection of the *suttas* ("sermons") contained in the Pāli Buddhist *Tipitaka* ("canon"[9]), is where we find the maxim that best approximates the Golden Rule as it is formulated in other traditions. The *Khuddaka Nikāya* exerts a powerful influence upon Buddhist thought and practice in spite of the misleading "minor" or "lesser" attribution of

[6] The dependent relationship between the "inspired utterance" and its narrative context is not always so obvious in the *Udāna vāggas* (sections). In the case of this first chapter of the *Udāna's* Sonavāgga (Section on the layman Sona), the relationship is unusually clear.
[7] William Scott Green, *Parsing Reciprocity: Questions for the Golden Rule*, p. 1.
[8] *dhamma* (Sanskrit, *dharma*) in the Buddhist context refers to the Buddha's teachings. In the pan-Indic context it conveys a vast semantic field meaning law, order, morality, righteousness, duty, responsibility, religion, etc.
[9] Whether or not the Pāli *Tipitaka* may be rightly called a canon is a matter of debate. The Christian concept carries with it a sense of holy scripture and of dogma that are different than what we find in Buddhism. That said, it is a collection of authoritative texts, commended by regular Buddhist councils beginning shortly after the death of the Buddha, and the *Tipitaka* texts convey both prescriptions and norms. For more on the canonicity of the Pāli *Tipitaka*, see Steven Collins, "On the Very Idea of the Pāli Canon," *Journal of the Pāli Text Society* 15 (1990), 89–126.

its title. Some of the best known Buddhist texts are among its collection. The *Dhammapāda*, perhaps one of the most translated and utilized texts from the Buddhist canon, precedes the *Udāna* in the Khuddaka collection, and the collection also includes the Jātaka and Buddhavamsa. As an anthology, the *Udāna* collects together vital texts that guide the practitioner in his or her practice of cultivating the moral self, and several of these texts can be found in other places in the Pāli canon as well.

Our verse is contained within this *Udāna*, a collection of eighty *suttas*. In spite of its canonical pedigree, and its ubiquity on websites dedicated to the Golden Rule in the world's religious traditions, the location of the formula is buried in the midst of a composite text from a bulky section of a bulkier canon. The sixth-century monk Dhammapāla's commentary on the *Udāna*, the Paramatthadipani, explains the semantic field of the term *Udāna* thus:

> In what sense is the word *udāna* used? It is the expiration of an accumulated thrill-wave of strong emotion (*piti*). Just as oil and such-like material for measurement, when it cannot occupy the measure (*māna*) oozes out, and that is called "the overflow"; and as the water which a reservoir cannot hold runs out, and that is called "flood-water," even so that accumulated thrill-wave of strong emotion, of thought directed and diffused (*vitakka-vipphāra*), which the heart cannot contain, when it grows to excess cannot stay within, but bursts forth by way of the door of speech, regardless of who receives it—in fact an extraordinary expiration (*udāhāra-viseso*)—that is called *udāna*.

The *Udāna*, thus, is an outpouring of emotional expression, an eruption of sorts into the world of the text of a truth that cannot be easily contained.

Each sutta in the *Udāna* follows a formula: it begins by the stock phrase "Thus have I heard," which signals its status as a full-fledged *sutta* text.[10] It then orients the occasion for the text vis-à-vis the Buddha proper, telling within the narrative where the Buddha was staying at that time and how the tale that would follow came to his attention, and how it provided him the opportunity to "breathe forth" (*udānesi*) the "inspired utterance" (*udānam*).[11] Once oriented, the text

---

[10] *Evam me suttam.* The *suttas* were initially orally transmitted, and this particular phrase carries with it the connection to the Buddha's legitimating authoritative teaching voice. The "I" in the formulation is none other than the Buddha's right hand man Ananda, who reportedly repeated each and every sermon he heard from the Buddha's own mouth to the first Buddhist council of 500 monks, convened in Rājagaha upon the Buddha's final *parinibbāna* (passing away). See John Brough, "Thus Have I Heard . . .," *Bulletin of the School of Oriental and African Studies*, University of London, (13) (2) (1950), 416–26.

[11] Each narrative section that precedes the utterance of uplift concludes with the same stock phrase, the repetition of which signifies to the reader that he is about to receive the *Udānam*, or "verse of uplift": "Then, on realizing its significance, the Lord uttered on that occasion this inspired utterance" (*atha kho bhagavā etam attham viditvā tāyam velāyam imam udānam udānesi*)." Quoted from Ireland, p. 1.

opens on a royal exchange between the Kosalan king Pasenadi and his main queen Mallika:

> Thus have I heard: On a certain occasion the Exalted One was staying near Sāvatthi, at Jeta Grove in Anāthapindika's Park.

> Now on that occasion the rājah Pasenādi, the Kosalan, had gone with the Queen Mallikā to the upper storey of the palace. Then the rājah Pasenādi, the Kosalan, said this to Mallikā the queen: "Tell me, Mallika, is there anyone dearer to you than the self?"[12]

> "To me, Mahārājah, there is no other dearer to myself than the self. But to you, Mahārājah, is there anyone dearer than the self?"

> "To me also, Mallikā, there is no other dearer than the self."

> Thereafter the rājah Pasenādi, the Kosalan, came down from the palace and went to see the Exalted One, and on coming to him saluted him and sat down at one side. So seated the rājah Pasenādi, the Kosalan, said this to the Exalted One: "Sir, I had gone with the queen Mallikā to the upper storey of the palace, and I said this to the queen Mallikā . . . (and he related the conversation).

Thereupon the Exalted One at that time, seeing the meaning of it, gave utterance to this verse of uplift:[13]

> *The whole wide world we traverse with our thought,*
> *Finding to man nought dearer than the self.*
> *Since aye so dear the self to others is,*
> *Let the self-lover harm no other man.*[14]

The translation of the *Udāna* verse rendered by John D. Ireland is less stilted and dated:

> *On traversing all directions with the mind*
> *One finds no one dearer than oneself.*
> *Likewise everyone holds himself most dear,*
> *Hence one who loves himself should not harm another.*[15]

---

[12] "*atthi nu kho te Mallike koc' añño attanā piyataro?*" *Udāna*, edited by Paul Steinthal (London: The Pāli Text Society, 1982), p. 47. "*Attana*" means "yourself".

[13] John D. Ireland translates *udānam udānesi* "inspired utterance." Ireland, p. 68 and throughout.

[14] F. L. Woodward (trans.), *The Minor Anthologies of the Pāli Canon, Part II: Udāna: Verses of Uplift and Ittivuttaka: As it was Said.* (London: Pāli Text Society, 1987), p. 56. (reprint)

[15] Ireland, p. 68.

To some degree, the literary context constrains an interpretation of the Golden Rule's meaning by embedding it in a particular narrative, namely an encounter with the Buddha himself. But as we see from the commentarial explanation of the term *udāna*, something so profound and emotionally rich is hardly able to be constrained, even by the arbiter of equanimity, the Buddha himself.

The underlying sentiment of reciprocity and respect in the *Udāna* formulation of the Golden Rule fuels the Theravādin interpretive tradition. To get a sense of its impact, we can look at other texts such as the *Dhammapāda* that operate in the same constellation of meaning and are collected in the same canonical grouping as the *Udāna*, to see how the ideas take alternate but resonant forms. We can look at the commentarial tradition, the evidence of a very active interpretive community, that seeks to explain and interpret the verse. And we might also profitably turn to a text of another genre entirely, the Pāli *Mahāvamsa*, that enshrines certain understandings of the value of selves regarding the directive to not harm others.

Another text from the *Khuddaka Nikāya*, the *Dhammapāda*, can be well mined to shed light on our verse as Charles Hallisey demonstrates in this volume's following chapter.[16] Chapter 10 of the Pāli *Dhammapāda* begins with the following verses:

> All tremble before violence.
> All fear death.
> Having done the same yourself,
> you should neither harm nor kill.

> All tremble before violence.
> Life is held dear by all.
> Having done the same yourself,
> you should neither harm nor kill.

> Whoever, through violence, does harm
> to living beings desiring ease,
> hoping for such ease himself,
> will not, when he dies, realize ease.

> Whoever does no harm through violence
> To living beings desiring ease,
> Hoping for such ease himself,
> Will, when he dies, realize ease.[17]

---

[16] See Charles Hallisey's contribution to this volume.
[17] Glenn Wallis (trans). *The Dhammapāda: Verses on the Way* (New York: The Modern Library, 2004), p. 29.

Both the *Udāna* and *Dhammapāda* represent the same orientation around the self as the moral agent. The meaning begins with self-conception and understanding. It appeals to common sense—Do unto others, since you understand the experience; you know what it would be like, so don't be violent. The *Dhammapāda* shows that there is a reward for right behavior (nonharm) toward others, and no such reward for those who transgress. There was no such incentive suggested in the *Udāna* verse; one is expected to act in the right way purely on recognition of the equal experiences of self-interest among all individuals.

This companion text within the *Khuddaka Nikāya* sheds light on the meaning of our Golden Rule by means of comparison. We can also probe the meaning by consulting the commentarial tradition on our *Udāna*. Commentaries are widely employed in the Theravādin interpretation of texts.

While we might consider the prose narrative about King Pasenadi that precedes the inspired utterance as functioning as a preemptive commentary to prime the reader for its full effect, there is in fact an extensive commentary that explains and expands the context for such an utterance as well as the profound dharma lesson within its brevity. This commentary on the *Udāna*, the *Paramatthadīpanī*, is attributed to the prolific sixth-century scholar-monk Achāriya Dhammapāla. In his commentary on what he refers to as "the Great Chapter,"[18] Dhammapāla parses the meaning of individual phrases and delivers further narrative context to help interpret the verse.

The narrative explains the origin of the relationship between queen Mallikā and the Kosala king Pasenādi, and is framed to answer the question, why did the king ask his queen if there is anyone else dearer than the self? The reciprocity implicit in the verse it seeks to explain finds a narrative precursor to prime the reader; in the prose we see that quite literally, one good turn deserves another. The story in the commentary goes as follows:

Mallikā had been the daughter of a lowly garland maker, who devotedly waited on the Buddha by offering him the cake she had intended to eat herself. After the Buddha had eaten, Ananda asked him "what ripening will there be of this gift of hers?"[19] The omniscient Buddha prognosticates that before the day is out she will become the chief consort of the reigning king, Pasenādi. Later, upon seeing the king return from a hard day's battle, "she did him a (good)

---

[18] Peter Masefield (trans.), *The Udāna Commentary* by Dhammapāla (Oxford: The Pāli Text Society, 1995) Vol. II, p. 729.

[19] Masefield, p. 729. Note that this question is phrased, characteristically, in terms of "ripening." In the realm of *karma*, actions are like seeds that are planted, only later (perhaps in future lifetimes) will bear fruit. This organic metaphor is very common; for example, *karmaphāla* are "the fruits of karma," or the results of previous actions. *vipāka* is both ripening of fruit and actions.

turn," presumably some good service.[20] "The king, finding satisfaction in that (good) turn of hers, sent for her father, invested (her) with great authority, had her subsequently conveyed to the inner palace, and installed her in the position of chief-consort."[21]

After a while, reflecting on the good he had done for her, the king begins to muse about how his queen might respond if he were to ask her "who is dear to you?" He anticipates that her response will be that she holds him most dear, which is his wishful thinking. As it turns out, because this queen was a savvy attendant on the Buddha and his *sangha*,[22] she responds truthfully, rather than capitulating to the king's obvious ego-driven compliment seeking. When she replies that there is no one more dear to her than herself, itself a challenge to the line of questioning initiated by the king, she goes further by turning the question back to him. He follows her lead and answers in the same fashion,[23] but then he reflects:

> I, who am king, ruler *of the earth, indwell, after conquering* it, this great circle of the earth as its owner. As far as I am concerned, it is fitting that I do not behold another dearer than the self. But this outcaste, being inferior from birth, (yet) who was installed by me in an exalted position, does not hold me, who am her lord, likewise dear. She says, face to face with me, that "The self alone is dearer." "How hard, truly, is this one," and, having lost his self-posses-sion, reproved her, saying: "Surely for you the Three Jewels are dearer."[24]

The queen's response is telling. Even good intentions that seem altruistic in fact have roots in self-preservation, self-interest, and self-cultivation. She explains that while she holds the Three Jewels dear, she ultimately does so to

---

[20] The Pāli used for "did him a (good) turn" is *vattam akāsi*, which carries the semantic range of performing a service, doing her duty, "or perhaps even 'proposed' (from 2.√ vri (SED), to woo)." Here it may be worth quoting at length from the footnote of the translator for edification if not entertainment:
"For at (Jātaka iii 406), she allows him to sleep with his head on her lap for awhile, after he had asked her whether or not she was married (Jātaka iii 406). She was to prove to be not always faithful, if the episode involving the dog in the bath-house is anything to go by, as a result of which she was reborn for seven days, immediately following her death, in hell, during which period the Buddha had to stall until he could truthfully announce to Pasenādi that she had been reborn in heaven."

[21] Masefield, pp. 729–30.

[22] Community of monks.

[23] The commentary suggests that the following rather conceited diatribe is due to the king's "slow-witted nature." (Masefield, 730). I can't help but wonder about the utility of such an observation for the audience of this text. As an intellectually challenged protagonist, per-haps the character of king Pasenādi works for the audience as a sort of straw horse. The audience might reflect "I am not like that king," . . . a good reader would want to count himself among the smart and virtuous.

[24] Masefield, pp. 729–30.

secure for herself the benefits of a better rebirth along the long pathway of self-cultivation that ideally results in "the bliss of freedom."[25]

And this whole world holds another dear solely out of self-interest—even in wishing for a son, it wishes (for same) thinking "This one will nourish me in my old age," for a daughter thinking "she will propagate the clan for me," for a wife thinking "She will wait upon me (hand and) foot," for other relatives, friends and kinsmen, too, by way of their various functions. Hence, it is in perceiving self-interest alone that this world holds another dear.[26]

To explain the concluding line of the verse of uplift, and to conclude the commentary, the text delves into the shared fundamental nature of all human experience, namely that of dukkha, or dis-ease:

> *Therefore one desiring self should not harm another* (*tasmā na himse param attakāmo*): since each being holds the self dear in that way, is one desiring happiness for that self, one for whom dukkha is repulsive, therefore one desiring self, in wanting well-being of and happiness for that self, should not harm, should not kill, should not even antagonize with the hand, a clod of earth or a stick and so on, another being, upwards from and including even a mere ant or (other) small insect. For when dukkha is caused by oneself to some other, that (dukkha) is, after an interval of time, observed in one's (own) self, as though it were passing over therefrom. For this is the law of *karma*.[27]

Achāriya Dhammapāla represents one particularly authoritative voice in a vast tradition of commentarial literature. While the Pāli *vāmsa* texts are generally considered chronicles, or Buddhist histories, they can also be considered to participate in the same domain as the commentarial literature insofar as they appeal to narrative to edify on points of *dhamma* as well as aid in the transformation of the audience into moral agents capable of cultivating their own perfections. The narrative works hard in the *vāmsas,* especially in the fifth century Pāli *Mahāvamsa,* a text that conveys the Buddhist history of a particular place (Sri Lanka). It is to this text that we now turn to see how another layer of the interpretive tradition makes sense of the underlying goals of the Golden Rule. While the way it is phrased in the *Udāna* suggests that the nonharm decree is a universal (that all others should not be harmed, in all the quadrants of the world), the doctrine of nonharm (*ahimsa*) comes with a caveat for Sinhalese Buddhists mining the *Mahāvamsa* for an escape clause to the Golden Rule.

---

[25] Masefield, p. 730.
[26] Masefield, p. 731.
[27] Masefield, pp. 731–32. In a footnote, the translator explains that the word in the passage for "kill," *haneyya,* is replaced in some manuscripts with the more general *hileyya,* "show hostility towards." (Masefield, footnote 25, p. 797).

In the twenty-fifth chapter ("The Victory of Dutthagāmani"), the conqueror-king Dutthagāmani has concluded a murderous battle against the Dāmila.[28] He begins to feel remorse at having killed so many people (other beings) in battle, and so he solicits the comfort and advice of some monks:

> "How will there be any comfort for me, venerable sirs, since the slaughter of a great many numbering millions was caused by me?"

> "From this act of yours there is no obstacle to the way to heaven. In this world the Lord of Men has slain only one and a half human beings. One was stead-fast in the Refuges, and the other the Five Precepts; the remainder were of bad character and wrong views, considered beasts. But in many ways you will cause the *buddhasāsana*[29] to shine, therefore, Lord of Men, drive out the perplexity from your mind!"[30]

The Golden Rule formulation in the *Udāna* can almost stand if the definition of a person is a narrow one, only a person who has entered the Buddhist path. The *Udāna* formula, "*On traversing all directions with the mind, one finds no one dearer than oneself*," does not specify the types of other beings to which it refers. Within the context of its narrative, we see that it most certainly includes women, but Queen Mallikā and King Pasenadi are both supporters of the Buddhist *sangha*. The fifth-century compiler of the *Mahāvamsa* appears to have found a loophole to the universal applicability of the Golden Rule.

How does the Golden Rule work?

We thus see that the social consequences of the Golden Rule formula depend on the operative definitions of self and other in each interpretive community. As we saw from the Paramathadipani commentary on the *Udāna* passage, the social consequence within the narrative is of central importance. In the narrative, the king is surprised that his beneficence toward one of a lower status, Mallikā, would not result in her finding him dear above herself. We see that the reason behind the nonharm statement crosses both social class and gender lines when Mallikā does not give the king the answer he anticipates. But Mallikā is not such an ordinary character because she is both a queen and a benefactor of the *sangha*. Can we deduce that the Golden Rule contained within the verse

---

[28] The text classifies the Dāmila as occupiers of what is rightfully a Buddhist land. Dāmila is often translated as Tamil, and this particular passage that eulogizes the violent victory of Dutthagāmani is still used as justification for the continued violence in contemporary Sri Lanka.

[29] *The tradition, teachings, and institutions of Buddhism.*

[30] *Mahāvamsa* XXV.108–111.

of uplift is intended to be applicable to all, regardless of caste or gender? As a sacred utterance, it carries the authority of the Buddha himself. We can only surmise it depends on the interpretation of self and other.

As we see from the *Mahāvamsa* passage, the universal applicability gleaned from within the *Udāna* text may not carry over into the interpretive communities of the text. Likewise, we should consider the location of these texts in the purview of monks. All sources consulted here are monastic in origin. The commentary that unlocks the social dimension of the *Udāna* was composed by a monk for consumption by monks. A monk by definition leaves behind markers of status upon his renunciation. Likewise, he no longer is bound to fulfill hereditary gender roles once his life is given over in service to the *sangha*. What might it mean that within the *Udāna* narrative there is a lay female protagonist, but it is a story that is to be read and interpreted by male, monastic virtuosi?

The Golden Rule of the *Udāna* assumes that "the actor is an autonomous moral agent whose subjective and individual desires are the basis for the actions taken toward the other."[31] To determine how he wants or would want to be treated, the actor looks within and considers his own self-interest. Once perceived, he can project the quality of his own self-interest onto others. If we recall that in the Theravādin weltanschauung, any moral action carries positive, negative, or neutral weight that directly impacts one's self-interest in this life or an other, we can understand that the reason to do good to others is that it has consequences for the doer and the receiver. Keown explains this in terms of the transitive and intransitive effects of *karma*. There is a transitive effect of an action, for example, if I hit someone, it has a very palpable effect on this other person. But there is an intransitive dimension to the action of hitting someone else for the actor, namely, the accrual of demerit (*pāpa*) for such an unskillful, unwholesome (*akusala*) action. How you treat others is an extension of compassion or loving kindness, and is an opportunity to cultivate the self.[32]

The Golden Rule as conveyed in the *Udāna* verse certainly includes reflexivity as a component of reciprocity, but in a less stable form than that found in the Judeo-Christian formulae. The reason is the unstable nature of the self. In Buddhism, the self is a conventional designation that is used in the texts to refer to the moral agent, but there is a highly articulated sense of nonself (*anatta*) at the heart of the tradition.[33] Each "self" is in fact a construct, a functional composite of the five aggregates. To simplify, there is no eternal or independent "self," the self is only a heuristically useful designation. Mapped onto

---

[31] From William Scott Green, *Parsing Reciprocity: Questions for the Golden Rule*, p. 1.

[32] Keown, *Buddhist Ethics: A Very Short Introduction*, (New York: Oxford University Press, 2005) p. 6.

[33] Nagasena's explanation of the difference between the parts of the chariot and the chariot itself from *Milindapanha* is an often cited example of a heuristcically useful designation (name).

the structure of *karma*, with all of the movement through various relationships a "self" will undergo, we see that the exchange of self and other is not a one-time proposition, but rather the nature of the universe. Constant change, flux, impermanence (*anicca*) applies to personhood as well as every other condition. The Golden Rule as it is formulated in the *Udāna* text represents a classic, middle way between deontology and utiltarianism, and within the context of *karma*, allows for the influence of both past and future actions and effects.[34]

In Theravāda Buddhism, the Golden Rule is not equivalent to the precept to "love your neighbor as yourself," but rather "do no harm to your neighbor as you would do no harm to yourself." Love and nonharm are separate paths of action, while they may stem from the same wellspring. The Golden Rule's basic reference point is the actor rather than the recipient of the action. It does pre-suppose or even require empathy, but empathy should be considered a natural effect of the karmic shuffle of relationships. It is important to note, however, that the verse itself is only partly a guide to action, and a general one at that. It is also a matter of fact, descriptive explanation of why one would act in non-harmful ways toward others.

The *Udāna*'s Golden Rule thus sanctions nonviolence, and the converse is anathema. Presumably, if one hated oneself, one might resort to violence against others. But the expectation is that the reader would want to associate himself with the right minded agent, the doer of good and the cultivator of self.

Conclusion: How does the Golden Rule matter?

While the particular utterance of the Golden Rule in the *Udāna* verse may not be central, it unquestionably captures the critical thread of the centrality of morality running through Theravāda thought and practice. The sentiment and moral lesson that can be drawn from the narrative context in which one finds the verse is also central, even if its particular articulation in the *Udāna* text

---

[34] Perhaps the Western philosophical category of virtue ethics comes closest to what is con-veyed in the Theravāda. Damien Keown writes:

> According to virtue ethics, of which Aristotle (384–22 B.C.E.) was a leading exponent, what is of primary importance in ethics are neither preexisting obligations nor pleasant outcomes, but the development of character so that a person becomes habitually and spontaneously good. Virtue ethics seeks a transformation of the personality through the development of correct habits over the course of time so that negative patterns of behavior are gradually replaced with positive and beneficial ones. The way to act rightly, according to virtue ethics, is not simply to follow certain kinds of rules, nor seek pleasant consequences, but first and foremost to *be* or *become* a certain kind of person. As this transformation proceeds, the virtuous person may well find that his or her behaviour spontaneously comes increasingly into line with conventional moral norms. (Keown, p. 23.)

seems to obscure it. As we saw in the introduction, the laws of *karma* and the workings of *samsāra*, the goal of eventual perfection, as well as the composite nature of the self are all prerequisite assumptions for the *Udāna* Golden Rule to make sense as a principle and a practice. The consequences of "ignoring, disobeying, or otherwise failing to implement the Golden Rule" are simple—the agent will pay for transgressions in future selfhoods. The benefits of following the Golden Rule may be eventual rather than immediate, but ultimately contributes to the perfection of the self and the opportunity of release from the binds of *samsāra* and continued rebirths.

The Golden Rule may be an admirable goal for all on their way through multiple lifetimes of cultivating the self, but it finds most resonance for the religious virtuosi, the monks for whom the texts are most readily accessible. The nonharm advocated in the Golden Rule resonates with a deontological aspect of Buddhist practice; taking the precepts marks one as a Buddhist, and the first precept is that of nonharm.[35] It is a formal, ritualized precept, an outward acknowledgement of the responsibilities of a moral agent, and a voiced, explicit commitment to follow what is the implicit requirement of *dhamma. Ahimsa,* literally "nonharm" or "nonviolence," is one of the most fundamental Buddhist virtues. As with other apophatically phrased prescriptions in Buddhist rhetoric, nonharm is not simply the lack of doing harm, but is an active requirement of a moral agent.

---

[35] "I undertake the precept to refrain from harming living creatures." The first virtue phrased in another way, quoted in Kalupahana, p. 73:

1. Refraining from taking life (*panatipata*), abandoning severe punishment (*danda*), and arms (*sattha*), being modest (*lajji*), and loving (*dayapanna*), extending friendliness and compassion to all living beings (*sabbabhutahitanukampi*).

Chapter 11

The Golden Rule in Buddhism [II]

Charles Hallisey
University of Wisconsin-Madison

As soon as we start to ask about what is the Golden Rule in Buddhism and what is its utility or significance for Buddhists, we find ourselves confronting the very same conundrum of sameness-and-difference[1] that we encounter whenever we explore the place of the Golden Rule more generally across the various religious traditions of the world: is the similarity among different versions of the Golden Rule more important than the differences among similar versions? Why are there differences, if there is similarity? Why is there similarity if there are differences? Is there a connection between the similarity and the differences? There should not be any surprise in this. On the contrary, we learn something important about the task at hand when we acknowledge that there is a parallelism between the study of the particular example of Buddhism and what we do as part of our comparative concerns. We see that there are challenges and responsibilities that we must take up if we are to do any sort of justice to our topic, whether we are considering the Golden Rule in a single religious tradition or whether we are considering the Golden Rule comparatively or philosophically.

What are we looking for when we look for the Golden Rule in Buddhism?

This conundrum of sameness-and-difference in the Golden Rule is, at one level, a descriptive issue and we can consider how this is so first. Buddhism, like the other religious traditions considered in this volume, is historically complex and internally diverse. The Buddhist traditions, now found globally, began approximately 2,500 years ago in India and gradually spread across Asia. As complex religious heritages, the Buddhist traditions (both in the past and in the present)

---

[1] I am adapting the expression "conundrum of sameness-and-difference" from Joseph Errington, *Linguistics in a Colonial World: A Story of Language, Meaning, and Power* (Oxford: Blackwell, 2008) especially Errington's presentation of the different frameworks for studying language recast questions about linguistic unity and diversity in human life.

encompass an astonishingly diverse set of religious aspirations, ideas, practices, and institutions. The complexity and diversity of Buddhist ideals and practices and the richness of their character in local settings are such that when Europeans first encountered Buddhists at the beginning of the colonial age, it took them quite a while to realize that the religion they saw in Sri Lanka was historically related to what they saw in Japan.

When we accept that historical and cultural diversity is actually constitutive of what we call Buddhism, we see that coming up with a single general description of the Golden Rule and its place in Buddhism—one that will be somehow uniquely representative of Buddhism as a whole or even as a system—is impossible. The textual evidence alone is too inconsistent or is too resistant to a single scheme of organization for any generalization to be adequately representative, and this is before we begin to consider the even more challenging historical issues of texts received and interpreted in multiple contexts. It may actually be a good thing, in fact, that in the different Buddhist traditions the Golden Rule has not been the subject of sustained reflection in its own right, as it was in Christianity and Confucianism, since it means that we cannot avoid grappling with the historical and cultural diversity of Buddhism even if we try to elucidate the Golden Rule in Buddhism by focusing only on one, albeit a systematic one, strand of thought about the Golden Rule.[2]

Relevant to coming to terms with the constitutive diversity of Buddhism is Jeffrey Wattle's suggestion that "[t]he golden rule, happily, has more than a single sense. It is not a static, one-dimensional proposition with a single meaning to be accepted or rejected, defended or refuted. Nor is its multiplicity chaotic. There is enough continuity of meaning in its varied uses to justify speaking of the Golden Rule."[3] That is to say, very different statements and practices, each, on first sight, enormously different from others, can also be perceived as resembling each other as objects which fall under a single, if multivalent common category. The perceived resemblance—Wattles' "continuity of meaning" in the Golden Rule—is, somewhat ironically, what grounds our interest in the differences among these examples, which are described, compared with, and presented in the image of more familiar examples, much as South Asian languages can be described and taught on a grammatical model adopted from Latin, because of the assumption of a shared resemblance among all languages.[4] What is perhaps most striking here is that when we see the Golden Rule in Buddhism, we can use the resemblance between what we see in Buddhist material and what we see in other religious traditions to draw attention to and to describe the

---

[2] On Christianity and Confucianism, see Jeffrey Wattles, *The Golden Rule* (New York: Oxford, 1996), p. 9.

[3] Wattles, p. 5; quoted in William Scott Green, "Parsing Reciprocity: Questions for the Golden Rule" (present volume), p. 1.

[4] See Errington, p. 3.

differences between Buddhism and these other religious traditions. Thus, in a basic way, what we are looking for when we ask about the Golden Rule in Buddhism is how Buddhism is different.

As was said above, problems of interpretation that are found in comparative studies of the Golden Rule obtain when considering Buddhist materials alone. A simple example found in two important texts can illustrate the more complex historical issues at work here, even as it introduces us to a significant example of a formulation of the Golden Rule in Buddhism. In the *Dhammapada*, a Pali-language anthology of verses attributed to the Buddha and preserved by the Theravada traditions of Sri Lanka and Southeast Asia, we find the following often-quoted verse:

> All are frightened of the rod.
> For all, life is dear.
> Having made oneself the example,
> One should neither slay nor cause to slay.[5]

The third line, "Having made oneself the example," is what marks this verse as an example of the Golden Rule,[6] but let us postpone for the moment further consideration of the content of this verse as an example of the Golden Rule in Buddhism, apart from simply noting that its formulation is in the negative. We will see below that there are also positive formulations of the Golden Rule in the Buddhist traditions, but it does seem that negative versions, as in this verse, do prevail. In fact, this prevalence is so marked that Lambert Schmithausen has made the observation that "[i]n the early canonical texts [of which the *Dhammapada* is one] . . ., the focus is on avoiding wrongdoing. In the verse texts, emphasis is on killing or injuring, and it is only in the prose texts that the rule is explicitly extended to a wider range of wrongdoing."[7]

Right now, however, let us simply note that an identical version of this verse occurs in the Sanskrit-language *Udanavarga*, which, like the Pali-language

[5] *Dhammapada* X.2, vs. 130. *The Dhammapada*, translated by John Ross Carter and Mahinda Palahawadana (New York: Oxford University Press, 1987), p. 203. An older translation by E. W. Burlingame generates an echo of formulations of the Golden Rule in Christianity explicitly:

> All men tremble at the rod; to all men, life is dear
> One should treat one's neighbor as oneself, and should neither strike nor kill.

(E. W. Burlingame, *Buddhist Legends* (Cambridge: Harvard University Press, 1921), p. 295.

[6] Wattles identifies this verse as an example of the Golden Rule in Buddhism; see Wattles, p. 194, n. 3.

[7] Lambert Schmithausen. "Problems with the Golden Rule in Buddhist Texts," in *Pramana-kirtih: Papers Dedicated to Ernst Steinkellner on the Occasion of his 70th Birthday*, Part 2, edited by Brigit Kellner, Helmut Krasser, Horst Lasic, Michael Torsten Much, and Helmut Tauscher, *Wiener Studien zur Tibetologie und Buddhismuskunde 70.2* (Vienna, 2007), p. 796. I would like to thank Parimal Patil for providing me with a copy of this excellent essay. My dependence on Schmithausen's work is basic throughout this essay.

Dhammapada, is an anthology of verses attributed to the Buddha.[8] The *Udana-varga* includes many of the same verses as the *Dhammapada* and was translated into both Tibetan and Chinese. Despite the overlap in verses included in both anthologies, the *Dhammapada* and the *Udanavarga* are each organized by quite different thematic structures. Thus we find this particular verse grouped in the Pali *Dhammapada* with other verses that refer to the use of "the rod" (*danda*), including the immediately following verse:

> Who with a rod does hurt
> Beings who desire ease,
> While himself looking for ease—
> He, having departed, ease does not get.

And then later in the same chapter:

> As with a rod a cowherd
> To the pasture goads his cows
> So does old age and death
> Goad the life of living beings.[9]

In the *Udanavarga*, this same verse is grouped with other verses that refer to what humans find "dear" (*priya*, as found in the second line, "For all, life is dear"), including the immediately following verses:

> He who has been to a great distance and who returns from afar without mishap, his assembled kinfolk and friends receive him with joyful cries of "Alala!"

> So likewise he who has been virtuous, on arriving from this world into another, his good works receive him like dear relatives and welcome him.[10]

As well as earlier in the chapter:

> From those things which are dear comes sorrow; from those things which are dear comes fear: if one casts off what is dear, he will be without sorrow, without fear.[11]

---

[8] *Udanavarga*, V.19. *Udanavarga*, edited by Franz Bernhard, *Sanskrittexte aus dem Turfenfunden X* (Göttingen: Vandenhoeck and Ruprecht, 1965), Vol I, p. 144.

[9] *Dhammapada* X.3, vs. 131; X.7, vs. 135. Carter and Palihawadana, pp. 203, 205.

[10] *Udanavarga*, V.20, 21. *Udanavarga: A Collection of Verses from the Buddhist Canon*, translated from the Tibetan by W. Woodville Rockhill (London: Trubner and Co, 1883), p. 27; translation slightly modified.

[11] Rockhill, p. 24; translation slightly modified.

Anthologies are one important strand of the Buddhist interpretive traditions, as important as commentaries, and it is worth noting that neither the *Dhammapada* nor the *Udanavarga* seem to take note of the third line of the verse, "having made oneself the example," as central to the lesson of the verse, even though, we with our interest in the Golden Rule here, may wish to focus on what Buddhists think about that notion. Rather than seeing the verse as providing instruction on how we can best take care of others, the anthologies, as interpretive traditions themselves, suggest that the verse was understood as having greater relevance to questions about how we can take care of ourselves. The pattern of sameness-and-difference that connects and distinguishes the *Dhammapada* and the *Udanavarga* in their placement of the verse in their thematic-defined chapters further suggests that our own generalizations and interpretations of the verse as an instance of the Golden Rule overlaps with the processes of generalization and interpretation engaged in by Buddhists themselves, even if particular generalizations themselves may be different.

The differences between the contextual import of this one verse in the *Dhammapada* and in the *Udanavarga* also reassures us that there is not an intrinsic problem with differences in generalizations and interpretations produced by contemporary students of Buddhism. Instead, these differences among Buddhist interpretations encourage us to expect confidently that generalizations about the Golden Rule in Buddhism, made by different contemporary students, will often, if not inevitably, yield quite distinct, but equally valid accounts of the available evidence, simply because each generalization depends on the specific and numerous choices that are made by the student about which examples to select and how to connect them to each other and to their contexts. Moreover, as suggested above, the differences reveal something important about the material itself. The inclusion in this volume of two essays about the Golden Rule in Buddhism, the previous one by Kristin Scheible and this one, hopefully makes this important point of historical hermeneutics tangible,[12] even as it reinforces the significance of Wattles' adverb "happily" in his more-general observation, "The golden rule, happily, has more than a single sense."[13]

The difference in implicit interpretation of the same verse in the *Dhammapada* and the *Udanavarga* reminds us further that the conundrum of sameness-and-difference in the Golden Rule is, at another level, a problem of the interpretive framework chosen and employed—hopefully, self-consciously—by Buddhist thinkers as well as contemporary students of Buddhism. As this level, the conundrum of sameness-and-difference is predescriptive. Indeed, it stands between and bridges our practices of description and analysis, belying any easy

---

[12] This point would be further reinforced by considering the generalizations about the Golden Rule found in Schmithausen, n. 3.

[13] Wattles, p. 5.

distinction that we might want to be able to make between them. This predescriptive level of the conundrum may be somewhat harder to see, but some
comments by Charles Darwin in his *Descent of Man* can help us bring it into
sufficient focus that we can describe its antipodes.

Darwin, early in a chapter in the *Descent of Man* on the "Moral Sense" among
humans and animals, says:

> The following proposition seems to me in a high degree probable—namely,
> that any animal whatever, endowed with well-marked social instincts, would
> inevitably acquire a moral sense or conscience, as soon as its intellectual pow-
> ers had become as well developed, or nearly as well developed as in man.

Darwin immediately adds that

> the social instincts lead an animal to take pleasure in the society of its fellows,
> to feel a certain amount of sympathy with them, and to perform various
> services for them.

After giving support for his proposition with a variety of examples from animal
life (as well as some racist asides typical of his day), Darwin then ends his discussion with the conclusion that

> the social instincts—the prime principle of man's moral condition—with the
> aid of active intellectual powers and the effects of habit, naturally lead to the
> golden rule, "As ye would that men should do to you, do ye to them likewise,"
> and this lies at the foundation of morality.[14]

What is significant about Darwin's proposition is not actually its content, interesting as that may be, but the interpretive framework within which the proposition has its cogency in so far as it turns our attention to "the foundation of
morality." That framework is foundational, in so far as it looks to the Golden
Rule, its ubiquity in human testimony, to provide a major piece of evidence
about the nature of human morality and especially to reveal a common foundation to human morality despite the obvious differences of ethical expression
in various times and places. Darwin's interpretive framework also seems to
assume that this foundation will ground the authority, if not the truth, of human
morality itself, and allow us to take it as a guide for our own reflections on how
to lead moral lives. It is the same interpretive framework, albeit one with a very
different content, that informs the work of more recent commentators on the
Golden Rule, such as Jeffrey Wattles and Donald Pfaff. Wattles says at the end of

---

[14] Charles Darwin, *The Descent of Man* (Princeton: Princeton University Press, 1981), pp. 71, 72,
106. Reference to this passage is from Mary Midgley, "The Origin of Ethics," in *A Companion
to Ethics*, edited by Peter Singer (Oxford: Blackwell, 1993), p. 10.

his book, *The Golden Rule*, that "The rule is an expression of human kinship, the most fundamental truth underlying morality."[15] And, in his recent book, *The Neuroscience of Fair Play: Why We (Usually) Follow the Golden Rule*, Pfaff says:

> For several years now, I have been reading far and wide in the literature of religions throughout the world, looking to answer just one question: "Can I find an ethical command that seems to be true of all religions, across continents and across centuries?" Well, I found one, and you'll recognize it instantly. You probably know it as the Golden Rule.

> Once I found abundant evidence for a universal ethical principle, I was convinced there must be a biological reason for it. My thinking ran like this: If this type of behavior takes place throughout human society, it must come from some trait in human biology—not something we tell another to do but a feature, or, in biological terms, a mechanism that exists in our physical being.[16]

For Darwin, Wattles, and Pfaff, the conundrum of sameness-and-difference in the Golden Rule is recast as a question about how the Golden Rule is the *expression* of a human trait that is manifested variously.

What are in play for us then are two different interpretive frameworks that can order our investigations of what is the Golden Rule in Buddhism and what is its utility or significance for Buddhists, each framework engaging the conundrum of sameness-and-difference in a distinct way. The first framework privileges difference and, looks to discover what is distinctively Buddhist about the Golden Rule as it is found in the Buddhist traditions, the second privileges sameness and looks to discover what is human about the Golden Rule as it is used by Buddhists. But perhaps the first framework can be used to temper the second: is it the case that Buddhists thought about "human kinship" in the same way that Wattles—as well as perhaps most of us in contemporary North America—does?

"Human kinship" and the community addressed by the Golden Rule

While it seems obvious that Buddhists made statements that can be described as examples of the Golden Rule, it seems less obvious that they always saw such statements as an expression of an already-given feeling of human kinship or

---

[15] n.b. how Wattles' notion of human kinship echoes, but is really quite different from Darwin's "social instincts." For Darwin, the social instincts are what keep us with our intimate others—our families—while for Wattles, what is at stake is the "human family," as such.

[16] Donald Pfaff, *The Neuroscience of Fair Play: Why We (Usually) Follow the Golden Rule* (New York: Dana Press, 2007), p. 3.

even addressing a straightforwardly-defined human community. Instead, textual evidence suggests that Buddhists sometimes saw such statements and the notions articulated by them as tools that could help build community and fellow-feeling in the face of all-too-common human traits that threaten kinship and community. In this sense, Buddhists seem to have engaged the Golden Rule not as an expression of "human kinship" but as a tool—in Darwin's terms, a "habit"—to create this feeling. But to see how they thought so, we must first consider that Buddhists also seem to have drawn the boundaries of who was included in "human kinship" in somewhat surprising ways.

The *Dhammapada* verse quoted above is one in a pair.[17] The preceding verse in the pair is identical in all but the second line and we might see the next verse with its second line that "life is dear to all" as a reaffirmation of the point of its counterpart:

> All are frightened of the rod.
> Of death all are afraid.
> Having made oneself the example,
> One should neither slay nor cause to slay.[18]

The Pali commentary on this verse explains the last two lines "Having made oneself the example" by glossing "'As I am, so are other beings,'—seeing thus, let one not strike another, nor get another struck [by someone else]."[19] This gloss does seem to presume an awareness of an underlying "kinship, sameness in a defining experience, that can be used as a guide for actions, such as we might expect in any example of the Golden Rule in any religious tradition. The commentarial gloss to the verse on the expression "of death," as something of which all are afraid, however, qualifies this idea of a "human kinship" in two, quite significant ways:

> In the discourse the wording admits of no exceptions, but the sense does. When a king proclaims by drumbeat that all should assemble, all do assemble except the princes and ministers of the state. In the same way, even though it is said that all fear [the rod and death], it must be understood that all are frightened except the following four; the thoroughbred horse, the thorough-bred elephant, the thoroughbred bull, and the influx-extinct [Arahant]. Of these, the influx-extinct does not fear [death and the like], not seeing a "being" that can die, due to the fact that the notion of a substantial being [or self] is extinct [in such a one]. The other three are not frightened, not seeing a being [that can] become an adversary to them, due to the fact that the notion of self is very strong [in them].[20]

---

[17] It is worthwhile noting, perhaps, that this pair is not found in the *Udanavarga*.
[18] *Dhammapada* X.1, vs. 129. Carter and Palihawadana, p. 202.
[19] Ibid.
[20] Ibid.

The commentarial gloss distinguishes between two categories of beings for which the putatively-universal fear of death does not apply. The first is a set of animals who do not fear attack. In one sense, their exclusion from the cohort of those who live in fear is because of fault of the consciousness (an excessively strong sense of the wrong-view of Self because they are not troubled by a fear of predators); here the *Dhammapada* commentary seems to be exploring the kind of worry raised by Wattles and Gert that any application of the Golden Rule should not require "an agent to identify with the other in a simplistic and uncritical way."[21] More pertinent to our purposes at the moment is to recognize that the exclusion here of the thoroughbred horse, elephant, and bull presupposes an inclusion that is not always made by other familiar versions of the Golden Rule. The *Dhammapada* commentary, in line with what is found in other Buddhist texts and also what is found in Hindu and Jain texts, includes within the objects of action based on the Golden Rule not just humans, but all sentient beings, including animals and sometimes even insects.[22]

The other exclusion is uniquely Buddhist, but rather than expanding the community of kinship presupposed by the Golden Rule, as happens with the inclusion of animals, it draws the boundaries of the human community closer by excluding a certain class of humans. The *Dhammapada* commentary in singling out the "influx-extinct" excludes enlightened persons from inclusion within this community of those who fear death. The enlightened person is someone who cannot reflexively "make himself into an example" as this version of the Golden Rule recommends. The enlightened person, or *Arahant*, is free from the wrong views of self and consequently is free of both desire and fear.[23] The inclusion of animals and the exclusion of the enlightened person addressed by the Golden Rule means that we cannot take this community to be, pure and simple, a human community. It is both more than human and less than human at the same time.

Precision about excluding the human Arahant from the community addressed by the Golden Rule is a frequent concern in the Buddhist commentarial traditions. The *Dhammapada* commentary on the other verse in the pair sees

---

[21] Wattles, p. 7; for Gert, see Green, p. 2.

[22] See, for example, Schmithausen's reference to the commentary on the *Udana*: "That even small animals like insects are included is confirmed by Ud-a 275, 23–24, where the range of beings not to be killed or injured expressedly includes even *kunthas* [a kind of small insect] and ants." (Schmithausen, pp. 798–99).

[23] There is a significant inconsistency in the texts here. This *Dhammapada* verse excludes the Arahant from having the requisite conditions for turning oneself into an example because the Arahant does not fear death. Other instances of Buddhist statements that can also be taken as instances of the Golden Rule do include "sages," that is Arahants, within community addressed by the Rule, simply by omitting fear of death or the dearness of life as the condition for the requisite empathy. For example, a verse common to both the Pali-language *Suttanipata* and the Sanskrit-language *Mahavastu* says:

Regarding others like yourself and yourself like others
Cause no one to be harmed or killed.

(*Suttanipata* vs. 705; *Mahavastu* III. p. 375).

nothing to add to what it said about the previous verse except to use the line "For all, life is dear" as an occasion to note that it does not include enlightened beings, an indication of the significance of this idea for the commentator:

> Life is dear and sweet to all beings other than the one in whom intoxicants [i.e. cognitive flaws and moral defilements] are extinct. The one in who intoxicants are extinct, indeed, is detached both in regard to life and in regard to death. The rest is as in the previous (stanza).[24]

We see this concern to exclude the enlightened person from the community assumed by the Golden Rule throughout the Buddhist interpretive traditions, no matter what the school.[25] What seems often to be at stake for Buddhist commentators on this version of the Golden Rule is the affirmation of a systematic consistency that will maintain other doctrinal positions on the nature of an enlightened person. This can be seen in the following exchange between a Buddhist monk (Nagasena) and a king in the Theravadin *Questions of King Milinda.* The King speaks first:

> Venerable Nagasena, this too was said by the Blessed One: "All men tremble at punishment, all are afraid of death." But again he said: "The Arahat has passed beyond all fear." How then, Nagasena? Does the arahat tremble with the fear of punishment? . . . If the Blessed One, Nagasena, really said that all men tremble at punishment, and all are afraid of death, then statement that the Arahat has passed beyond fear must be false. But if that last statement is really by him, then the other must be false. This doubled-headed problem is now put to you, and you have to solve it.

> It was not said with regard to Arahats, O king, that the Blessed One spake when he said: "All men tremble at punishment, all are afraid of death." The Arahat is an exception to that statement, for all cause for fear has been removed from the Arahat. He spoke of those beings in whom evil still existed, who are still infatuated with the delusion of self, who are still to be lifted up and cast down by pleasures and pains.[26]

---

[24] Carter and Palihawadana, p. 203.

[25] Schmithausen provides a valuable account of discussions in Mahayana texts, in particular, including the Chinese *Mahaprajnaparamita Upadesa* and the *Mahaparinirvanasutra* in its Tibetan and various Chinese versions, on the undesired consequences implied by the expression of the Golden Rule in *Dhammapada* 129 and 130. It is obvious from these discussions that commentators were at pains to exclude the enlightened person from the cohort of those who might use this version of the Golden Rule to guide action and also from the cohort of those who might be the objects of actions guided by the same version of Golden Rule. The Mahayana *Mahaparinirvanasutra* goes so far as to portray Manjusri criticizing the Buddha for using in *Dhammapada* 129/130 universal, unrestricted statements when there are exceptions (Schmithausen, p. 804).

[26] *Milindapanha*, 145. Translation from *The Questions of King Milinda*, translated from the Pali by T. W. Rhys Davids (New York: Dover, 1963), I. pp. 206–207.

Schmithausen makes an important observation that this discussion in the *Questions of King Milinda* does not indicate whether there are ethical implications from excluding the premises of the Golden Rule with respect to the enlightened person. It may be the case, however, that this discussion about a particular Buddhist doctrinal point displays something quite critical about the ethical utility of the Golden Rule for Buddhists.

The Golden Rule's assumed community

To see this utility we need to be sure that we are clear about the community assumed by the Golden Rule in the Buddha's statements in the *Dhammapada/ Udanavarga* verses. It is not only a question of who is in or who is out of this community, it is also a question about what do the members of this community have in common. It is telling that the discussion about the verse in the *Questions of King Milinda*, as part of its exclusion of the enlightened person from the community to which the Golden Rule was addressed, says that the statement was made with reference to "those beings in whom evil still existed." What we want to note carefully here is that the agent who is to use the Golden Rule is not one without natural dispositions, beyond perhaps reason, and definitely not one defined by good dispositions, as a simple appeal to our "social instincts" or "human kinship" might incline us to expect. Those who are to use the Golden Rule are defined by their cognitive flaws (which lead them to misunderstand themselves and others) and moral defilements (which make them willing to harm themselves and others). The vision of moral persons that seems assumed here is one of moral egoists as ardent in their pursuits as anything envisioned by Thomas Hobbes. Those who are not defined by this ardent egoism, namely enlightened persons, have no need of the Golden Rule; the foundation of their morality is otherwise, nor can their morality serve as a model for the rest of us.

Buddhist commentaries routinely provide a context for when the Buddha first taught a particular idea, and frequently the circumstances of teaching shed important light on how the idea is to be understood and applied. The background context provided for this verse from the *Dhammapada* follows in the same vein as what we have just seen in the *Questions of King Milinda*, explaining that the verse was addressed to obviously imperfect people. Moreover, the contextual narrative construes an occasion that is not one in which people are asking what they should do, but one in which people have already harmed others:

All are frightened. This religious instruction was given by the Teacher while he was in residence at Jetavana with reference to the monks of the Band of Six.

For once upon a time, when lodging had been made ready by the monks of the Band of Seventeen, the monks of the Band of Six said to the former,

"We are older; this belongs to us." The Band of Seventeen replied, "We will not give it to you; we were the first to make it ready." Then the Band of Six struck their brother monks. The Band of Seventeen, terrified by the fear of death, screamed at the top of their lungs. The Teacher, hearing the outcry, asked, "What was that?" When they told him, he promulgated the precept regarding the delivering of blows, saying, "Monks, henceforth a monk must not do this; whoever does this is guilty of sin." Having done so, he said, "Monks, one should say to oneself, 'As I do, so do others tremble at the rod and fear death.' Therefore one should not strike another or kill another." So saying, he joined the connection, and preaching the Law, pronounced the following stanza,

> All men tremble at the rod, all men fear death.
> One should treat one's neighbor as oneself and therefore neither strike
> nor kill.[27]

Given what we have seen about the exclusion of the enlightened person from the cohort of people who use the Golden Rule, it is not surprising that this explanation of the Buddha's initial preaching of this verse does not say that the Buddha, using the Golden Rule himself, promulgated the precept against violence between monks. There could be any number of reasons why the Buddha promulgated this precept; from his own annoyance at being disturbed to a concern at what others might say about his monastic order. It is also worth noting that the verse is not taught as an action guide. The precept itself is the action guide. Rather, what we see in this account is that the verse is addressed to a group of people as something they can use to help them to observe this precept when they have already demonstrated their inclination to violate it out of their own self-interest. In other words, the verse is offered as a kind of "imaginative role reversal," to use Wattle's terms,[28] to aid adherence to a precept by persons whose dispositions direct them differently. The Golden Rule is not an aid to decision-making, but is a device used in moral formation.

It is worthwhile making two further observations about this account before continuing with a consideration of how the Golden Rule is utilized in moral formation. First is the manner in which a particular law is supported, practically, by an appeal to a moral universal. There is a curious relationship between legality and morality here. It is not that the law is an expression of the universal moral position, since the precept is promulgated quite specifically as being addressed to monks. It would seem then, and this is the second observation, that this lack of isomorphism between precept and imaginative role reversal allows for critical exceptions to the moral position that the imaginative role

[27] Burlingame, 2.294.
[28] Wattles, p. 132.

reversal suggests. Monks are not to hit other monks, but that is not the same as saying people are not to hit other people. In fact, some people are expected to hit other people in the world as Buddhists often imagined it, and preeminently kings and their agents were expected to do so. A king who drew the moral conclusion that the verse recommends eschewing violent punishment because they themselves fear violence would be an ineffective king. Indeed, it is a king's exploitation of his subjects' fear of royal violence that allows him to use violence less than he might otherwise.[29]

The Golden Rule and an active interest in the well-being of others

To this point, we have only discussed instances of the Golden Rule in Buddhist texts that are formulated negatively. There are also instances where the Golden Rule is formulated positively. One of the most important examples for our purposes here is found in the *Visuddhimagga*, a fifth-century manual for monks composed by the preeminent Theravadin thinker, Buddhaghosa. Looking at this example will help us to see that the manner in which the Golden Rule is embedded in a practical context of moral cultivation seems to take the practitioner beyond what might be taken as the commonsense implications of the Golden Rule:

> [R]eflecting, "I am happy," and "just as I desire to be happy, just as I am averse to suffering, just as I desire to live, as I desire not to die, so do other beings." So having made himself into the example, a mind that has happiness and concern for other beings arises. This method is made clear by the following statement by the Lord:
>
>> Having gone all around the world with the mind,
>> No one more dear than myself was ever found.
>> It's the same for others, the self is dear,
>> That's why anyone who loves himself will not harm another.[30]

The practical context for this instance of the Golden Rule in the *Visuddhimagga* is a meditation that seems to recreate imaginatively a version of the contextual setting of the preaching of the verse from the *Dhammapada*, with its angry confrontation between two groups of monks. In the *Visuddhimagga*, this positive formulation of the Golden Rule occurs in a chapter that provides instructions

---

[29] On the normative violence of kings in Buddhism, see Steven Collins, *Nirvana, and Other Buddhist Felicities* (Cambridge: Cambridge University Press, 1998), Chapter 6.
[30] *Visuddhimagga* IX.10; the verse quoted is found at *Samyutta* I.75 and *Udana* 47.

on how to cultivate "an active interest in others" or "loving kindness" toward others (*metta*). Curiously, Buddhaghosa seems most interested in the chapter with how to dispel one's anger toward a particular other that is an obstacle to the cultivation of feelings of universally directed feelings of kindness and interest:

> It should be known by a beginner even at the start that there are differences among persons, as it is said, "An active interest (metta) in these persons should not be cultivated first, and an active interest should never be culti-vated in these."

> Indeed, this active interest in others (metta) should not be cultivated at first with respect to four kinds of persons: a disliked person, a very dear person, someone toward whom one is indifferent, and an enemy. Nor should it be cultivated with respect to a particular person of the opposite sex. Nor with someone deceased.

> Why shouldn't an active interest in others be cultivated with respect to disliked persons first? Pretending to like someone who is disliked is exhaust-ing. Pretending that a very dear friend is someone you have no feelings for is exhausting too, and when some suffering happens to him, it's as if you could start crying. Putting someone you are indifferent to in a position of being respected or loved is exhausting. Anger arises just remembering an enemy. That's why an active interest in others is not to be cultivated first with respect to disliked persons, etc.[31]

Buddhaghosa structures his instructions on how to cultivate an active interest in others on a model of beginning with what is easy and then extending the moral emotions generated there to someone for whom it is difficult to have any feelings of interest in their happiness or to feel any kindness toward them. It is easy to wish good things for oneself, and Buddhaghosa recommends that a meditator begin with such wishes, but then use the imaginative role reversal that is part of the Golden Rule to extend these good wishes to others. Above all, what we see Buddhaghosa recommending here is to use the practice of an imaginative role reversal as a device to cultivate a habit of wishing others well, even—or, perhaps better, especially—those whom one does not like.

The Golden Rule here then is a mechanism utilized in a kind of moral engi-neering. It is not an expression of moral intuition grounded in human kinship nor a guide to action. This mechanism is employed precisely by persons who have dispositions and habits of the heart that actively prevent them from being well-disposed toward others.

---

[31] *Visuddhimagga* IX.4–5.

Do unto others as they would have you do unto them

The pragmatic employment of a positively formulated Golden Rule in Buddhaghosa's instructions on cultivating an active interest in the well-being of others seems to suggest that here the Golden Rule should be understood as integrated in a much larger moral framework—much as the Golden Rule, in some Christian interpretations, is integrated in an ethical framework of Love. To this extent, it seems that the actual rule that is operative is not one of reciprocity or fairness, but one of extravagant and unreciprocated generosity toward the other: "Do unto others what will make them happy." The apparent problem is not with the intellectual cogency of the rule, but with the practical problem that the agent who aspires to this is also an ardent egoist, and can not help but pursue his own desires and wishes. It is the latter problem that Buddhaghosa addresses in his instructions on how to cultivate an active interest in others, and the imaginative role reversal is used as a device to know what will make others happy.

A moral logic of extravagant generosity which goes far beyond the fairness that common sense generally attributes to the Golden Rule seems at work in another Buddhist thinker's instructions on how to get an ardent egoist to pursue the well-being of others.

Santideva is an early eighth-century Indian Buddhist thinker generally associated with the Mahayana traditions of Buddhism. His great work is the *Bodhicaryavatara* (Entering the Path of Enlightenment), and like the *Visuddhimagga*, it is a manual of training: And like the *Visuddhimagga*, the *Bodhicaryavatara* is addressed to ardent and self-destructive egoists, those who can ask, with Santideva,

> Where can fish and other creatures be taken where I might not kill them?

And also conclude with him,

> Though I have somehow come to a nigh unattainable place of advantage, and though I understand this, still I am led back to those selfsame hells once more.
>
> I have no will in this matter, as if bewildered by spells. I do not understand. By what am I perplexed? Who dwells here within me?[32]

Santideva's concern in the *Bodhicaryavatara* is to give advice on how to transform oneself from a being destined for hell as punishment for one's actions,

---

[32] Santideva, *Bodhicaryavatara*, translated by Kate Crosby and Andrew Skilton (Oxford: Oxford University Press, 1998), pp. 34, 27.

and he recommends that one begin the process of transformation by reflecting on the equality between self and other that is the foundation of the Golden Rule. In the process, he suggests that the kinship between beings in the world is defined by the commonality of suffering and happiness:

> At first one should meditate intently on the equality of oneself and others as follows: "All equally experience suffering and happiness. I should look after them as I do myself.
>
> Just as the body, with its many parts from division into hands and other limbs, should be protected as a single entity, so too should this entire world which is divided, but undivided in its nature to suffer and be happy.
>
> I should dispel the suffering of others because it is suffering like my own suffering. I should help others too because of their nature as beings, which is like my own being.
>
> When happiness is liked by me and others equally, what is so special about me that I strive after happiness only for myself?
>
> When fear and suffering are disliked by me and others equally, what is so special about me that I protect myself and not the other?"[33]

Santideva takes the insights that reflection on the commonality of suffering and the desire for happiness as a guide for action when he gives his version of the Golden Rule, "All beings equally experience suffering and happiness. I should look after them as I do myself," and we should note that this formulation includes reflexivity without any expectation of reciprocity. Santideva is acutely aware, however, that this action guide is to be employed by an agent who is very skilled in taking care of himself and incapable of taking care of others. Santideva's moral anthropology does not allow him to suggest otherwise, that a being defined by ignorance and evil disposition could suddenly become capable of acting in accordance with the insights of the Golden Rule. Instead, he recommends another practice of moral engineering, something which he calls, "the supreme mystery": "the exchange of self and other." "The exchange of self and other" is an intensification of the imaginative role reversal we have already identified in Buddhaghosa's use of the Golden Rule in the cultivation of an active interest in others and which others have seen in various utilizations of the Golden Rule in non-Buddhist traditions. It encourages the practitioner to simply take as literal fact the perspective afforded by the imaginative role reversal and to substitute the identity of another for one's own. One remains the ardent egoist, but now all one's cunning and energy in pursuing one's own

---

[33] Crosby and Skilton, p. 96.

desires and interest are put in the service of another. We can see the results in the following verse, but it is important to remember that the "you" that is addressed is the person speaking, as is the "he" that is described, and the "I" is another, on behalf of whom the agent is only acting:

> Do this! Stay like that! You must not do this! This is how he should be subjugated and punished if he disobeys.
>
> Where are you off to? I can see you. I shall knock all the insolence out of you. Things were different before, when I was ruined by you.
>
> Give up any hope that you will still get your own way. Unworried as you are by repeated molestations, I have sold you to others.[34]

What we see in Santideva's hyperbole is a moral logic of extravagant generosity, one which seems very far from the moral logic of the Golden Rule itself, at least as it is conventionally understood. Despite all its extravagance, however, Santideva's use of the Golden Rule is consonant with much else that we have seen from the Buddhist traditions. Used by beings with intrinsic flaws, the Golden Rule helps them to become better than they have a right to be.

---

[34] Crosby and Skilton, p. 103.

Chapter 12

A Hindu Golden Rule, in Context

Richard H. Davis
Bard College

"The Golden Rule or the ethic of reciprocity is found in the scriptures of nearly every religion," we are told in the anthology, *World Scriptures* (1991: 114). This hefty volume, a project of the International Religious Foundation published in 1991, provides an assemblage of quotations from diverse religious texts and teachings from many of the world's religions, arranged in a topical format. So under the rubric "Golden Rule," one may find the most familiar formulation from the Christian gospel of *Matthew*, "Whatever you wish that men would do to you, do so to them," along with similar quotations from Judaic, Islamic, Confucian, and Yoruba scriptures.

Within this framework, we learn that India of the classical period also had the Golden Rule, for the anthology provides quotations from early Jain, Buddhist, and Hindu texts. According to the ancient Jain collection, the *Sutrakritanga*, "A man should wander about treating all creatures as he himself would be treated (1.11.33)." The early Buddhists are represented by a passage from the *Sutta-nipata*, one of the earliest compilations of teachings ascribed to the Buddha, which asserts: "Comparing oneself to others in such terms as 'just as I am so are they, just as they are do am I,' he should neither kill nor cause others to kill." And for the Hindus, a passage from the vast epic poem *Mahabharata* is offered: "One should not behave towards others in a way which is disagreeable to oneself. This is the essence of morality. All other activities are due to selfish desire" (*Anusasana-parvan* 113.8). All these passages extol a reflection on the identity or equality of other beings and oneself, and promote a course of conduct toward others that is nonharmful based on that understanding of identification.

When we consider the role of the Golden Rule in the world religions, however, determining that these religions *have* such a statement somewhere within their copious textual canons is less important than assessing *what* role such statements might play within their dominant ethical formulations and commitments. We may gain perspective on this if we keep in mind that all statements such as those collected in the *World Scriptures* are made by particular speakers in the course of longer discourses, addressed to specific audiences. The speakers articulate these discourses within, and sometimes against, the normative background of their own societies and their broader understandings of the world.

Indic formulations of the Golden Rule such as those collected in the *World Scriptures* anthology repeatedly point toward an ethical principle that is much more significant within classical Indic ethical discourse, namely the principle of *ahimsa*, nonharming or nonviolence. To apprehend the other as oneself, for Indian religious thinkers of this time, leads to conduct that avoids actions harmful to others. The anthology cites another early Buddhist text that spells this out quite clearly:

> The Ariyan disciple thus reflects, Here I am, fond of my life, not wanting to die, fond of pleasure and averse from pain. Suppose someone should rob me of my life. . . It would not be a thing pleasing and delightful to me. If I, in my turn, should rob of his life, one fond of his life, not wanting to die, one fond of pleasure and averse to pain, it would not be a thing pleasing or delightful to him. For a state that is not pleasant or delightful to me must also be to him also; and a state that is not pleasing or delightful to me, how could I inflict that upon another?
>
> As a result of such reflections he himself abstains from taking the life of creatures and he encourages others so to abstain, and speaks in praise of so abstaining. (*Samyutta Nikaya* 353, cited in *World Scriptures* 1991: 115)

So the Buddha advises his audience, here the "Ariyan disciple" or one who has renounced society to become a follower of the Buddha. The principle of *ahimsa* certainly is fundamental within the ethical universe of the Jains, and to a large extent this is shared by the Buddhists. However, for Hindus *ahimsa* is a more problematic notion, one that cannot be easily taken as a universal normative ethical principle.

In this paper I will take the quotation from the *Mahabharata* offered by the *World Scriptures* as the representative Hindu formulation of the Golden Rule, and sketch out its location within the text from which the anthology has isolated it. I do this not to undercut the value of the anthology, but to show how the contextual understanding of the passage can lead us to a more complex understanding of how the Golden Rule may have operated within a classical Hindu setting. Before we return to the *Mahabharata*, however, I will make a few preliminary remarks about Hindu ethical discourse.

Hindu *dharma* and hierarchical ethics

The dominant mode of ethical thinking in classical India revolves around the term *dharma*, a word that takes on a variety of meanings. It can be construed both as an overarching cosmic order and as a set of guidelines for proper righteous conduct by individual persons. Hindu formulations pertaining to *dharma* assume a hierarchical social order, in which segmented social groups (later called "castes" by Western observers) are differentiated and ranked according to various criteria. In such a social setting, the primary goal of ethical thinking does not involve egalitarian reciprocity as an ideal. Rather, the challenge for ethical discourse is to determine the proper modes of interpersonal conduct in the myriad situations arising in everyday living where persons of differing ranks come into relation with one another. What are one's duties or responsibilities toward another person of different social status? Considerations of age, gender, and social rank must all be taken into complex consideration. Reciprocity cannot be a reliable guide when one person's responsibilities toward another are determined or inflected by an unequal relationship.

To illustrate hierarchical ethical thinking, I will look at one brief example, namely Manu's treatment of marital relations. One of the finest and most influential presentations of orthodox or brahmanical hierarchical ethics may be found in the *Manavadharmasastra*, "Manu's treatise on *dharma*." Roughly contemporary with the *Mahabharata*, this work presents an orthodox brahmanical vision of *dharma* as an overriding cosmic principle that shapes the social order as an organic whole, and it provides detailed guidance for persons of all classes in how they ought best to act within this ideal social world. It presents social divisions of age, gender, and class as aspects of the natural order that ultimately derives from the shape of creation.

According to Manu, a female should never enjoy an independent status.

> A girl, a young woman, or even an old woman should not do anything independently, even in her own house. In childhood a woman should be under her father's control, in youth under her husband's, and when her husband is dead, under her sons'. She should not have independence. (*MS* 5.147–148)

Manu's assertion is reinforced later when he considers the respective *dharma* of husband and wife:

> I will tell the eternal duties of a man and wife who stay on the path of duty both in union and separation, Men must make their women dependent day and night, and keep under their own control those who are attached to sensory objects. Her father guards her in childhood, her husband guards her in youth, and her sons guard her in old age. A woman is not fit for independence. (*MS* 9.1–3)

Passages such as these illustrate the element of misogyny in Manu, but they also point to a conception of marital relations that involves both inequality and unity. The wife, in Manu's vision of *dharma*, is subordinate and subservient to her husband. He is her lord (*pati*), and she considers service to her lord as her vow (*pativrata*). Reciprocally, the husband is required to offer protection to his wife:

> Regarding this as the supreme duty of all classes, husbands, even weak ones, try to guard their wives. For by zealously guarding his wife he guards his own descendents, practices, family, and himself, as well as his own duty. (*MS* 6.6–7)

Through the observance of these mutual and complementary duties toward one another, husband and wife become one:

> When a woman is joined with a husband in accordance with the rules, she takes on the very same qualities that he has, just like a river flowing down into the ocean. (*MS* 9.22)

Male and female are different categories of beings, whose duties derive from the positions their gender assigns them. Yet these unequal duties form an organic whole, in this case the marital unit, the basis of the household. So too, in Manu's treatise on *dharma*, members of different classes (*varna*) have unequal status and distinct social duties, which together compose an integrated hierarchical social order. Along the same lines, kings and subjects have complementary functions that allow a harmonious state. Manu outlines the necessary role of the king, as lord (*pati*), in protecting the realm and maintaining an orderly society:

> A ruler who has undergone his transformative Vedic ritual in accordance with the rules should protect this entire (realm) properly. For when this world was without a king and people ran about in all directions out of fear, the Lord emitted a king in order to guard this entire (realm), taking lasting elements from Indra, the Wind; Yama, the Sun, Fire, Varuna, the Moon, and (Kubera) the Lord of Wealth. Because a king is made from particles of these lords of the gods, therefore he surpasses all living beings in brilliant energy, and, like the Sun, he burns eyes and hearts, and no one is able to even look at him. (*MS* 7.2–6)

The social world envisioned by Manu is thoroughly hierarchical. Harmonious order arises when the various categories of beings recognize and conduct themselves according to the own proper responsibilities within this integral world. The aim of Manu's treatise, accordingly, is to set out those differentiated principles and guidelines that constitute *dharma*.

Within the hierarchical ethical framework outlined by Manu, especially for male members of the brahmin class but also pertinent to all others, the Golden

Rule does not make much sense. It is not useful for a husband, in Manu's world, to use the principle of reciprocity in doing to his wife as she would do to him, for their duties and responsibilities toward one another are incommensurate.

Yudhisthira's dilemma and Brhaspati's unhelpful response

If that is the general case, then where does the teaching of the Golden Rule articulated in the *Mahabharata* and cited by *World Scriptures* fit in?

The quotation comes in the context of a lengthy instructional session involving Yudhisthira, Bhisma, Brhaspati, and several other teachers, at the conclusion of the great eighteen-day war at the center of the *Mahabharata*. Yudhisthira is the eldest of the five Pandava brothers, and Bhisma stands as surrogate grandfather to him. (The actual relationship between the two is too complex to spell out here.) Both are members of the ruling warrior class, *ksatriyas*. Although kinsmen, they have fought on opposite sides in the war, with Bhisma serving as general for the enemy Kaurava forces during the first nine days of the battle. The third member of the discussion, Brhaspati, is identified as the priest of the gods, and appears only briefly within the session. Brhaspati, we will see, is the one who articulates the Golden Rule.

At the conclusion of the hostilities the five Pandava brothers have emerged victorious but at a terrible cost. Nearly the entire *ksatriya* class of India has been exterminated in battle. By one estimate, some five million warriors have died over the course of the eighteen days. The eldest Pandava, Yudhisthira, counts himself personally responsible for the war and for the deaths of all these noble warriors. What makes this even more devastating for him is that among the victims are many of his closest relations, such as his cousins, his sons, his uncles, and his teachers. One of the defeated warriors on the other side, Bhisma, lies dying on a bed of arrows. Earlier, however, he has received a boon from the gods that allows him to choose the time of his final demise. At first Yudhisthira is so overcome with grief (*soka*) that he refuses to assume the sovereignty that he has won through the war. Instead, he proposes to become a renouncer and retire to the mountains to expiate his terrible guilt. Others persuade him to accept the burden of kingship. However, he continues to mope about in despair until finally his friend Krishna persuades him to ask Bhisma for advice. Yudhisthira states his dilemma succinctly for Bhisma: "Those who know *dharma* hold that kingly rule is the very highest *dharma*, but I think it is a great burden" (*MBh* 12.56.2).

Close as he is to death, Bhisma nevertheless agrees to speak with Yudhisthira, in hopes of pacifying the ruler's debilitating grief. Bhimsa's teachings are extensive. They occupy two books in the *Mahabharata*, the *Santiparvan* and the *Anusasanaparvan*, and run to some 37,800 lines of verse—roughly equal to

the length of the complete Christian Bible. Initially Bhisma instructs Yudhisthira
in the duties of kingship (*rajadharma*). Here he seeks to persuade Yudhisthira
that kingship is necessary to the order of the world, and that violence, while
regrettable, is a necessary part of a king's responsibilities. However, even at the
conclusion of Bhisma's lengthy teachings on kingship, Yudhisthira declares that
he still has not regained peace of mind. His conscience is still full of guilt on
account of the terrific violence of the great battle between Pandavas and Kaura-
vas. Bhisma continues his discourse, therefore, and seeks with a new set of more
religious teachings to bring some sort of solace to his morose interlocutor.

In the course of these teachings, Yudhisthira asks Bhisma questions of
eschatology. What determines where humans go after they die, he wonders?
When one's soul abandons the dead body like a piece of wood or a clod of
earth, he asks, what is it that transmigrates to the next world? At just this moment
the preceptor of the gods, Brhaspati, appears on the scene, and so Bhisma
respectfully proposes that they pose this question to their distinguished visitor.

Brhaspati initially stresses that a person is born alone and dies alone. Through
all the vicissitudes of life, one has no ultimate companion. When a man dies,
observes Brhaspati, all his relatives may mourn the deceased for a moment but
then they quickly turn around and go their own ways. Relatives clearly do not
follow one into the next life. Here Brhaspati's teachings appear to be aimed at
the special grief Yudhisthira feels about the death of his own kinsmen in the war.
The ties of family relationship, Brhaspati emphasizes, are not ultimate ones.

However, one thing does accompany the transmigrating soul, Brhaspati continues, and that is *dharma*. The moral quality of one's actions in one lifetime
follow one to the next, and determine what that next one will be. This is the
classical Indic notion of *karma* (a term that denotes both a person's actions and
the moral consequences of those acts that may adhere to one), and in the world
of the *Mahabharata* it is broadly accepted as part of the world order. A living
being who has acted according to *dharma* will go to the highest heaven (*svarga*),
Brhaspati stresses, while one without *dharma* will go to a hell (*naraka*).

This cannot be a great reassurance to Yudhisthira, who continues to believe
that he has committed extremely sinful actions in the course of the war.
Therefore Yudhisthira immediately asks Brhaspati how one may become freed
from past sins. Brhaspati proposes gift giving as one way of repenting, and
thereby gaining an auspicious end, but this still does not satisfy Yudhisthira.
So the Pandava king lists several different proposals for virtuous expiatory
action and asks Brhaspati to advise him which is best. "Non-violence (*ahimsa*),
Vedic rites, meditation, restraint of the senses, asceticism, and service to one's
teacher—which of these is best for the soul?" (*Mbh* 13.114.1) Brhaspati begins
by asserting that all six are good:

All of these individually are doors of *dharma*, completely; all six of them
are praiseworthy. But now listen, and I will tell you what is the highest most

excellent route for the living being. That man who follows the *dharma* taking recourse to non-violence (*ahimsa*) attains the highest end. (*Mbh* 13.114.2–3)

Among all virtuous "doors of *dharma*," Brhaspati singles out the first in the list, *ahimsa*, and goes on to articulate his version of the nonviolent Golden Rule:

A person who strikes down non-violent creatures (*bhuta*) with his weapon, out of a desire for his own happiness, does not go to a happy end when he passes on. But a person who adopts towards all creatures the attitude that they are similar to oneself (*atmopama*), who puts down his weapon and conquers his anger, does obtain happiness when he passes on to the next life. (*Mbh* 13.114. 5–6)

Let us pause here to note one important extension in the Indic theory of non-violence. Much like the contemporary Jains, Brhaspati does not restrict the Golden Rule principle of reciprocity and nonviolence to human creatures; this rule encompasses *all* creatures. This is a natural extension of the idea of transmigration, since all living creatures are believed to be linked in a fluctuating cycle of transmigration (*samsara*). In fact, Brhaspati has explained in considerable detail just previously how sinful acts in this lifetime may lead to rebirth as animals. Brhaspati is quite strict about this, especially with brahmins who fail in their duties. For instance, a Vedic brahmin who offers sacrifices on behalf of someone who is not qualified for this, becomes, in his next life, a worm for fifteen years. Then he is born for five years as an ass, then as a hog, a cock, and a jackal. Next he is born as a dog, and finally he regains in the following life his status as a human. Such a viewpoint is certainly intended to make the brahmin careful in calculating those for whom he offers his sacrifices, but it also leads one to see the worm, ass, hog, cock, jackal, and dog as bearing a soul that may well have been human, even a brahmin, in the past and may in the future become human once again.

Brhaspati goes on to spell out the full implications of this principle of "similarity to self" (*atmopama*):

That which is contrary to oneself, one should not do to another. This is the rule of *dharma* in its brief form. Other actions derive from selfish desire (*kama*). In making gifts and in denying them to others, in pleasure and in pain, in what is agreeable and what is not agreeable, a person should evaluate one's actions through comparison with one's self. As one may behave towards another, so the other behaves towards the first. In the world of the soul (*jiva*), let the other person be the likeness (*upama*) of yourself. Thus *dharma* is conveyed completely. (*Mbh* 13.114.8–10)

Here Brhaspati appears to adopt a formulation of reciprocity that parallels the various versions of the Golden Rule found around the world: one should regard the other as like oneself, and use this as a guide to one's own conduct toward that other. This is the formulation that the *World Scriptures* anthology has singled out as the Hindu Golden Rule. And Brhaspati makes it clear by his final statement that he sees this teaching as a self-sufficient and universal principle for virtuous conduct.

Brhaspati contrasts actions based on similarity to self, which he considers *dharma*, with other actions deriving from *kama*. Here Brhaspati restates an ethical premise widely shared in classical Indian discourse. Selfish or self-interested desire (*kama*) is the adversary of righteous or responsible moral conduct. Although ethical instructors like Manu recognize the fundamental role of self-interest in motivating action, none would advocate self-interest as a sufficient guide for conduct or as the basis for a system of morality. Rather, Manu and others point to the relentless power of *kama* especially when it is indulged:

> Desire is never extinguished by the enjoyment of what is desired; it just grows stronger, like a fire that flares up with the oblation (of butter) and burns a dark path. (*MS* 2.94)

Manu, Brhaspati, and other Hindu moralists, along with their Jain and Buddhist counterparts, all advocate restraint (*tyaga*) of *kama* as the foundation of righteous action or *dharma*. Brhaspati's distinctive position is to suggest "similarity to self" as the basis for this self-restraint.

In the context of a social ethics generally grounded on an assumption of hierarchy among living creatures, however, this teaching is bound to appear radical. If the social order is profoundly hierarchical, what can be the basis for regarding others as similar to oneself? Brhaspati's use of the two terms *atman* and *jiva*, both of which are often used in early Hindu texts to designate the transmigrating soul or spirit, point to a deeper level of similarity or equality. While orthodox brahmin treatises on *dharma* like that of Manu presuppose the stratified order in which humans must act as social beings, classical philosophical texts such as those of the Upanisads and the *Vedanta-sutras* of Badarayana provide on a more profound analysis of the human situation. These texts seek to identify the most fundamental aspect of the human being, and they use terms like *atman* and *jiva* to designate an underlying animating spirit that inhabits a body, transmigrates from that body upon death, and then comes to be reborn into a new body. This transmigrating *atman*, they postulate, cannot be identified with any of the material or worldly aspects of the body or its social situation. Some Indian philosophers push this idea toward a monist metaphysical position. There are not multiple monad-like spirits, but rather a single imperishable and universally shared Self (called *brahman*), of which all individually-embodied souls (*atman*) are aspects. Social differences are extrinsic, socially constructed. This nondualistic philosophical position, later articulated within the Advaita Vedanta school of thought, provides the basis for a deeply reciprocal principle of conduct, which Brhaspati presents in his teachings as the idea of "similarity to self."

It should be noted that philosophical teachings of the imperishability of the transmigrating soul do not necessarily lead to an ethics of nonviolence. In an earlier set of teachings in the *Mahabharata* that takes place just before the war, namely the *Bhagavad Gita,* Krishna uses the same idea to separate the Pandava warrior Arjuna from his disinclination to fight. Arjuna is concerned precisely with the prospect of having to face his own relatives in battle and threatens to put down his weapons. To persuade Arjuna to fight, Krishna stresses that he will not be killing the souls or spirits of the opposing warriors. Those souls are imperishable and will move on to other bodies in other worlds according to their own conduct within this world. All a warrior can destroy in battle are the bodies of his enemies. He need not grieve over his actions. The idea of a permanent transmigrating soul and of a universally shared Self can lead to a redefinition of death that reduces or relativizes moral culpability in the act of killing. Brhaspati's teachings, however, draw on the same underlying soul-theory to support an ethic of reciprocal nonviolence.

Lest we rest on Brhaspati's teachings of reciprocity and nonviolence, compelling as they are, as constituting a Hindu Golden Rule of universal application, let us return to the scene as the *Mahabharata* relates it. When Brhaspati has conveyed *dharma* completely, at least from his own point of view, he abruptly takes leave of Yudhisthira and Bhisma and rises upwards into the sky. He is, after all, preceptor to the gods and must return to continue his services there. Yudhisthira makes it clear that Brhaspati's teachings have made a strong impression on him:

Sages, brahmins, and gods in their great wisdom all praise that *dharma* characterized by non-violence, on account of its Vedic authority. (*Mbh* 13.115.2)

But Yudhisthira also indicates that Brhaspati's instructions have not spoken to his own concerns. The teachings of nonviolence may be all well and good for gods, sages, and brahmins but they do not suffice for a *ksatriya* ruler who necessarily performs violent duties in the interest of preserving the social order:

However, how does a person who has committed violence through actions, words, or thoughts free himself from sorrow? (*Mbh* 13.115.3)

Yudhisthira seems to view Brhaspati's speech as that of a visiting lecturer who has given a very impressive talk which has failed to address his own burning question. Brhaspati's intervention is like that of a pacifist lecturing soldiers suffering from posttraumatic stress disorder on the ethics of nonviolence, when what the soldiers need is a way to pacify their anxiety and guilt. Like a hospitalized soldier, Yudhisthira has committed violent atrocities (according to his own understanding) and Brhaspati's articulation of the Golden Rule does not help him gain liberation from the remorse that fills his being.

As a *ksatriya* and powerful warrior responsible for the death of many opponents, Bhisma has a better grip on the particular ethical quandaries of rulers and warriors than does a priest, even the preceptor of the gods. Renunciation of worldly responsibilities is not an appropriate response, Bhisma argues, for rulers must act in order to protect their subjects and maintain the social order. That is their duty, their particular *dharma*. Such action will inevitably involve violence and harm to some creatures. Yudhisthira's dilemma is how to gain respite from the grief arising from the violent actions he and his brothers have committed in pursuit of what they considered their duty as *ksatriyas*. Bhisma's answer, once Brhaspati is safely out of the way, is to advocate a more limited form of *ahimsa* which even worldly rulers can safely observe: one should avoid eating meat. Eating the meat of other creatures, Bhisma explains, is like eating the flesh of one's own son. (Here too transmigratory thinking seems to underlie Bhisma's hyperbole.) The problem lies not just with the violence entailed in killing other living beings for food, he goes on, but also in the way meat-eating engenders attachment:

> As the tongue is the cause of the knowledge or sensation of taste, so, the scriptures declare, attachment proceeds from taste. Well-dressed, cooked with salt or without salt, meat, in whatever form one may take it, gradually attracts the mind and enslaves it. (*Mbh* 13.115.11–12)

To renounce the eating of meat, therefore, allows one to avoid enslavement to sensory desire, and Bhisma suggests it is a practical way for a *ksatriya* ruler to expiate the emotional pangs he may feel over the other acts of violence he necessarily commits in the course of his royal duties.

Conclusion

When we look at this formulation of the Hindu Golden Rule in its larger textual setting, we see that Brhaspati's teaching connects the principle of reciprocity with other key ideas in classical Hindu discourse, such as transmigration, nonviolence, and the metaphysics of the *atman*. We see also that, in its broader context, his teaching is a radical one, and not universal in its application.

Brhaspati grounds his teaching of ethical reciprocity in the concept of a transmigrating soul or spirit, whose destiny is determined by the moral quality of the person's conduct. Among the various forms of virtuous conduct, Brhaspati singles out nonviolence or *ahimsa* as the most efficacious. One should regard others as "similar to oneself," and avoid doing harm to them on the basis of that similarity. Harmful actions grow out of selfish desire, and desire is the great enemy of *dharma*. The recognition that others are like to oneself, on the other hand, rests of a deeper understanding of the similarity or (in its Advaita formulation) unity of transmigrating souls, all equally caught up in the fluctuating world-process.

As preceptor to the gods, Brhaspati is an authoritative instructor in *dharma*, and his audience recognizes the virtue in his teaching. However, Yudhisthira and Bhisma also consider that it is limited in its scope of application. The burden of Bhisma's lengthy session with Yudhisthira is to provide guidance for a ruler to exercise sovereignty in a nonegalitarian social world. This requires nonreciprocal actions where a sovereign treats subjects and other rulers in ways he would definitely not have himself treated. It requires violence to preserve order. There may indeed be some—"gods, sages, and brahmins," as Yudhisthira puts it—who are in a position to conduct themselves according to a disciplined principle of reciprocity and nonviolence toward all other creatures. This is a radical extension of common Hindu ethical teachings. For most persons caught up in worldly pursuits, however, other moral teachings are more pertinent: the avoidance of desire-based conduct, the minimization of injury toward others, and the recognition of *dharma* in all interpersonal encounters.

Chapter 13

The Golden Rule in Confucianism

Mark A. Csikszentmihalyi
University of Wisconsin-Madison

Theologians and scholars have often cited Chinese versions of the "Golden Rule" to make arguments about comparative religious ethics or the existence of universal moral rules. The existence of passages similar to Biblical formulations of the rule, however, does not mean that the Chinese examples form a cohesive set that served as a cardinal moral imperative. Different voices within the Confucian tradition have made different kinds of arguments about the moral reflectivity that is at the heart of the Golden Rule. The earliest Chinese expressions of Golden Rule-style injunctions existed somewhat uneasily within a system that otherwise emphasized acting out of a set of virtues. While post-Buddhist Confucians were better able to integrate the general principle of reflexivity into their moral system, they still had difficulty reconciling it with classical aspects of their tradition. A close examination of both early and late traditional writing on Golden Rule passages in the Confucian canon reveals that the scope of the application of the rule was often restricted, sometimes even to the point of being used as a metaphor for reflexivity in action rather than as a moral imperative.

The most commonly cited examples of the Golden Rule in China are from the *Analects* (Lunyu 論語), the work that is today most widely seen as representative of the thought of Confucius. Discussions of the Golden Rule's formulations in the *Analects* usually have been explicitly framed as comparable to formulations in other cultures. Jesuit missionaries as early as Matteo Ricci (1551–1610) cited parallels between Chinese versions of the Golden Rule and formulations in the books of Matthew (7.12) and Luke (6.31) as evidence of a relatively unpolluted link to an early shared "Natural Law."[1] Later, the connection is also mentioned by Thomas Thornton, author of the eight-volume *A History of China, From the Earliest Records, To the Treaty With Great Britain* published in 1844:

It may excite surprise, and probably incredulity, to state the golden rule of our Saviour, "Do unto others as you would that they should do unto you,"

---

[1] Donald E. Mungello, *Curious Land: Jesuit Accomodation and the Origins of Sinology* (Honolulu: University of Hawai'i Press, 1989), p. 63.

which Mr. Locke designates as "the most unshaken rule of morality, and foundation of all social virtue," had been inculcated by Confucius, almost in the same words, four centuries before.[2]

Whether the surprise is due to the parallel across cultures or the fact that the Chinese version was earlier is not specified by the author.

While writers like Ricci and Thornton emphasized similarities between China and Christendom, later writers were more intent on drawing contrasts between the two. In the nineteenth century, many were more concerned with the "negative formulation" of China's "Silver Rule." The Scottish Nonconformist missionary and translator James Legge compared the "golden" and "silver" rules in this way:

> The lesson of the gospel commands men to do what they feel to be right and good. It requires them to commence a course of such conduct, without regard to the conduct of others to themselves. The lesson of Confucius only forbids men to do what they feel to be wrong and hurtful.[3]

Legge highlights the difference between the "positive" moral injunction "do unto others as you would that they should do unto you," and the "negative" one that he translates "[do] not do to others as you would not wish done to yourself," and finds the positive formulation superior. Bracketing the question of the relevance of the formulation of the Golden Rule for now, it is worth noting that Legge's condemnation of the negative formulation is not the subject of universal agreement. Robert E. Allinson argues that the "negative" formulation is superior:

> If we take an illustration from modern history, the notion of making the world safe for democracy arises naturally from the background of the affirmative formulation, but would not be a natural deduction from the negative formulation. If I am to avoid harming another, it does not follow that I should attempt to impose a political system on him that I find desirable for myself.[4]

---

[2] Thornton, *History of China*, volume 1, page 209, quoted in James Legge, *The Chinese Classics* (Oxford: Oxford University Press, 1895), v. 1, p. 109. The Locke quotation is also cited by the Rev. Hampden C. DuBose in 1886, who contrasts Locke's "foundation" to Confucius's "keystone in the arch of Chinese ethics" (see *The Dragon, Image and Demon: Or, The Three Religions of China* (New York: A.C. Armstrong and Son, 1887), p. 107.)

[3] Legge, Ibid. Norman J. Girardot, in his study of Legge, points out that Legge originally judged Confucius as being inferior to Jesus in a number of areas, resulting in barriers to conversion: "it was the influence of the Master's [i.e., Confucius'] unreligion that caused later generations of Chinese to respond so unfavorably to the 'ardent religious feeling' displayed by Evangelical Protestantism." See Girardot, *The Victorian Translation of China: James Legge's Oriental Pilgrimage* (Berkeley: University of California Press, 2002), p. 60.

[4] Allinson, "The Golden Rule as the Core Value in Confucianism and Christianity: Ethical Similarities and Differences." *Asian Philosophy* 2.2 (1992): 173–85, p. 179. Allison adds, point-

Historically, the question of negative or positive formulation is often tied to just such normative statements. Allinson lacks Legge's missionary imperative, and as a result he reverses his predecessor's valuation of the imposition of "positive" reforms on others.

Beyond the way that the terms "golden" and "silver" establish a hierarchy of value, the excessive concern with "Chinese" versus "Western" formulations obscures the fact that myriads of different formulations bear each of these labels. The latter category includes "all things whatsoever ye would that men should do to you, do ye even so to them" (Mt. 6:31), "do unto others as an impartial rational observer would have you do unto them" (Marcus Singer), and often even "act so that I can also will my maxim to become a universal law" (Immanuel Kant). This chapter looks carefully at four early Chinese formulations of the Golden Rule. While the analytic focus in many previous studies of the Golden Rule in Confucianism has been on the negative formulations of the *Analects*, a close look at other early texts shows that positive formulations also existed in China, and that the use of positive and negative formulations somewhat interchangeably implies that the earliest applications of the Golden Rule in China were perhaps not as literal as contemporary philosophers are wont to read them.

What does the Golden Rule say?

The core of Golden Rule, to borrow William Green's minimal definition, is "a general statement that instructs us to treat others as we want, and would want, others to treat us." Minimally, the Golden Rule requires a type of reflexivity to be applied by the agent of an action with respect to another person, bringing the agent into the picture, and implicitly drawing an analogy between the agent and the other person. Strictly speaking, the Golden Rule does not tell us what we can or should do, but rather provides a standard for comparing two courses of action based on the desires of the other person. Further, for the purpose of the following discussion, I would like to pay particular attention to the continuum of metaphorical to concrete invocations of the Golden Rule. A metaphorical invocation is one that uses the Golden Rule as a cultural referent to illustrate other instances of reflexivity. A concrete invocation is one that actually contains an imperative that the Golden Rule should guide actions. In China, as it turns out, at least half the canonical invocations of the Golden Rule in China are of the metaphorical variety.

The two *Analects* passages that mention the Golden Rule are usually numbered 12.2 and 15.24, and connect the core notion of reversibility to the concepts of

edly, "It may be simply coincidental that the notion of being the moral policeman or the moral guardian of the world has arisen from the Christian West, but I do not think that it is an accident."

benevolence (ren 仁) and reciprocity (shu 恕), respectively. Both *Analects* passages say that a person's desires may serve as a guide for how to treat others, but are phrased in such a way as to emphasize the nonperformance of actions that one does not oneself desire: "do not impose upon others those things that you yourself do not desire." In *Analects* 12.2, the injunction is part of a description of benevolence:

仲弓問仁。子曰：「出門如見大賓，使民如承大祭。己所不欲，勿施於人。在邦無怨，在家無怨。」仲弓曰：「雍雖不敏，請事斯語矣！」

Zhonggong asked about benevolence.

The Master [i.e., Confucius] said:

"Although you have left your home, still behave as if you are receiving important guests. Although you are delegating commoners, still behave as if you are undertaking great sacrifices. Do not impose upon others those things that you yourself do not desire. If in your state you generate no resentment, then in your clan you generate no resentment."

Zhonggong said:

"Although I am not clever, I will attempt to put these words into practice!"[5]

Here Confucius tells his disciple Zhonggong 仲弓 to treat people respectfully even if they are outside his kinship group or social class, to use his own desires as guide for how to treat others, and that resentment created elsewhere can follow you home. As many commentators have pointed out, this is not the general definition of benevolence. In fact, this dialog is only one of six in the *Analects* that begins with a disciple asking about benevolence. Of these six, only this one mentions reflexivity in any form. More generally, benevolence itself is mentioned in over 50 passages in the *Analects*, and, as we shall see below, later Confucians argued that the Master's particular answer in 12.2 was geared to the particular case of the disciple Zhonggong.[6]

---

[5] Yang Bojun 楊伯峻, *Lunyu yihuzhu* 論語譯注 (Hong Kong: Zhonghua, 1984), pp. 123–24.

[6] For example, the influential Song dynasty commentator Zhu Xi 朱熹 (1130–1200) compares Confucius' answer in *Analects* 12.1 to the one in 12.2, and argues that the two answers to the same question are a matter of something like a Buddhist "expediency" (fangbian 方便). He uses the dual principle of *yin* and *yang* (as expressed by their counterpart hexagrams in the *Book of Changes*, *kun* 坤 and *qian* 乾) to reconcile the different answers into a single overarching scheme: 克己復禮，乾道也；主敬行恕，坤道也。顏、冉之學，其高下淺深，於此可見。然學者誠能從事於敬恕之間而有得焉，亦將無己之可克矣 "To 'observe the rites by overcoming the self' [i.e., the answer in 12.1] is the *qian* Way. To 'emphasize reverence and act with reciprocity' [i.e., the answer in 12.2] is the *kun* Way. The types of learning that Yan and Ran [i.e., the disciples Yan Yuan and Zhonggong] were engaged in, their strengths and weaknesses, talents and deficiencies, can all be seen from this comparison. Thus students can sincerely attend to affairs in reverence and reciprocity and benefit from it, and also will end up without a self to overcome." See Zhu Xi, *Sishu zhangju jizhu* 四書章句集注 (Beijing: Zhonghua, 1983), pp. 132–33.

In this light, it is interesting that the second instance in the *Analects* does not contain a reference to benevolence. *Analects* 15.24 provides the other occurrence of the Golden Rule:

子貢問曰：「有一言而可以終身行之者乎」子曰：「其『恕』乎！己所不欲，勿施於人。

> Zigong asked:
>
> "Is there a single doctrine that one may put into practice throughout one's life?'
>
> The Master [i.e., Confucius] said:
>
> "It is 'reciprocity.' Do not impose upon others those things that you yourself do not desire."[7]

This passage would appear to place the concept of reciprocity and the Golden Rule at the center of Confucius' teachings. However, numerous interpreters have argued there are good reasons to be skeptical about either the claim that reciprocity is so central or the original nature of the passage itself. In particular, Bryan Van Norden's recent work *Virtue Ethics and Consequentialism in Early Chinese Philosophy* argues that this passage was a later interpolation and further that it is inconsistent with the virtue ethics approach of the *Analects* in general.[8] E. Bruce Brooks goes even further to dismiss both *Analects* passages as interpolations, saying the Golden Rule is "notable as *not* a saying of Confucius. Its laterality (there are no sacred or other verbal sanctions), and its basis in desire (the appeal is exclusively to feelings; compare 5:11), imply an origin outside the Analects itself."[9] These reactions underscore the extent to which the concrete invocation of Golden Rule does not fit easily into the modified "Virtue Ethics" of early Confucianism. As Van Norden notes, the measure of a good action is generally whether it is an expression of the relevant virtue on the part of the actor, and this does not take into account the desires of the other person. Indeed, an action that expresses the actor's ritual propriety would be determined by the social role of the other person involved, and not, as Brooks points out, their desires. Yet this raises a question which is a more significant comparative issue than the issue of formulation. If the Golden Rule in the *Analects* is not to be read as a concrete, universal moral imperative, are there other ways to read it?

Metaphorical readings of the Golden Rule are clearly intended if we move beyond the *Analects* to the early Confucian text *Record of Rites* (*Liji* 禮記). The *Record of Rites* contains rather different versions of the Golden Rule, including

---

[7] Yang, 166–67. "Reciprocity" is paired with "loyalty" in *Analects* 4.15.

[8] See chapter two of his *Virtue Ethics* (New York: Cambridge, 2007).

[9] *The Original Analects: Sayings of Confucius and His Successors* (New York: Columbia University Press, 1998), p. 24.

a positive formulation. From the perspective of the entire history of Confucianism, these instances are very important, since they come from the two chapters of the *Record of Rites* that are singled out by Zhu Xi in the Song dynasty to become part of the canonical "Four Books" (sishu 四書) that supplanted the "Five Classics" (wujing 五經). The titles of these two chapters are commonly rendered into English as the "Doctrine of the Mean" (*Zhongyong* 中庸) and "Great Learning" (*Daxue* 大學), and originated as chapters 31 and 42 of the *Record of Rites*, respectively. In the twelfth century, however, Zhu Xi identified the former as the work of Confucius' disciple Zengzi 曾子 and Zengzi's disciples, and the latter as the work of Confucius' disciple Zisi 子思. Zhu Xi also placed these two works on the same footing as the *Analects*. The "Doctrine of the Mean" is explicit about identifying its formulation of the Golden Rule not as a saying of Confucius, but as commentary on one of his sayings:

子曰：「道不遠人。人之為道而遠人，不可以為道。」

《詩》云：『伐柯伐柯，其則不遠。』執柯以伐柯，睨而視之，猶以為遠。

故君子以人治人，改而止。忠恕違道不遠，施諸己而不願，亦勿施於人。

The Master said:

    "The Way is accessible to people. If a person acts a certain way, but it is inaccessible to others, then it cannot be *the* Way."

    The *Book of Odes* says: "'When carving an axe-handle, its design is accessible.' You grasp an axe's handle when you carve another axe-handle, but if you only see it out of the corner of your eye, it is *as if* it is inaccessible."

    So when a Gentleman governs people, once he reforms them then he stops. Loyalty and reciprocity ensure access to the Way. Do not impose on others what you do not want done to yourself.[10]

This version of the Golden Rule differs from the *Analects* passages in several ways. First, it is clearly intended as advice to a ruler. In light of the passage from the *Book of Odes*, the ruler's perfected state is the handle of the axe that is being wielded to carve the unfinished blocks of the subjects' raw states. Because the axe being wielded provides a blueprint for the axe being fashioned, the reversibility of the process is analogized to a ruler's examination of their own nature as a model for their subjects. The second difference arises from its use as an illustration of a principle that is slightly different from the Golden Rule in the abstract. This passage is usually explained in terms of the ruler's bringing people into conformity with their natures, but going no further. It is not defining moral action in general, but is used to explain how far a ruler goes in transforming his subjects.

---

[10] Wang Wenjin 王文錦, *Liji yijie* 禮記譯解 (Beijing, Zhonghua, 2001) 31.778.

As such, it appears that this citation of the Golden Rule is to invoke a general *reflexivity*, but not specifically an injunction against doing to others as one does not oneself desire. Instead, it is much more specific. It concerns not shaping one's subordinates in ways that embellish the blueprint of the exemplar that one is using. Another passage, from the "Great Learning," that is often cited as a Chinese formulation of the Golden Rule is similar to the previous one in several ways:

堯舜率天下以仁, 而民從之。桀紂率天下以暴, 而民從之。其所令反其所好, 而民不從。是故君子, 有諸己, 而後求諸人。無諸己, 而後非諸人。所藏乎身不恕, 而能喻諸人者, 未之有也。

Yao and Shun led the people of the world through benevolence, and the common people followed their example. Jie and Zhou led the people of the world through violence, and the common people followed their example. It is when their commands ran counter to what they enjoyed that the people did not follow them. That is why the Gentleman possesses something himself and only then seeks it in others. He does not possess it himself, only then does he condemn it in others. There has never yet been anyone who lacked their own store of reciprocity, yet was able to convey it to others.[11]

As with the passage in the "Doctrine of the Mean" this "Great Learning" passage is really more about the way in which the ruler inculcates values in his subjects than about moral action in general. It differs from the usual reading of Golden Rule passages in the *Analects* in that it is not a universal moral principle, it only applies to the ruler's ability to morally transform the population of the state. That process requires a comparison of the ruler's own qualities to those he seeks to inculcate in the people.[12] Significantly, there is both a *positive* and a *negative* aspect of this reflexive action. But its close relation to the "Doctrine of the Mean" passage implies that while the formulation is not the same as in the *Analects*, the positive and negative formulation may have been seen as mutually implying each other.

In all of these occurrences, *reflexivity* is key to the Golden Rule in early Confucian classics. While it is impossible to say whether *Analects* 15.24 is an

---

[11] *Liji zhengyi* 42.986.

[12] This passage, perhaps written by Zisi, is similar in many respects to one attributed to his student Mengzi 孟子 (fl. fourth century B.C.E.) The latter reads: 「桀紂之失天下也, 失其民也。失其民者, 失其心也。得天下有道 : 得其民斯得天下矣。得其民有道, 得其心斯得民矣。得其心有道 : 所欲, 與之聚之 ; 所惡, 勿施爾也。民之歸仁也, 猶水之就下, 獸之走壙也。。。」 "The reason that Jie and Zhou lost the people of the world is that they lost the common people. The reason that they lost the common people was that they lost their hearts and minds. There is a way of gaining the people of the world: what you desire you give to them and so collect them, what you hate you do not impose on them. The common people return to benevolence like water flowing downward, or as beasts flee to open spaces." See *Mengzi* 孟子 section 4A9, see Zhu, *Sizhu zhangju jizhu*, pp. 280–81.

interpolation, the arguments for its inconsistency with the moral system of the text as a whole say quite a bit about how well it fits with the Confucian system as a whole. The other instances apply the reflexive principle in a particular context. In *Analects* 12.2 the principle is applied by a person who performs ritual, and it allows that person to treat people outside his affiliation group in the same way that the person treats people inside that group. In the "Doctrine of the Mean" and "Great Learning" passages, the principle is applied by a ruler in the context of the transformation of the ruler's subjects by the power of charismatic authority. In these last three cases, the application of the Golden Rule is not universal, but is instead limited to particular interactions, and the rule seems to be invoked at least partly as a metaphor to talk about more limited moral imperatives.

What does the Golden Rule mean?

Early Confucian instances of the Golden Rule include what seem to be full-fledged moral imperatives (e.g., *Analects* 15.24) as well as invocations of the imperative as a metaphor for reflexive comparison of self and other (e.g., "Doctrine of the Mean"). Attention has primarily been paid to the question of whether the "negative formulation" means something different than the positive formulation. In the end, were the Chinese formulations of the Golden Rule interpreted to mean something different from Western formulations?

Out of deference to the exalted position of the controversy about the relative merits of the positive and negative formulations, it is necessary to begin by pointing out the ultimate similarity of these two versions of the Golden Rule. As demonstrated in the previous section, the positive statement of the Golden Rule in the "Great Learning" plays a functionally similar role to the negative one in the "Doctrine of the Mean." Not all Chinese formulations of the Golden Rule are negative, and indeed the negative and positive seem to imply one another in the minds of those writers. Heiner Roetz makes this argument in his *Confucian Ethics of the Axial Age*: "the ethically essential abstraction represented by the Golden Rule, the establishment of a reciprocal relation between the self and the other is also established by the negative version."[13] Second, as philosopher David S. Nivison has argued:

> If, having promised to appear this evening, I had not done so, I still would have done something, namely breaking a promise. Not doing something to another is always, under another description, doing something to that person, and conversely.[14]

---

[13] Roetz, *Confucian Ethics of the Axial Age* (Albany: State University of New York Press, 1993), p. 134.

Indeed, the conflict between the "golden" and "silver" rules seems to largely disappear once the need to assert the superiority of one system is put aside.

The specific implications of these early texts are worked out by later writers in different ways. In most readings of the *Analects*, the Golden Rule is associated with the virtue of benevolence, and indeed later writers try to work out what the implications of the rule are in the context of interpersonal interactions. Generally, benevolence was seen as rooted in natural feelings of compassion (literally, sharing another's suffering), and feelings that were extended through moral self-cultivation to reach all other persons.

In the metaphorical readings of the "Doctrine of the Mean" and "Great Learning," the Golden Rule is used as a guide for more specific actions that feature an aspect of the reflexivity that it embodies.[15] The Song Confucian Zhu Xi's comment to the "Great Learning" passage explored above is a case in point. Zhu connects it to a subsequent passage about the ruler's ability to unify the country:

> 有善於己，然後可以責人之善；無惡於己，然後可以正人之惡。皆推己以及
> 人，所謂恕也，不如是，則所令反其所好，而民不從矣。

> Only when one has a good point may one charge others with that good point, only when one lacks a fault may one correct that fault in another. This is extending oneself in order to reach others, otherwise called "reciprocity." If one does not proceed in this way, then "one's commands ran counter to what they enjoyed so the people did not follow them."[16]

In early Confucian texts, then, sometimes the Golden Rule was subordinated to the virtue of benevolence, but other times was used in a looser, metaphorical way to illustrate correct political action.

It was not until after Buddhism came to China that Neo-Confucians gave these classical expressions of the Golden Rule a more important role in their ethical systems. Examples of Neo-Confucians who did this are Yamaga Sokô 山鹿素行 (1622–85) in Japan and Dai Zhen 戴震 (1723–77) in China. Fumihiko Takahashi has explored the way that the "Ancient Learning" school in Japan expanded the role of the Golden Rule in Confucianism.[17] A short time later,

---

[14] Nivison, "Golden Rule Arguments in Chinese Moral Philosophy" in *The Ways of Confucianism: Investigations in Chinese Philosophy*, ed. Bryan Van Norden (Chicago and La Salle: Open Court, 1996), pp. 59–76; p. 62.

[15] The "Banfa jie" 版法解 chapter of the Warring States *Guanzi* 管子 (p. 340) uses the Golden Rule as a metaphor for reflexivity in an economic context: 己之所不安，勿施於人。故曰：「審用財，慎施報，察稱量。」 "Do not impose on others what makes you uneasy. Therefore it is said: 'Be careful about using your resources, pay attention to what you give to others in return, and investigate into the weights of the balance.'"

[16] Zhu, *Sizhu zhangju jizhu*, p. 9.

[17] Takahashi, "The Confucian Golden Rule: Chu Hsi's Neo-Confucian Interpretation and the Critical Arguments by Japanese Confucianists in the Seventeenth and Eighteenth Centuries" *Jarbuch-fuer-Recht-und-Ethik* (2008.8): 315–41.

Dai Zhen also turned to the general principle as a means of rejecting the radical intuitionism of Wang Yangming 王陽明 (1472–1529). Philip J. Ivanhoe describes Dai's moral theory:

> It is the orderly pattern of the universe which we can come to understand through careful examination and study. It is not *within us* already; it is something we come to realize through acquiring certain kinds of knowledge and augmenting this with a systematic application of the Confucian Golden Rule.[18]

In contrast to earlier Confucian commentators, then, Dai Zhen did not just treat the Golden Rule in the context of commenting on specific passages in the canon that contained its formulations, but foregrounded it in his discussion of the entire corpus.

In a sense both Yamaga and Dai were following the lead of Zhu Xi (1130–1200) who attempted to systematize Confucianism and ended up giving the Golden Rule a larger role in its moral theory. Zhu noticed the difference between the different formulations of the Golden Rule in the early classics, and argued that the "Great Learning" formulation was the "reciprocity of giving someone responsibility" (*zeren zhi shu* 是責人之恕) while the *Analects* formulation was the "reciprocity of taking care of someone" (*airen zhi shu* 是愛人之恕).[19] By making a modal distinction (to use John Henderson's term), he makes "reciprocity" a multifaceted and therefore more central concept in Confucian ethics. The more important role that Golden Rule formulations played in Neo-Confucian thinking is perhaps a result of the way that Confucianism had moved from a developmental model of virtue acquisition to a discovery model, to use Ivanhoe's terminology. As such, good actions were not defined in terms of particular contexts as much as in terms of abstract principles. While early Confucianism was not especially compatible with the Golden Rule, later Confucianism was more so.

How does the Golden Rule work?

Of particular interest to philosophers are the myriad ways of repairing the formal principle of the Golden Rule. For Confucians, too, it appears to have been implicit that application of the formulations of the Golden Rule meant embedding the principle in a broader system. This contextualization, already noted above, was noticed by the missionary James Legge:

> Still, Confucius delivered his rule to his countrymen only, and only for their guidance in their [five archetypal social] relations of which I have had so

[18] Ivanhoe, *Confucian Moral Self Cultivation*, 2nd edn. (Cambridge: Hackett, 2002), p. 95.
[19] Zhu Xi, *Zhuzi yulei* 朱子語類 16.70.

much occasion to speak. The rule of Christ is for man as man, having to do with other men, all with himself on the same platform, as the children and subjects of the one God and Father in heaven.[20]

Indeed, Legge's critique is another way of saying that the Golden Rule was subordinated to the general Confucian social system. Indeed, in most Confucian contexts proper ritual action is indexed to one's place in the social hierarchy, and so it is hard to imagine the application of an unrepaired version of the Golden Rule not eliciting harsh punishment.

Yet this obscures the way that early Chinese society imposed a web of obligations on the moral actor, making it difficult to meaningfully compare the place of the Golden Rule in early Chinese ethics with its role in other religious contexts. Legge's direct comparison obscures the ways in which Confucianism was a hybrid system that relied on the authority of the classics, on conceptions of human nature, on sacred ritual practices, and on the historical precedents of the Sage-kings. So the Golden Rule is perhaps best seen as an existing resource in early Chinese culture that was selectively incorporated into Confucianism.

We may take Bernard Gert's objections to the Golden Rule as a guide for conduct as a starting point to answer the question of how the Golden Rule worked contextually in China. Gert argues that: "The Golden Rule also requires, and students might like this, that teachers not give flunking grades to students even if they deserve it."[21] Here, the analysis of the Confucian use of the Golden Mean by philosopher Herbert Fingarette directly addresses Gert's perceived shortcoming. Fingarette argues that the Golden Rule in Confucianism offers a chance to reflect on our role or roles in the social system, and take a "detached" view of ourselves. Fingarette, in fact, draws a different conclusion about the paradigmatic case raised by Gert when he limns the Golden Rule's considerations about a student who requests a better grade to get into Law School:

> [M]y better judgment as I contemplate myself leads me to wish that, were this really me, the instructor would not indulge my panic-induced escapism, would confront me with the fact that instead of trying to learn from my error I was starting my college career by blaming the "system," and that I was undermining my capacity to act responsibly and to learn how to succeed in classwork legitimately.

The answer to the student is the opposite of what Gert says it would be.

Fingarette's reading of the implications of the Chinese Golden Rule in this situation is based on the concept of "reciprocity" in early Confucian texts. He writes: "What [shu] does is to require that I not make that ultimate judgment

---

[20] Legge, op. cit., p. 110.
[21] Cf. William Scott Green's essay in this volume, page 3.

except as I concurrently make the effort to appreciate, imaginatively, as if I were he, the consequences and meaning of my act for the other person."[22] Indeed, while the application of the Golden Rule in classical texts was more often than not indexed to particular positions *vis a vis* a kinship group or the ritual/political hierarchy, there is not fundamentally a difference in the basic reflexive principle behind the evaluation of actions. Further, the difference in roles and differences in life experience are often *key* to properly assessing a situation and applying the Golden Rule in a more reasonable way. Gert's critique of an unrepaired version of the Golden Rule clearly would not apply to the more sophisticated interpretation of the Confucian Golden Rule that Fingarette provides.

How does the Golden Rule matter?

In Confucianism, the Golden Rule is fundamentally the idea of reversibility as a guide for action. It is therefore a "method" integrated into the practice of benevolence (in the *Analects*) into good government (in the *Records of Ritual*), and into a theoretical antidote for intuitionist approaches to ethics (for later writers like Dai Zhen). It is not—at least not for the earliest Confucians—consistently seen as a universal guide to moral action. This fact provides a much more substantive basis to ask whether the formulations of the Golden Rule in China first pointed out by the Jesuit Matteo Ricci actually should be called "Golden Rule" than the historically more controversial issue of "Silver Rule" formulation ever did. To the extent that the classical expression of Golden Rule–style statements were applied more widely and more universally by post-Buddhist Confucians, the role of these expressions within the Chinese cultural system changed over time, and it can be said the Golden Rule "mattered" more to later writers.

Yet describing the nature of the relation of the Golden Rule to broader moral or cultural systems is a complex task. A measure of the high degree of embeddedness of the Golden Rule within the Chinese cultural system is that questions about consequences for violating the Golden Rule cannot be answered in a general way. It is not clear that social roles always trumped reflexivity in moral decision-making, nor is the opposite unambiguously true. Instead, in a way that is perhaps more suitable to a Virtue Ethics system than a Consequentialist one, the balance is a matter to be determined by the morally cultivated individual. The Chinese situation is closer to how Ernest D. Burton once described the Golden Rule in general as "not in actual application a rule at all. It is a principle of wide application, and in the actual relations of life, because they are so complex, difficult to apply."[23]

---

[22] Herbert Fingarette, "Following the 'One Thread' of the *Analects*," *Journal of the American Academy of Religion*, thematic issue S (Sept. 1980): pp. 373–405, p. 387.

What this means is that Legge is not strictly right to assert that Confucius only taught people to apply reflexivity for "guidance in their [five archetypal social] relations." A counterexample is the *Analects* 12.2 imperative: "although you are delegating commoners, still behave as if you are undertaking great sacrifices." In 12.2, the treatment being described appears to cross the lines of social class. A modern version of Legge's criticism is that unless the formulation of the Golden Rule explicitly advocates social leveling, it is incomplete. Martha C. Nussbaum reacts to Nivison's assertion that the Chinese version of the Golden Rule is "the very ground of community, without which no morality could develop at all . . . reassuring both that person and myself of our common humanity" with skepticism because of the hierarchical framework to which the maxim is indexed. She argues that there is no sense of shared humanity implied by an argument that says "[t]reat your dogs the way you'd like to be treated by the gods" because such a thought does not involve questioning the hierarchy between dogs and people.[24] Nussbaum faults the "missing thought" in Chinese moral philosophy as a concept of moral luck, "the thought that many of the most important distinctions among human beings are the work of fortune, unconnected to human dessert."[25]

It is possible to fault both Nivison and Nussbaum for assuming that formulations of the Golden Rule are either quieted by social hierarchies or drown them out in a blast of moral universalism. Instead, it is probably wiser to align the classical formulations of the Golden Rule in China with those premodern religious imperatives that were not absolute in the sense of the Kant's "Categorical Imperative." This is consistent with the fact that the earliest instances are a mixture of a situationally appropriate moral imperative and a metaphorical tool for talking about reflexivity. It also illustrates the way in which the early Chinese Golden Rule played a role in moral systems, but was a far cry from Locke's "foundation of all social virtue."

---

[23] Burton, "Is the Golden Rule Workable Between Nations?" *The Biblical World* (1918): pp. 131–41, p. 131.

[24] The Nivison quotation is from Nivison, "Golden Rule Arguments in Chinese Moral Philosophy," *ibid.* See Nussbaum, "Golden Rule Arguments: A Missing Thought?" in *The Moral Circle and the Self: Chinese and Western Approaches*, ed. Kim-chong Chong, Sor-hoon Tan, and C. L. Ten. (Chicago and LaSalle: Open Court, 2003), p. 7.

[25] Ibid. Nussbaum, who appears to be operating simply from Nivison's article and a set of assumptions about the nature of Chinese religion, fails to appreciate the degree to which the *Analects* does indeed have a strong notion of moral luck. A famous example is 12.5: "Life and death are a matter of *ming*, while riches and nobility are a matter of *tian*," 死生有命 富貴在天.

Chapter 14

"Wired for Reciprocity": Some Concluding Reflections

William Scott Green
University of Miami

The first half of the title of this concluding chapter comes from neuroscientist Donald W. Pfaff, whose work has been cited by some contributors to this volume. Pfaff's valuable book, *The Neuroscience of Fair Play: Why We (Usually) Follow the Golden Rule,*[1] postulates "that we are born with mechanisms inherent in our forebrains that dispose us toward behaving in accordance with an ethical universal . . . I propose that we have an inherent capacity for fair play. I say we are wired for reciprocity."[2] If so, then the essays collected below suggest at the very least that religion and culture complement nature. Maxims about reciprocity, about treating others in terms of oneself, are present in every major world religion, both historical and contemporary. Although these maxims are formalized differently in the discrete religions—sometimes explicitly stated as a central principle, sometimes unstated but assumed and suffused in other teachings and practices—the materials presented here show that in some fundamental respect reciprocity is basic to the world's religions. While this claim in itself may be neither novel nor controversial, the papers in this book present a distinctively rich and full picture of the range of ways reciprocity emerges in humanity's religious life.

The confluence of these two sets of evidence helps explain why reciprocity, in the form of the Golden Rule, is so commonplace across religions. As humans, we have, if not a natural inclination, then at least a natural potential, toward reciprocal action. On the basis of our physiological constitution, it seems neither strange nor unusual that we do. Seen this way, the Golden Rule not only complements nature, it extends it. In all the religions examined below, the Golden Rule appears as the consequence not of accidental behavior, but of human consciousness, deliberation, and self-control. Perhaps it is not too much to suggest that the religious articulation of the Golden Rule, in whatever form, turns an

---

[1] Donald W. Pfaff, *The Neuroscience of Fair Play: Why We (Usually) Follow the Golden Rule,* Dana Press (New York, 2007)
[2] Ibid., p. 206

instinct into a learned behavior and thereby does for human collective life what genetic predisposition alone either could not achieve or could not achieve as effectively and extensively. Seeing the Golden Rule as an extension of our genetic construction enriches the Rule's context and helps us see the high stakes it represents. If reciprocity is fundamental to human nature, then some teachings of the world's religions must be as well.

This book may suggest something more. If, as Pfaff asserts, we have an "inherent capacity for fair play," then nature tells us *that* we will practice reciprocity, but it does not necessarily tell us *how* we will practice reciprocity. Reciprocity may indeed be basic to the human character, but, as the papers below demonstrate, the way in which it will be understood and exercised is not uniform across religions. One useful way to think of the range of religious conceptions of reciprocity might be to employ some contemporary social scientific rubrics for discussing human capital: bonding and bridging. These categories represent conceptual poles in understanding different sorts of social networks that often, sometimes typically, exhibit reciprocity within groups. Bonding usually refers to social networks within culturally homogeneous groups. Bridging refers to social networks between culturally distinct or differentiated groups. Two examples from the essays gathered in this book help to illustrate these categories.

Ancient Israelite scripture, as analyzed by Baruch Levine, exhibits elements of both bridging and bonding reciprocity. As Levine shows, the classic maxim of Lev. 19.18 to "love your fellow as yourself" applies only to other Israelites. This seems to fall into the category of bonding. Lev. 19.33 and Deut. 10.19, however, apply the same language to the *ger* ("resident alien"), who is not a member of the native Israelite community. Exod. 23:9 applies the same principle, but not in the same language. As Levine explains:

> To love someone, in these terms, means to be kind and caring, and to be fair. It should strike us as significant that in the very commandment to love the resident alien the Torah is mandating reciprocity; the Israelites might have perished as a group had the Egyptians not granted them the basics of life, at least for a time. In effect, an Israelite who did what the Holiness Code prescribed, and avoided doing what it prohibited, was acting with love toward his fellow Israelite, and toward the resident alien, as well.

The explicit focus on the *ger* is instructive because it uses the presumption of a shared experience, rather than a shared lineage or cultural heritage, as the grounds for reciprocity. In the language of Exod. 23:9, the Israelites "know the feelings" of the *ger*. So although it does not represent a bonding reciprocity between autonomous culturally distinct groups, because the alien resides among the Israelites, the Hebrew Bible explicitly, even graphically, lays the foundation for finding experiential commonality—and thereby building bridging relationships—between culturally distinct groups. The focus is on collective rather than individual experience, and the experiential similarity is important precisely because the groups are culturally dissimilar.

An alternative conception may be at work in some of the materials from Greco-Roman philosophy and religion, as described by Robert Berchman. In Berchman's analysis of Aristotle, reciprocity is cast as a matter of friendship and operates within a community of people who are essentially like one another. The passage he cites from Aristotle appears to suggest as much:

> Perfect friendship is the friendship of good men and of men who are similar according to their virtue. For they wish things that are good similarly to each other as good men they are essentially good.

As Berchman explains:

> The type of friendship Aristotle has in mind is that which embodies a shared recognition and pursuit of several goals. It is this sharing which is essential and primary to the constitution of any form of self and community, whether household or city.

Friendship requires a shared active intellect and freedom. Thus, slaves, for example, seem excluded from the purview of Aristotle's Golden Rule.

The other papers in this volume exhibit a stunning range of sophisticated speculation and reflection on how reciprocity is to work in discrete religions and to whom it is directed. No two of them are precisely alike. We might see these speculations and reflections as operating along a continuum between bonding and bridging—from reciprocity that operates within a defined community to reciprocity that collapse bridging into bonding by imagining all human beings as undifferentiated and atomistic members of a single human community. Now that we have tracked and described these differences, we can raise another set of analytical questions to account for them.

The rich variations of reciprocity described below show that the world's great religions contain abundant resources on the importance of seeing others in terms of ourselves in the development of human community. We should be realistic—rather than smug and celebratory—about these religious resources. As Pfaff's book reminds us, culture can subvert and misdirect our natural inclinations toward reciprocity as well as extend it. The resources of the world's religions can point to what we can be and help us create a sustained global life with one another.

Bibliography

Chapter 3

Donlan, W. 1998. "Political Reciprocity in Dark Age Greece: Odysseus and His Hetairoi," in Gill, Postlethwaite, and Seaford *Reciprocity in Ancient Greece*. Oxford: Clarendon Press, pp. 51–71.

—. 1999. *The Aristocratic Ideal and Selected Papers*. Wauconda: Bolchazy-Carducci.

Dover, K. 1974. *Greek Popular Morality in the Time of Plato and Aristotle*. Indianapolis: Hackett.

Edmonds, J., trans. *Greek Elegy and Iambus I*. Cambridge, MA: Harvard University Press (Loeb Library).

Evelyn-White, H., trans. *Hesiod. The Homeric Hymns and Homerica*. Cambridge, MA: Harvard University Press (Loeb Library).

Fagles, R., trans., *Sophocles. The Three Theban Plays. Antigone, Oedipus the King, Oedipus at Colonus*. London and Harmondsworth: Penguin Books.

Farenga, V. 2006. *Citizen and Self in Ancient Greece. Individuals Performing Justice and the Law*. Cambridge: Cambridge University Press.

Gill, C. 1996. *Personality in Greek Epic, Tragedy, and Philosophy. The Self in Dialogue*. Oxford: Clarendon Press.

—. 1998. "Altruism or Reciprocity in Greek Ethical Philosophy?" in Gill, Postlethwaite, and Seaford (1998), pp. 303–28.

Gill, C., Postlethwaite, N., and Seaford, R., eds. 1998. *Reciprocity in Ancient Greece*. Oxford: Clarendon Press.

Herman, G. 1987. *Ritualised Friendship and the Greek City*. Cambridge, MA: Cambridge University Press.

—. 1998. "Reciprocity, Altruism, and the Prisoner's Dilemma: The Special Case of Classical Athens," in Gill, Postlethwaite, and Seaford (1998), pp. 200–25.

Lamb, W. R. M., trans. 1930. *Lysias*. Cambridge MA: Harvard University Press (Loeb Library).

Lattimore, R., trans. 1951. *The Iliad of Homer*. Chicago: University of Chicago Press.

Konstan, D. 1997. *Friendship in the Classical World*. Cambridge, MA: Cambridge University Press.

—. 1998. "Reciprocity and Friendship," in Gill, Postlethwaite, and Seaford (1998), pp. 279–301.

—. 2006. *The Emotions of the Ancient Greeks. Studies in Aristotle and Classical Literature*. Toronto: University of Toronto Press.

Missiou, A. 1998. "Reciprocal Generosity in the Foreign Affairs of Fifth-Century Athens and Sparta," in Gill, Postlethwaite, and Seaford, pp. 181–97.

Ostwald, M., trans. 1963. *Aristotle. Nicomachean Ethics.* Upper Saddle River, NJ: Prentice Hall.

Pearson, L. 1962. *Popular Ethics in Ancient Greece.* Stanford: Stanford University Press.

Postlethwaite, N. 1998. "Akhilleus and Agamemnon: Generalized Reciprocity," in Gill, Postlethwaite, and Seaford (1998), pp. 93–104.

Sahlins, M. 1965/1972. "On the Sociology of Primitive Exchange," in Sahlins (1972), *Stone Age Economics.* Chicago: Aldine-Atherton.

van Wees, H. 1998. "The Law of Gratitude: Reciprocity in Anthropological Theory," in Gill, Postlethwaite, and Seaford (1998), pp. 13–49.

Warner, R., trans. 1972. *Thucydides. History of the Peloponnesian War.* London and Harmondsworth: Penguin Books.

Watkins, C. 2000. *The American Heritage Dictionary of Indo-European Roots* (2nd ed.). Boston: Houghton Mifflin.

West, M. L. 1994. *Greek Lyric Poetry. A New Translation by M .L. West.* Oxford: Oxford University Press.

Zanker, G. 1998. "Beyond Reciprocity: The Akhilleus-Priam Scene in *Iliad* 24," in Gill, Postlethwaite, and Seaford (1998), pp. 73–92.

Chapter 6

Bailey, H. W. 1943. *Zoroastrian Problems in the Ninth-Century Books*, 1st ed. Oxford: The Clarendon Press, repr.1971.

Boyce, M. 1968. "Middle Persian Literature," in *Handbuch der Orientalistik, Iranistik, Literatur, Abt.* 1, Bd. IV. Leiden: E. J. Brill.

Darmesteter, J. 1960. *Le Zend Avesta.* Annales du Musée Guimet, 3 vols. Paris: Librairie d'Amérique et d'Orient Adrien-Maisonneuve, 1st ed. 1892–93, repr. 1960.

De Blois, F. 1984. "The Admonitions of Ādurbād and Their Relationship to the Aïqar Legend," in *Journal of the Royal Asiatic Society of Great Britain and Ireland* 1(1984), pp. 41–55.

De Menasce, J. P. 1945. *Une apologétique mazdéenne du IXe siècle: Škand-Gumānīk Vičār. La solution décisive des doutes.* Fribourg en Suisse: Librairie de l'Université.

—. 1958. *Une encyclopédie mazdéenne: Le Dēnkart.* Paris: Presses Universitaires de France.

—. 1973. *Le troisième livre du Dēnkart.* Paris: C. Klincksieck.

Dhabhar, E. B. N., ed. 1932. *The Persian Rivayats of Hormazyar Framarz and others.* Bombay: The K. R. Cama Oriental Institute.

JamaspAsa, K. M. 1970. "The Pahlavi Text of Vicīrīhā ī dēn ī wēh ī Mazdayasnān", in *W. B. Henning Memorial Volume*, eds. M. Boyce and I. Gershevitch. London: Lund Humphries, pp. 201–18.

JamaspAsana, D. J. M., ed. 1913. *The Pahlavi Texts II.* Bombay: Fort Printing Press.

Kanga, E. M. F., ed. 1960. *Čitak Handarz ī Pōryōtkēšān.* Bombay.

Kotwal, F. M. P. 1969. *The Supplementary Texts to Šāyest nē-Šāyest.* København: Munksgaard.

Madan, D. M. 1911. *The Complete Text of the Pahlavi Dinkard (Dēnkard)*, 2 vols. Bombay: The Society for the Promotion of Researches Into the Zoroastrian Religion.

Molé, M. 1967. *La Legende de Zoroastre Selon Les Textes Pehlevis.* Paris: C. Klincksieck.

Sanjana, P. 1895. *The Dînâ î Maînû î Khrat. The Religious Decisions of the Spirit of Wisdom.* Bombay: Printed at the Duftur Ashkara and the Education Society's Steam Press.

Shaked, S. 1969. "Esoteric Trends in Zoroastrianism," in *Proceedings of the Israel Academy of Sciences and Humanities,* III (7), pp. 175–221.

—. 1979. *The Wisdom of the Sasanian Sages (Dēnkard VI) by Aturpāt-ī Ēmētān.* Boulder (Colorado): Westview Press.

—. 1987a. "Andarz and Andarz Literature in Pre-Islamic Iran," in *Encyclopaedia Iranica,* vol. I. London: Routledge & Kegan Paul, pp. 11–16.

—. 1987b. "Paymān: An Iranian Idea in Contact with Greek Thought and Islam," in *Transition Periods in Iranian History, Actes du Symposium de Fribourg-en-Brisgau (22–24 Mai 1985).* Leuven Belgique: Association pour l'avancement des études iraniennes, pp. 217–40.

Skjaervø, P. O. 1997. "Counter-Manichean Elements in Kerdir's Inscriptions. Irano-Manichaica II," in *Manichaean Studies III,* eds. L. Cirillo and A. van Tongerloo. Brepols, Belgium: International Association of Manichaean Studies and the Center of the History of Religions, pp. 313–42.

Tarapore, J. C. 1933. *Pahlavi Andarz-Nāmak containing Chitak Andarz ī Pōryōtkaēshān.* Bombay: J. F. Bulsara for the Trustees of the Parsee Punchayet Funds and Properties.

Williams, A. V. 1990. *The Pahlavi Rivāyat Accompanying the Dādestān ī Dēnīg,* 2 vols. The Royal Danish Academy of Sciences and Letters, Copenhagen: Munksgard.

Zaehner, R. C. 1955. *Zurvan. A Zoroastrian Dilemma.* Oxford: Clarendon Press.

—. 1976. *The Teaching of the Magi: A Compendium of Zoroastrian Beliefs.* New York: Oxford University Press.

Index

order of the universe (*dike*) 45
Origen of Alexandria 88–99
Osama Bin Laden 114

pagan authors, on natural law 98
Pahlavi Rivayat, questions to Adurbad 71
Pahlavi texts 65
Pāli *Dhammapāda* 121, 122
Pāli *Tipitaka* 118
paradise, ways to reach 73
Patristic exegesis on Jesus teaching 77
patronage and the sage (*sapiens*) 52
payback 99
payman, right measure 72, 73
peace and understanding 115
perfections, ten, in Buddhism 116
Pericles, Thucydides funeral oration 38
persecution
    of Manicheans 71
    for righteousness' sake 86
Pfaff, Donald W., neuroscientist 170
    on universal ethical princple 135
Pharisees, Jesus disputes with 82
philanthropy 52
Philo of Alexandria, natural law 96
philosophy, Golden Rule in 1
piety 42, 43
    in Zoroastrianism Golden Rule 74
Plato
    Golden Rule 45
    on happiness in virtuous action 42
    Phaedrus 30
    on reciprocity of virtue 44 on
    Republic 44
Plotinus 50, 51
political obligations 41
poor, giving to 101
Pope Benedict XVI 78
    letter to, from Muslim clerics 115
Porphyry on Egyptian priesthood 53
positive and negatives 159, 163
positive good in Christian gospel 158
Potiphar's wife, and Joseph 16, 17
power relations, reinforcement 30
Priam 30, 31
    with Hector's body 33–5
priests, power of, and Jesus 82

Prisoner's Dilemma 29
"pro-life" versus "pro-choice", abortions 4
Providence as healer 51
Psalm 15
    ethical agenda 19–20
Pseudo-Clementines, natural law
        doctrine 90
Pufendorf, Samuel, Freiherr von *De Iure
        naturae et Gentium* 98
punishment and payback 20
purity 65
    and Jesus 82

quid pro quo 29
Qur'ān 100

rebirth
    as animals 152
    release from 128
recipient of Golden Rule 6
reciprocal bond, Covenant as 20–5
reciprocal violence, Bin Laden 114
reciprocity 2, 4, 13, 14, 25
    and altruism in ancient Greece 28
    based on justice 42
    and biblical law 11, 12, 14, 15
    in Confucian ethics 161, 166
    of divine Providence 51
    empathetic, to enemy 36
    of giving favors 34, 35
    in kindness 18–19
    Muslim positive call 115
    and nonviolence 154
    retaliation or reconciliation 113–16
    wired for 170
    wisdom tradition 19
Recognitiones, Pseudo-Clementine 96
reflexivity 61, 163
    and reciprocity 7, 126
regard for other, and self-esteem 64
Reiner, Hans 88
relationships, unequal, Hinduism 148
religion
    central role in Sasanian Iran 70
    five best things 70
    Golden Rule in 1, 2
    and reciprocity 170